Classic Car Collection

By Jordan Biggio

Thank you for purchasing a copy of my book. I had a great time creating this book for you and I would to see what you do with the designs. Feel free to email me images of what you have colored. My email address is:

jordanbiggio@gmail.com

If you enjoyed coloring my designs, then please leave a review to let others know what you thought, be it good or bad. Leaving a review is the single best way to help support me and my art. Leaving a review is easy and don't forget to post a completed colored page with your review.

Thanks again!

Jordan

ISBN-13: 978-1-945803-14-7
ISBN-10: 1-945803-14-2

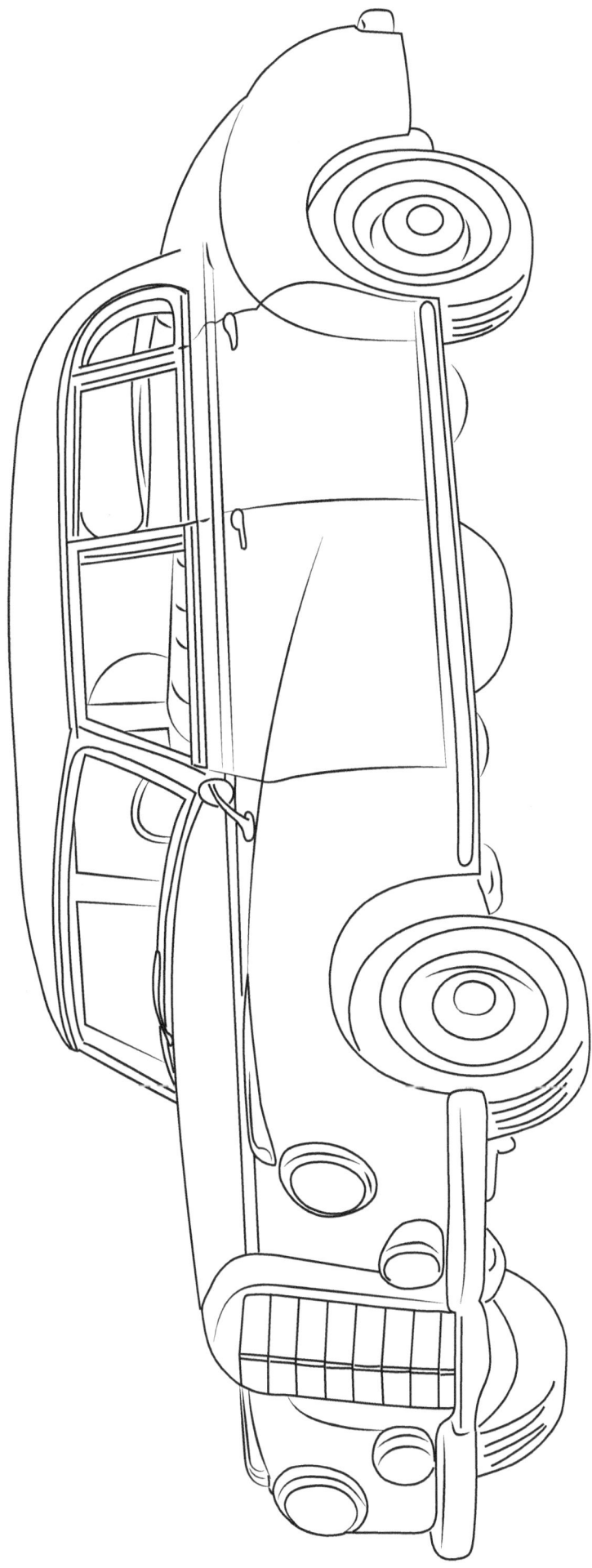

1951 Mercedes Benz Type 300

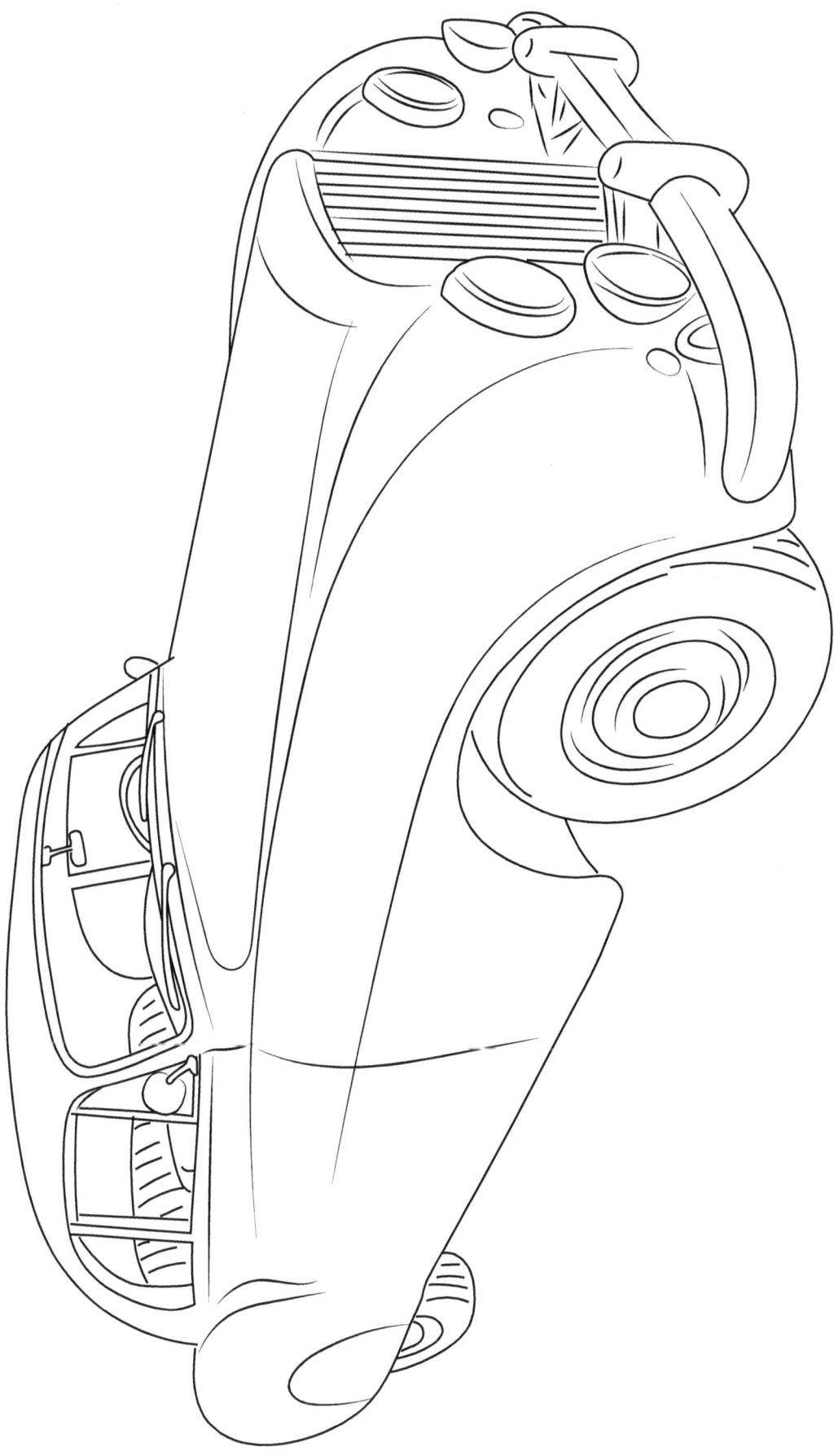

1952 Bentley R Type Continental

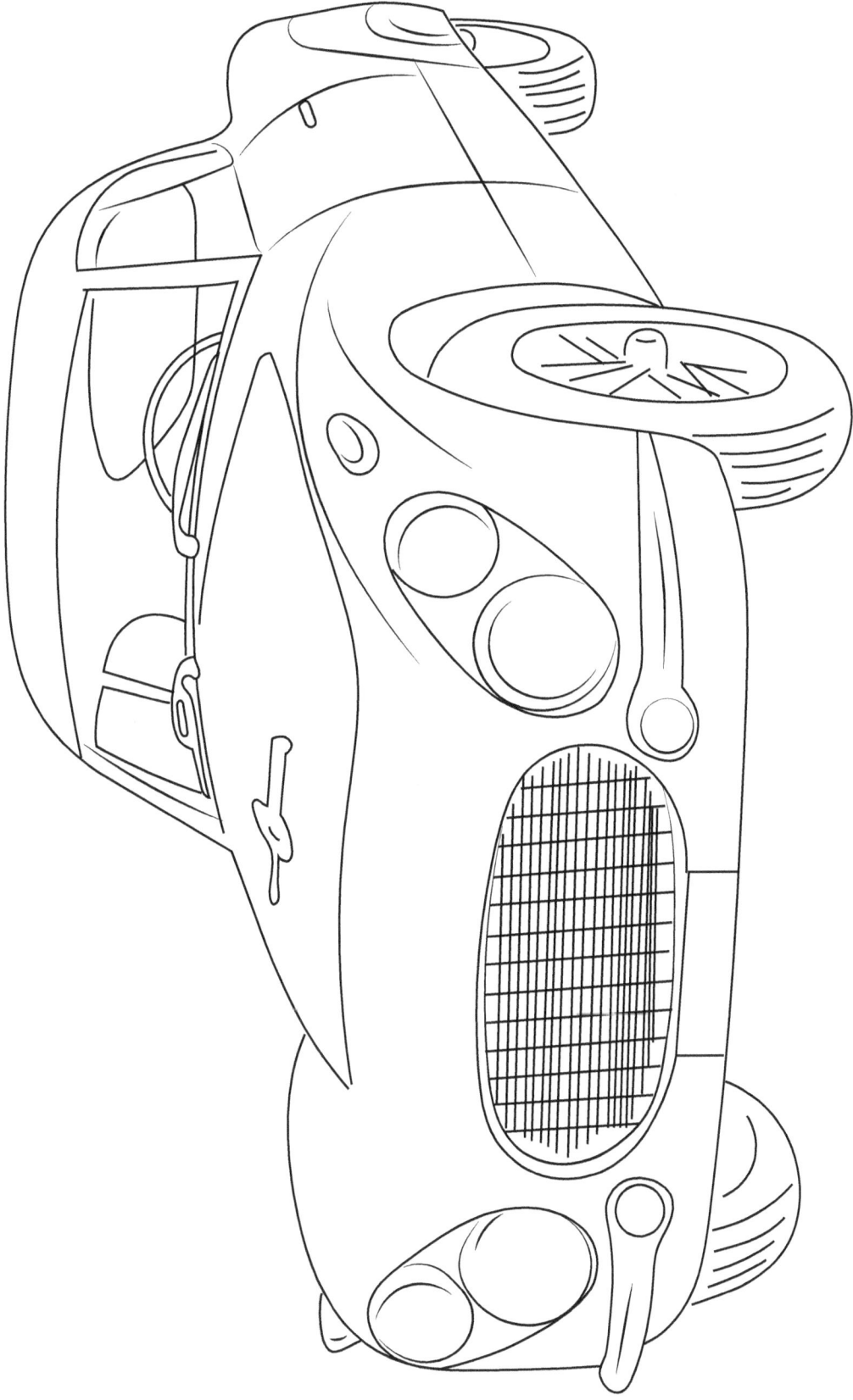

1952 FIAT 8V

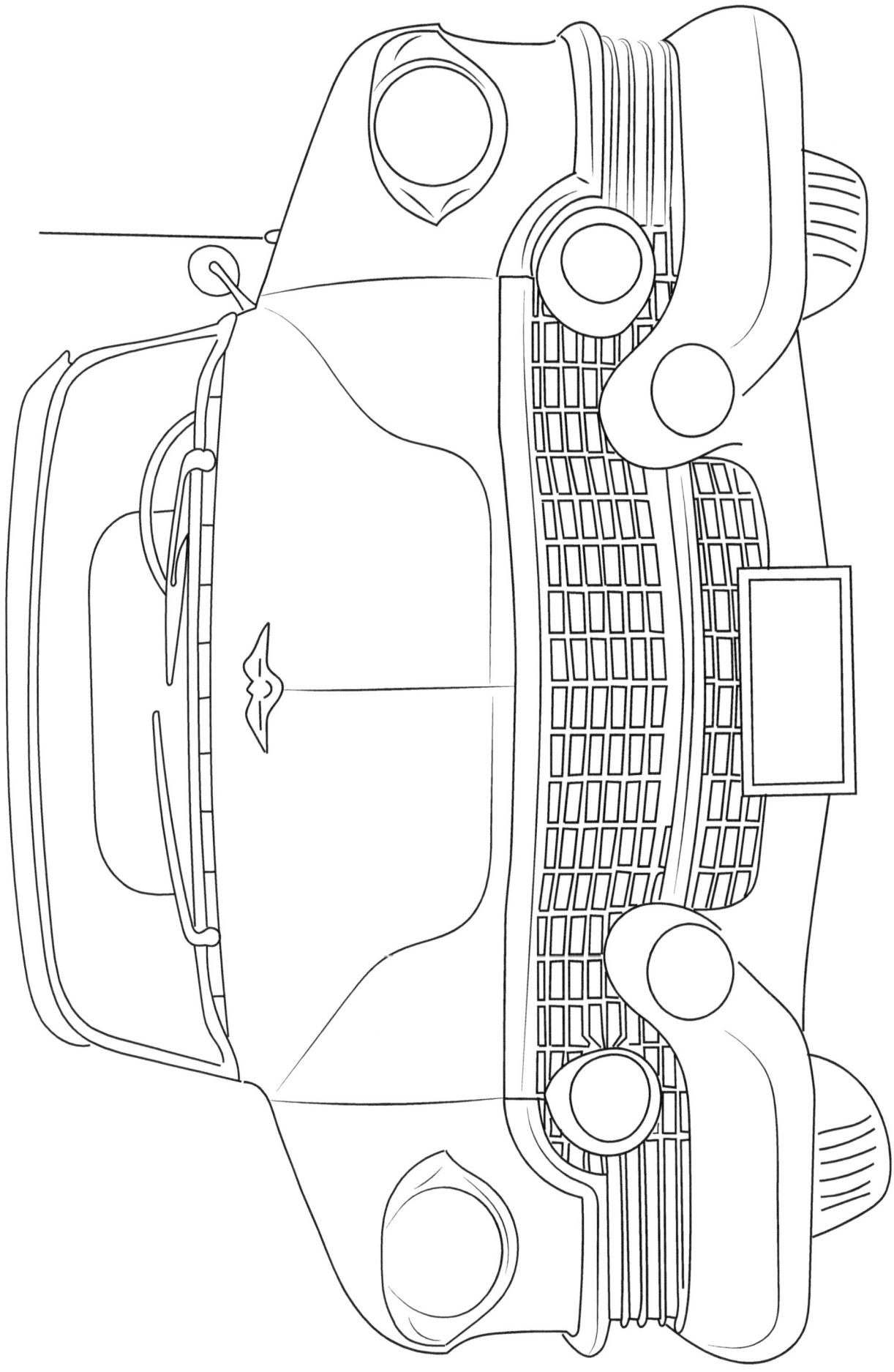

1954 Cadillac Eldorado

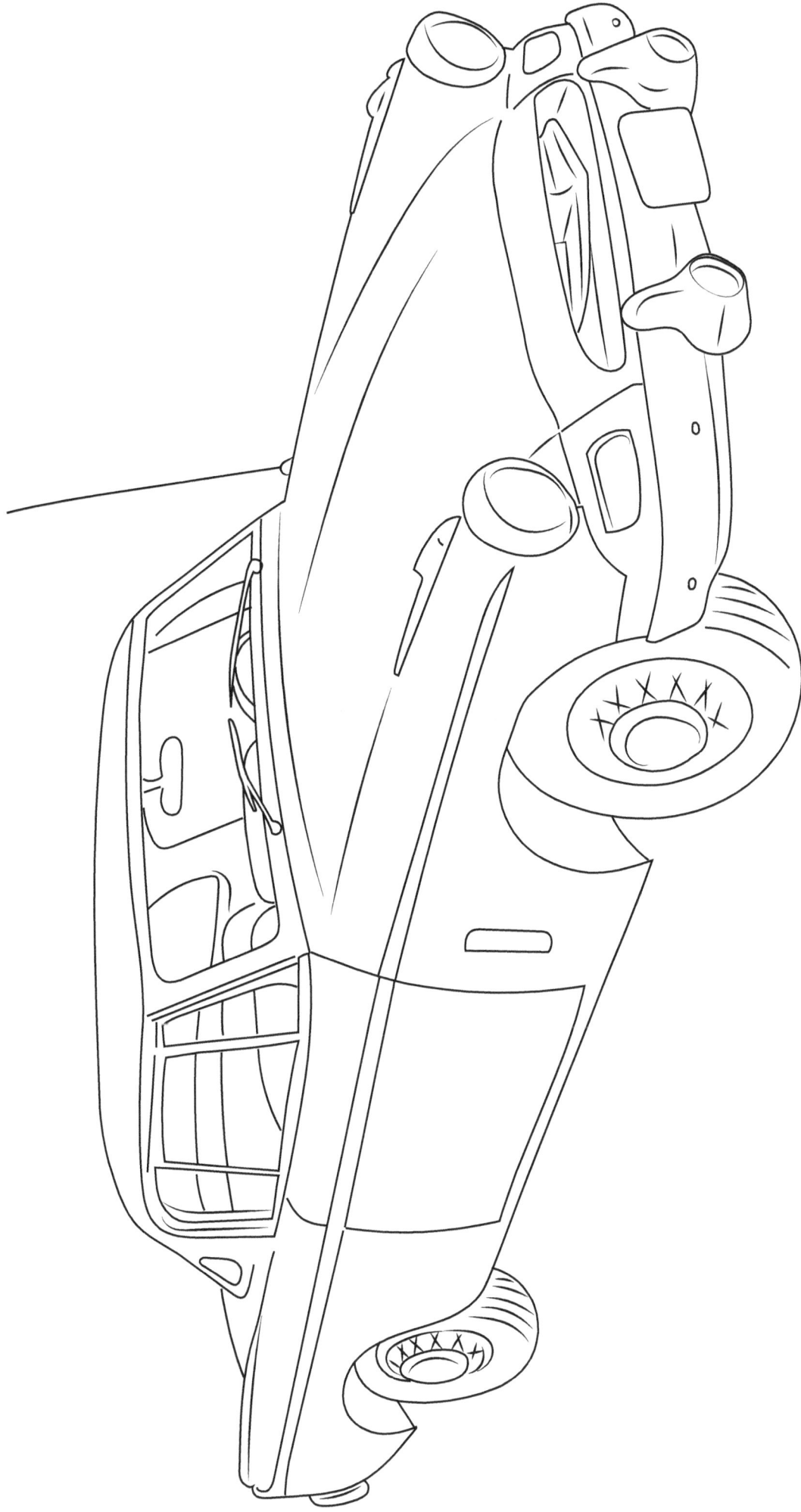

1955 Studebaker President Speedster

1955 Buick Skylark

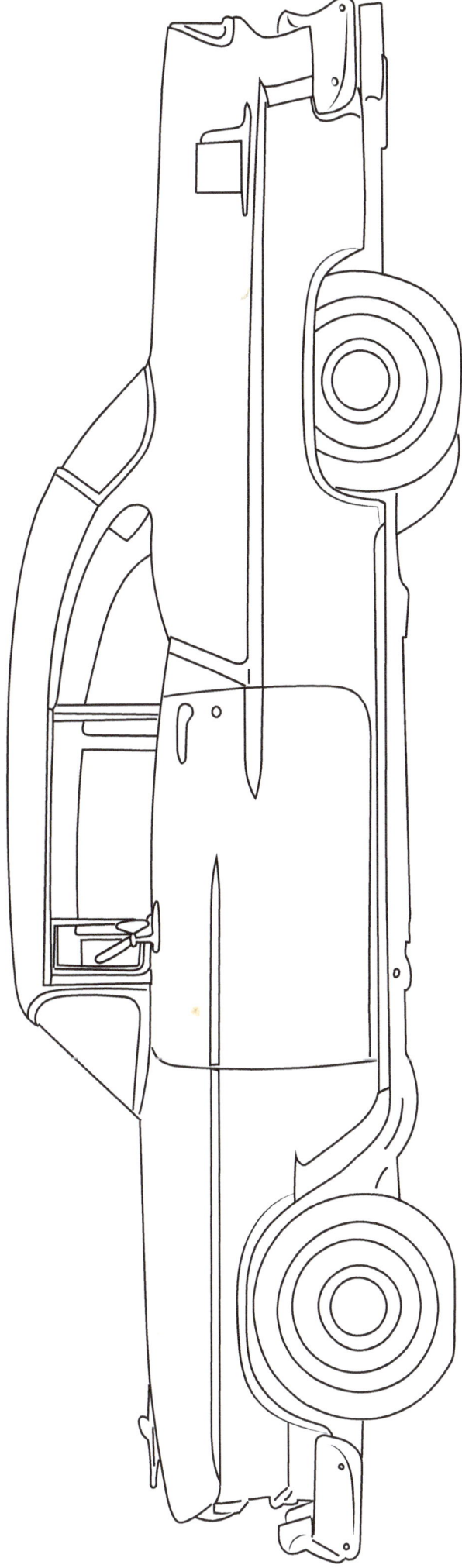

1955 Chevy Bel Air

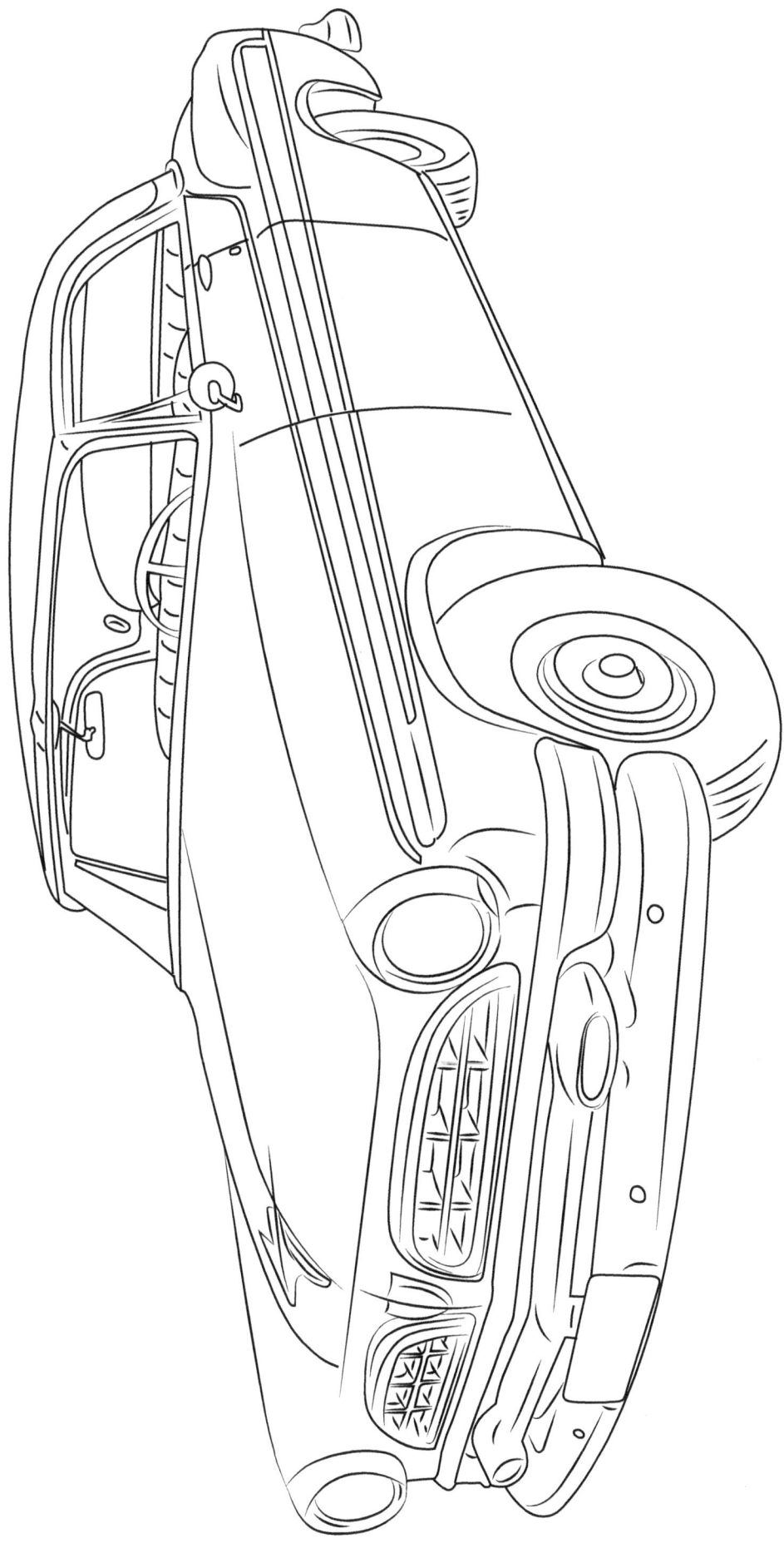

1955 Chrysler New Yorker

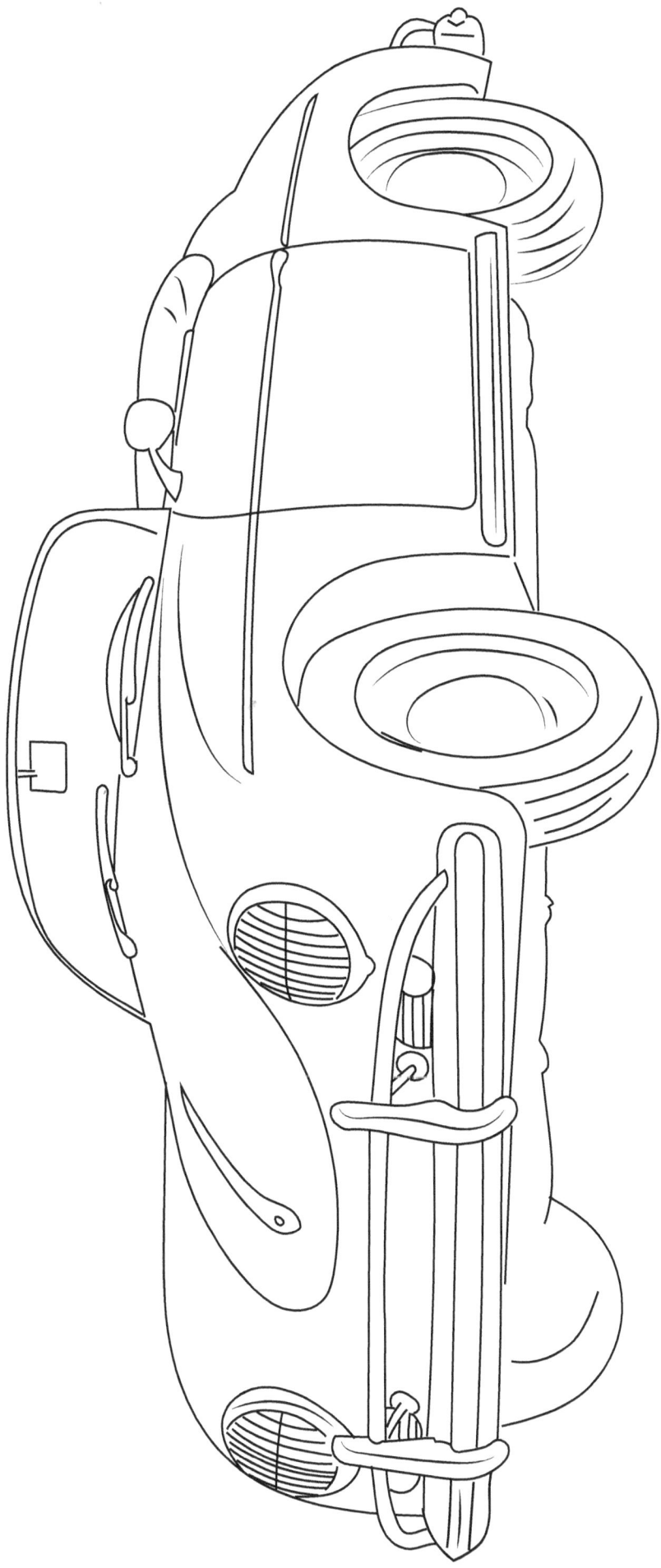

1955 Porsche 356 Roadster

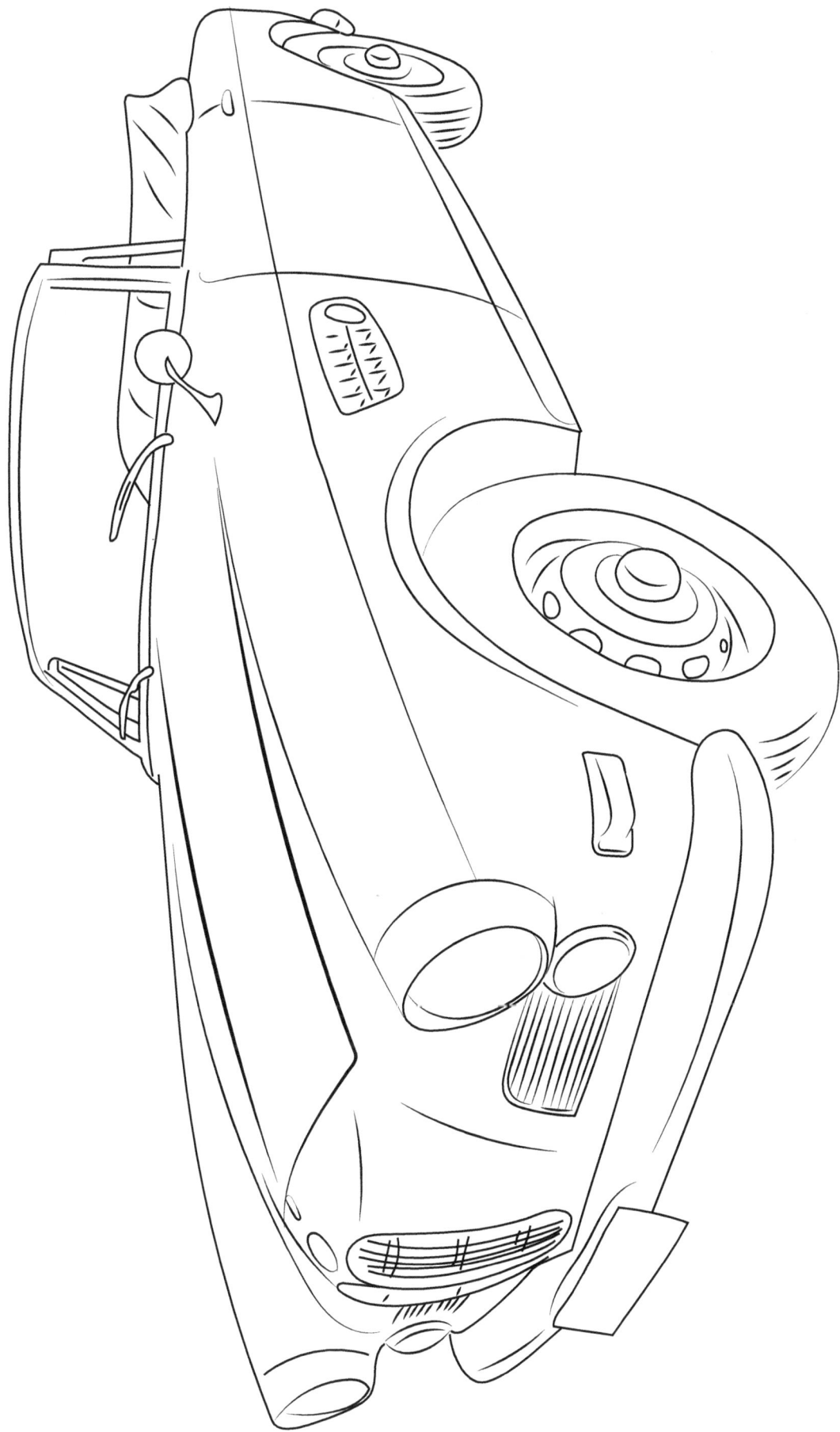

1956 BMW 503

1956 Chrysler Imperial

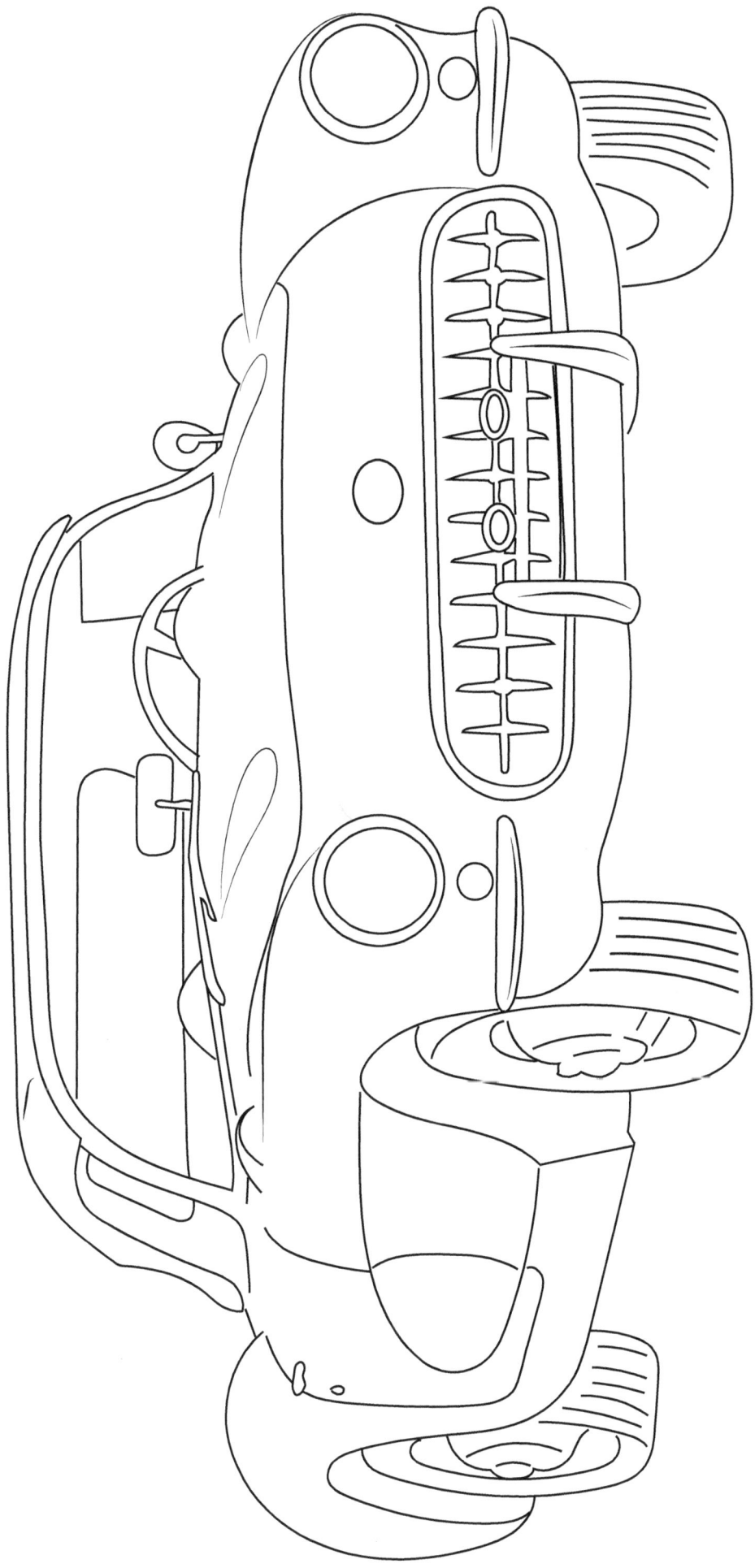

1957 Chevy Corvette

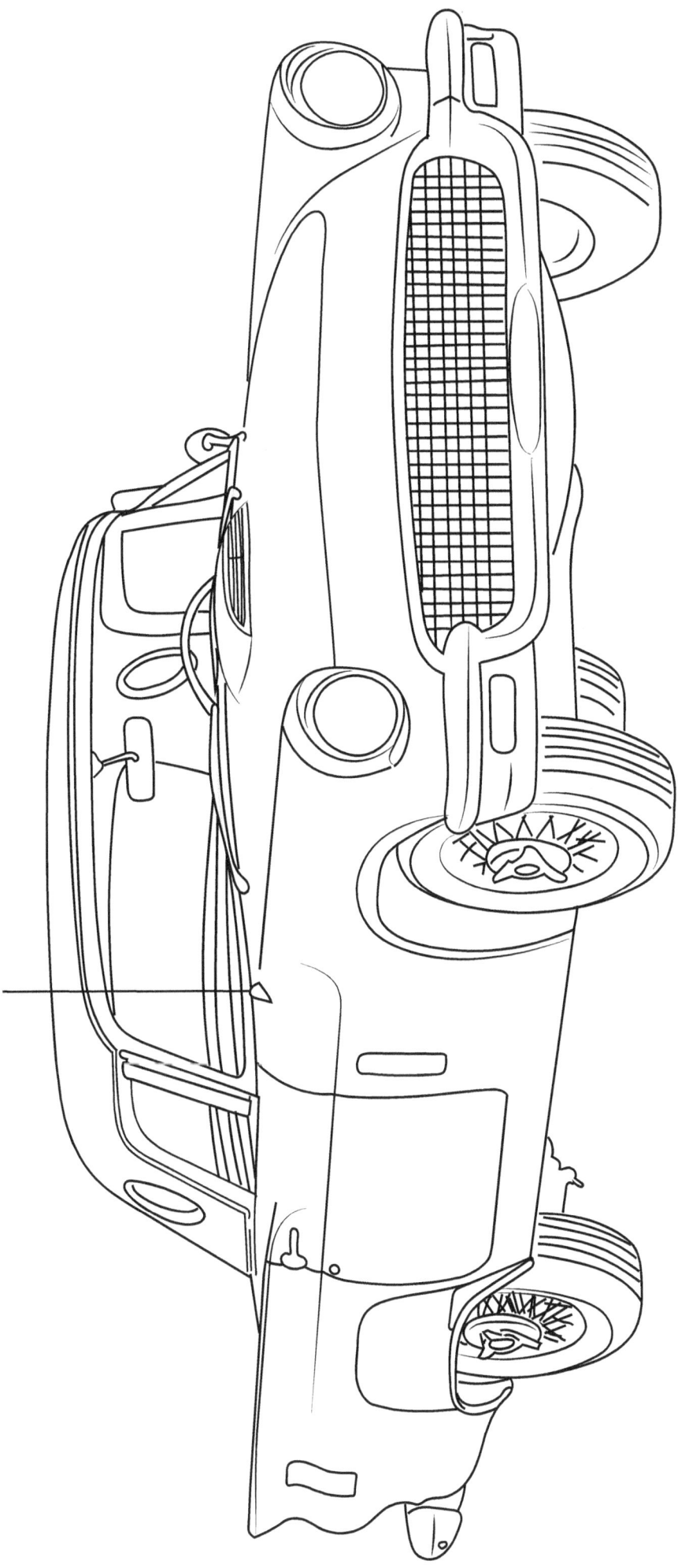

1957 Ford Thunderbird

1958 Buick Limited

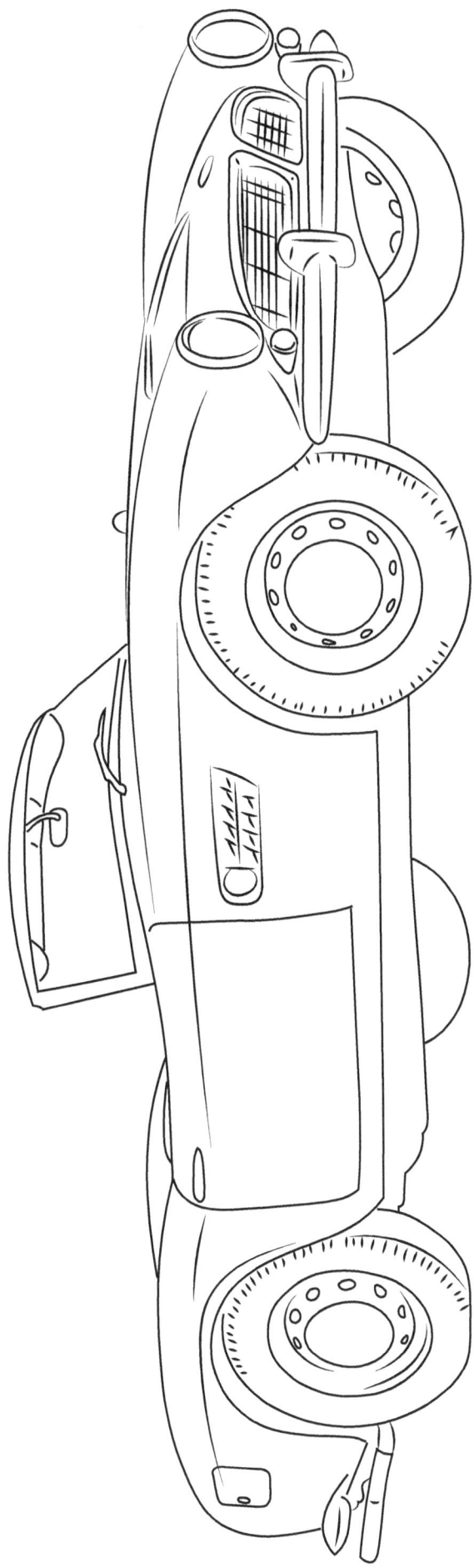

1958 BMW 507 Roadster

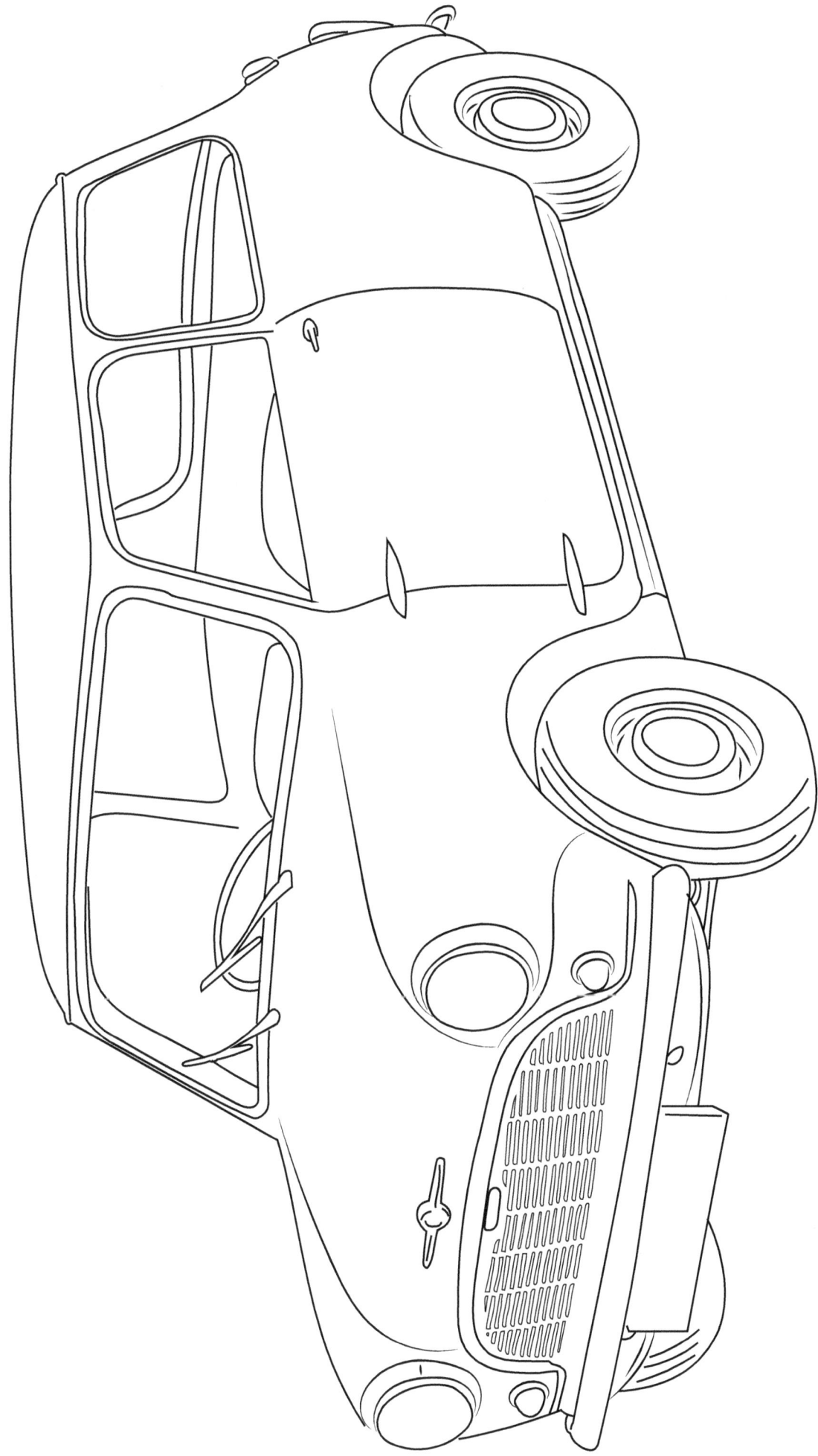

1959 Austin Mini

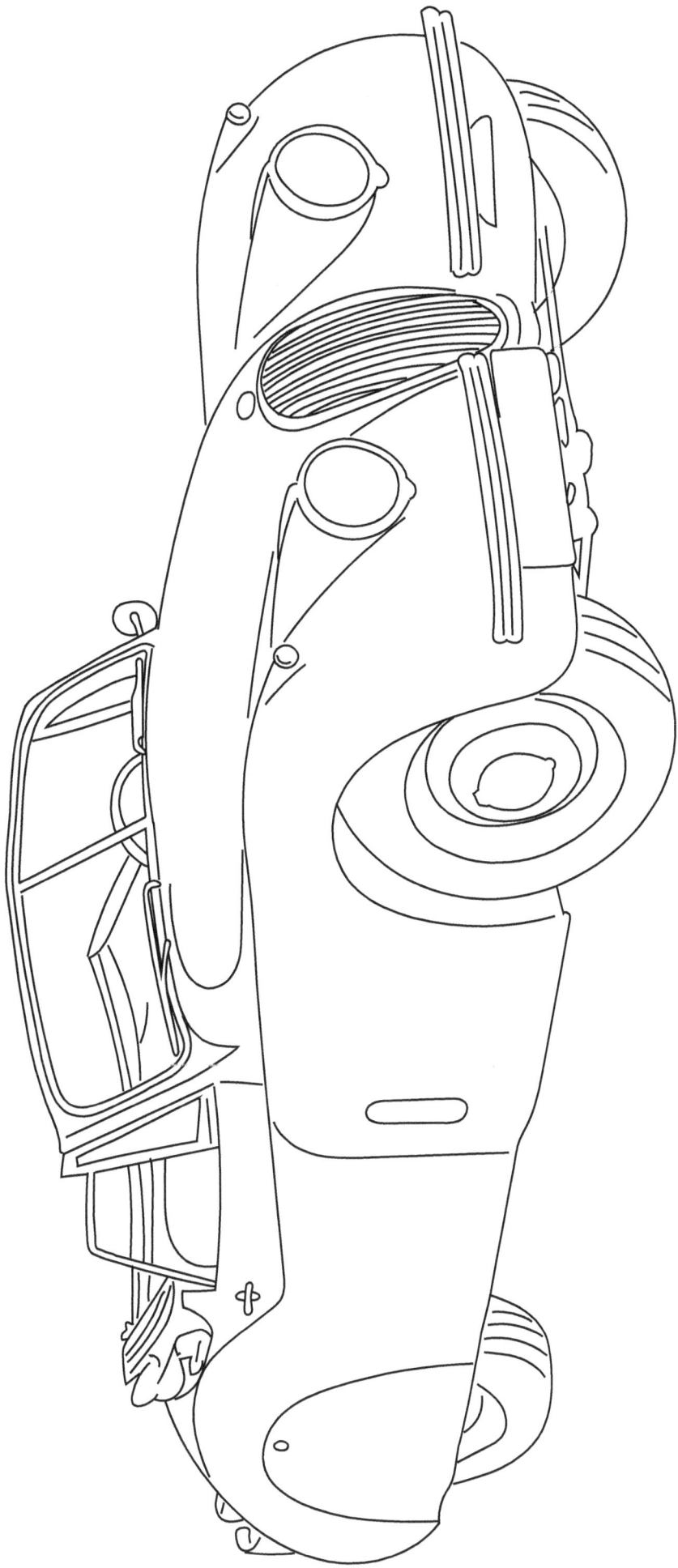

1953 Jaguar XK

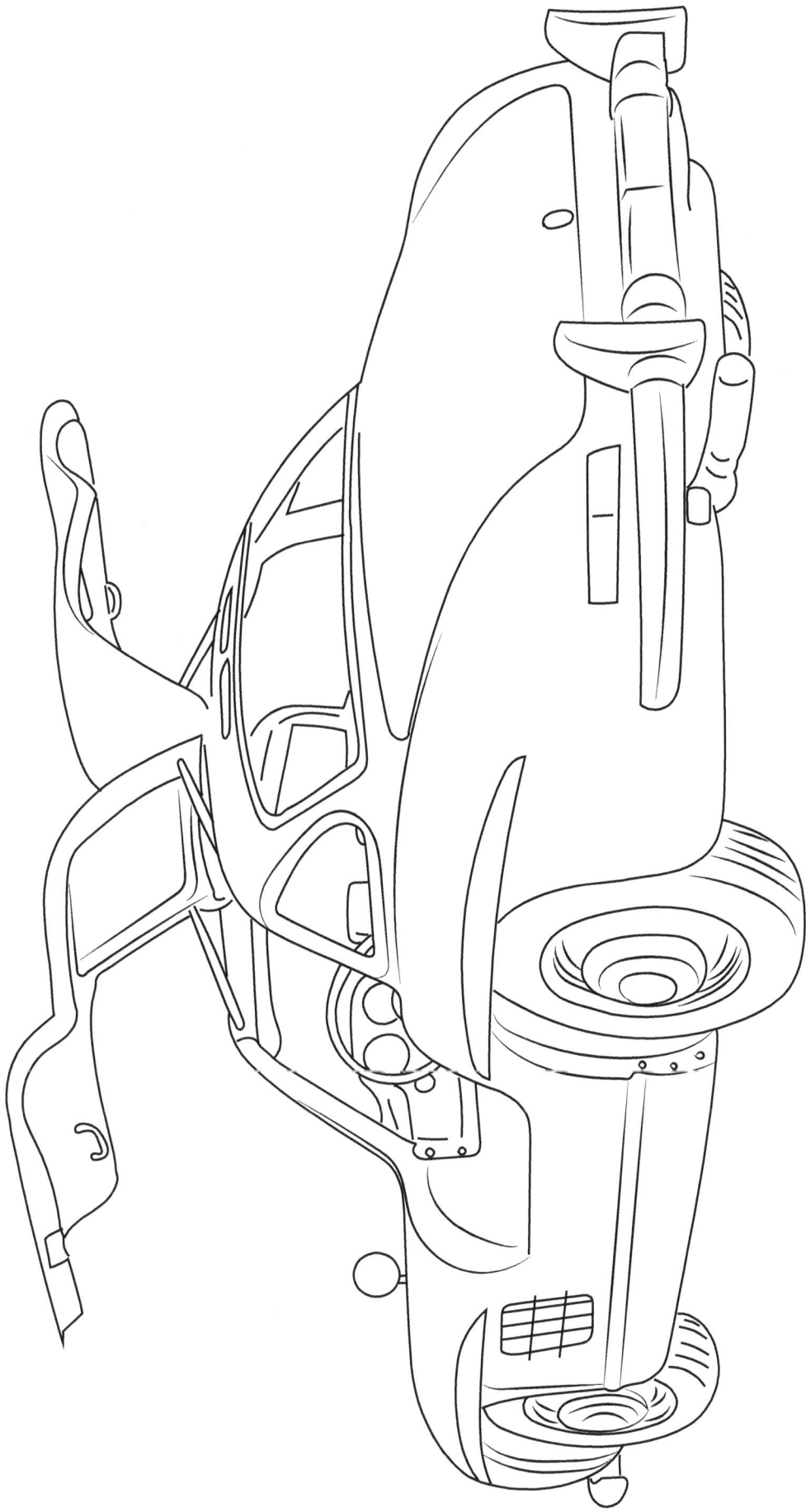

1955 Mercedes Benz 300SL Gullwing Coupe

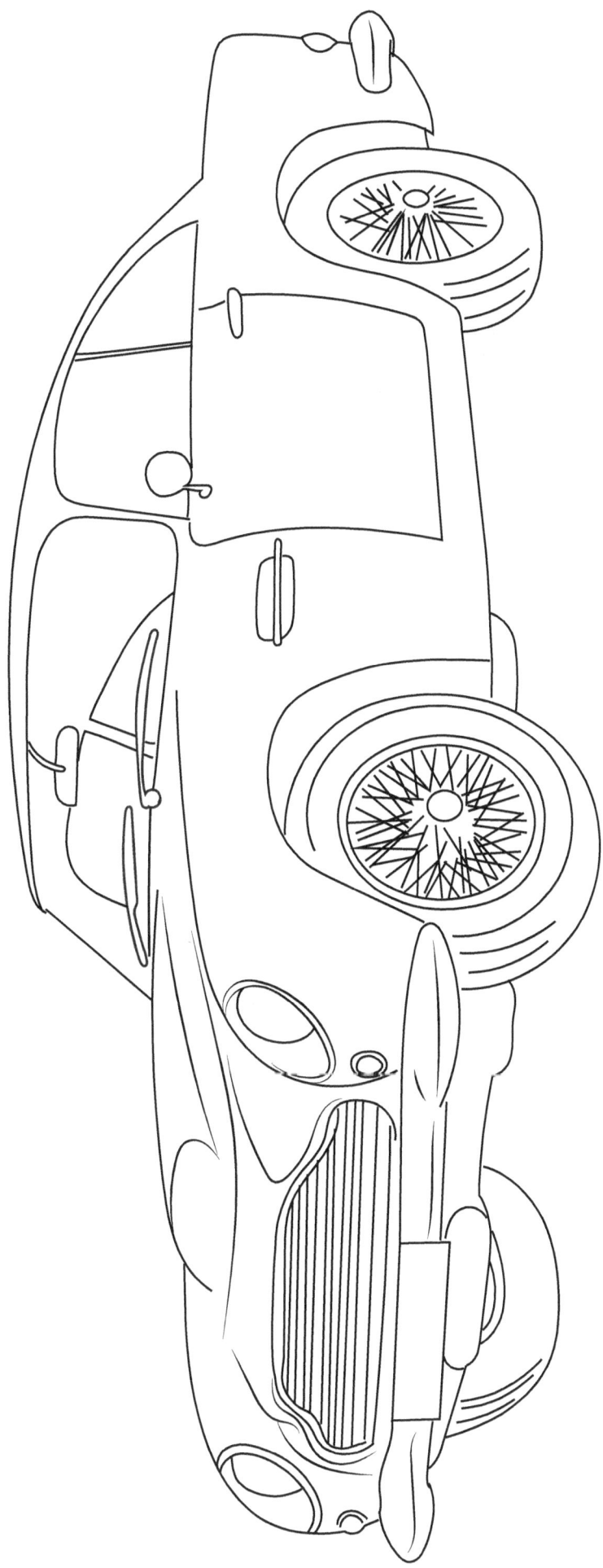

1959 Aston Martin DB4 GT Zagato

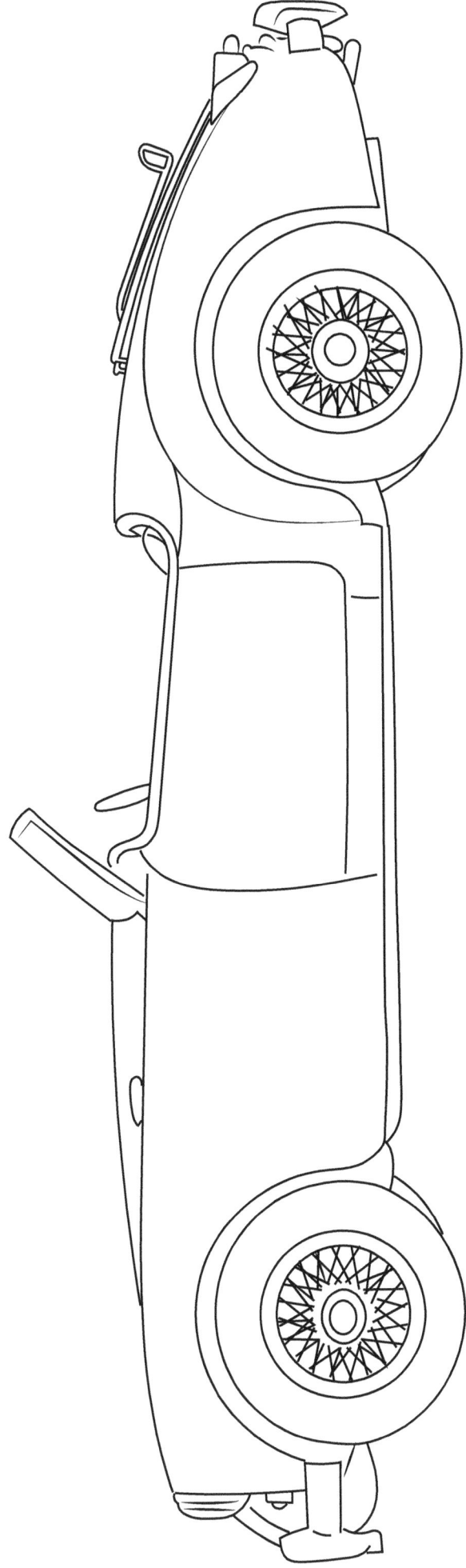

1959 MG MGS 1500

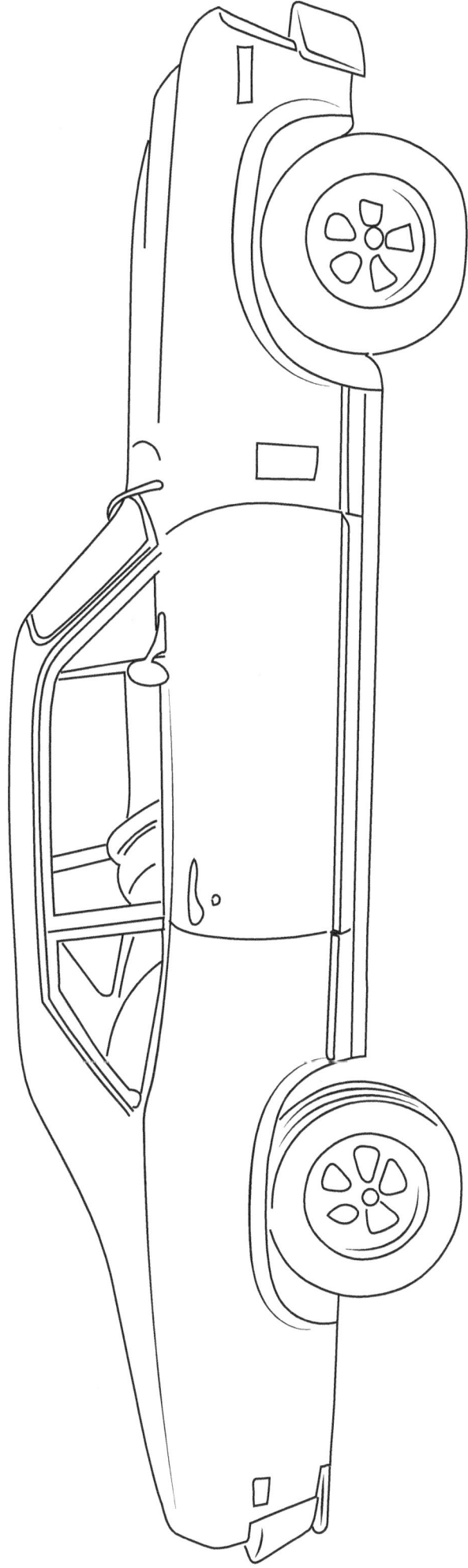

1968 Chevy Nova

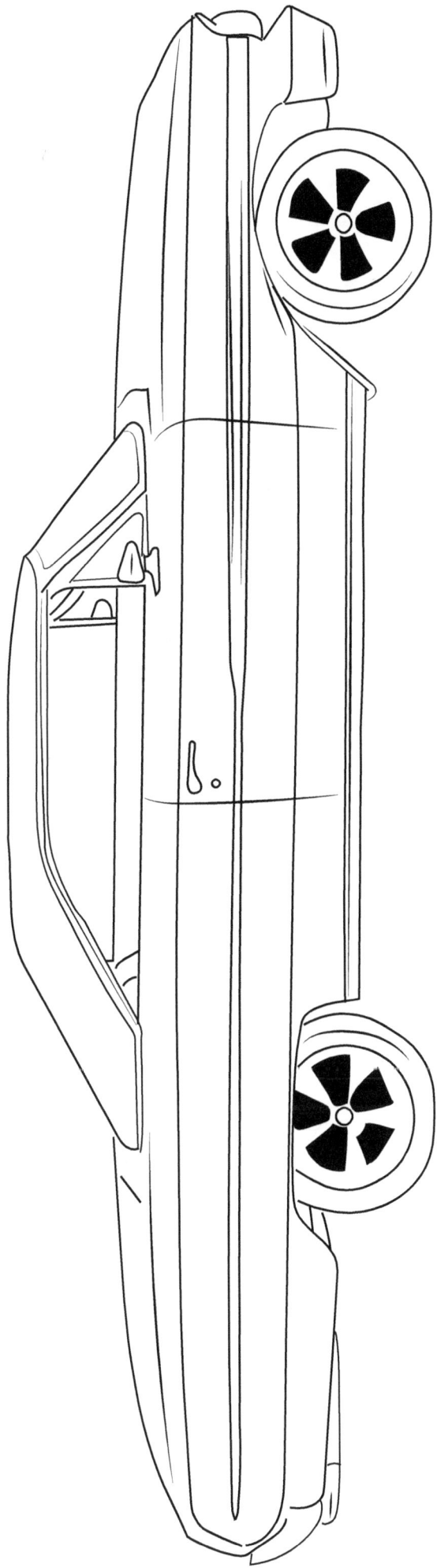

1964 Ford Galaxie

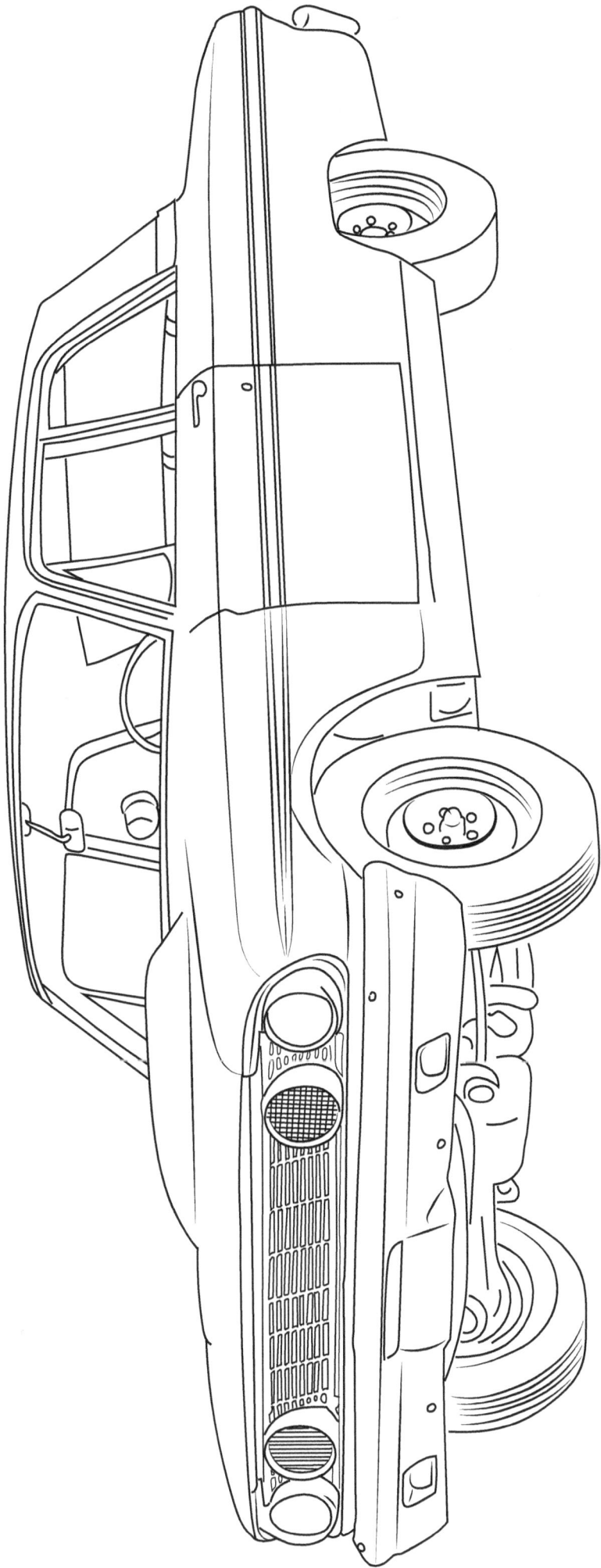

1964 Ford Thunderbolt

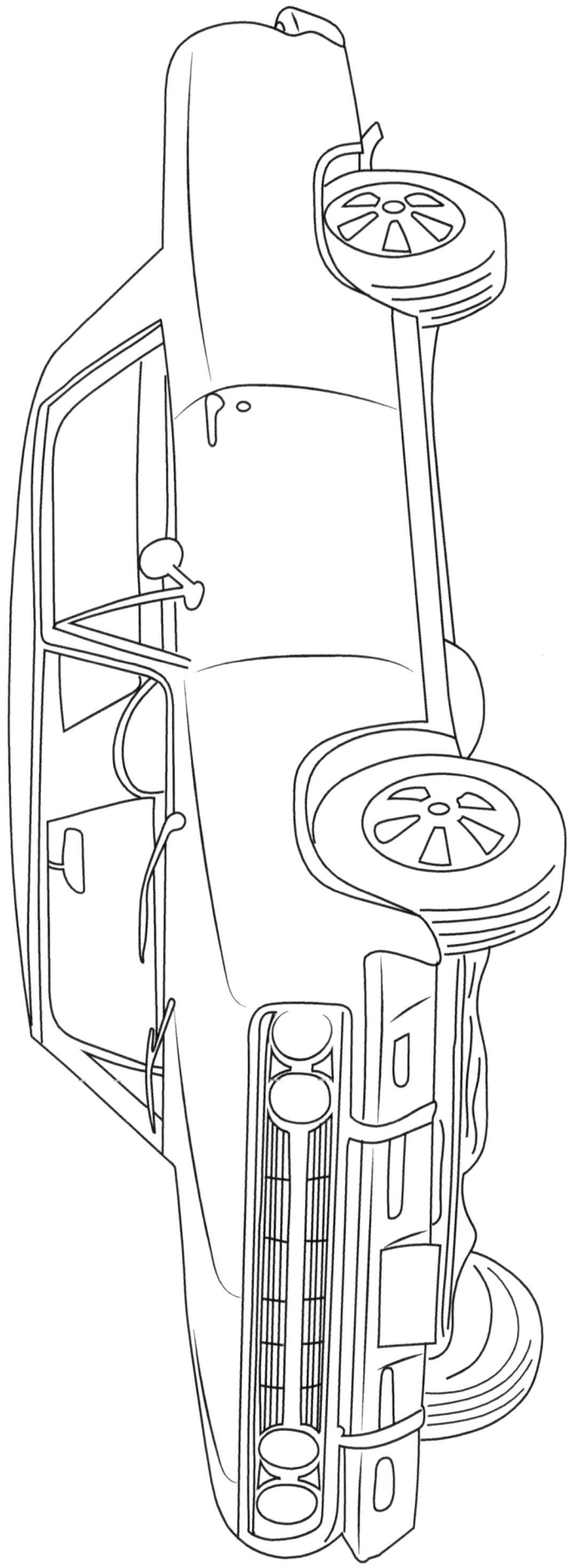

1965 Chevy Chevelle SS

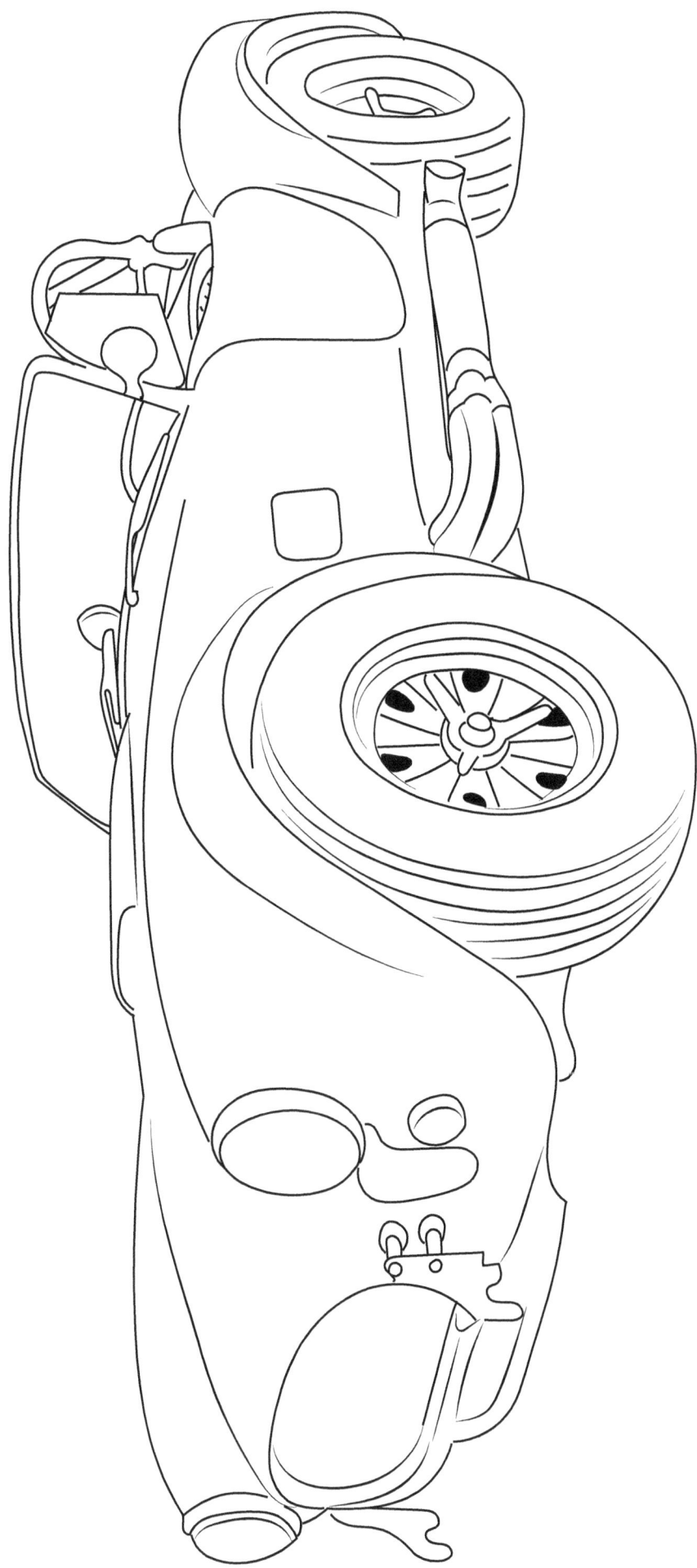

1965 Ford Shelby Cobra

1965 Pontiac GTO

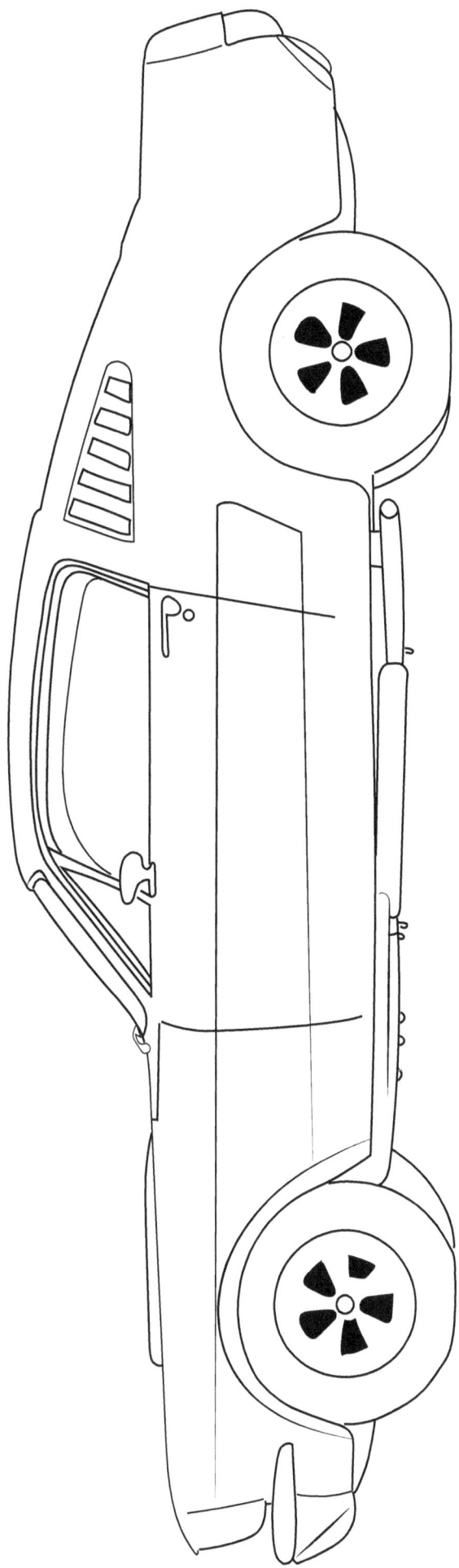

1965 Shelby Mustang 350

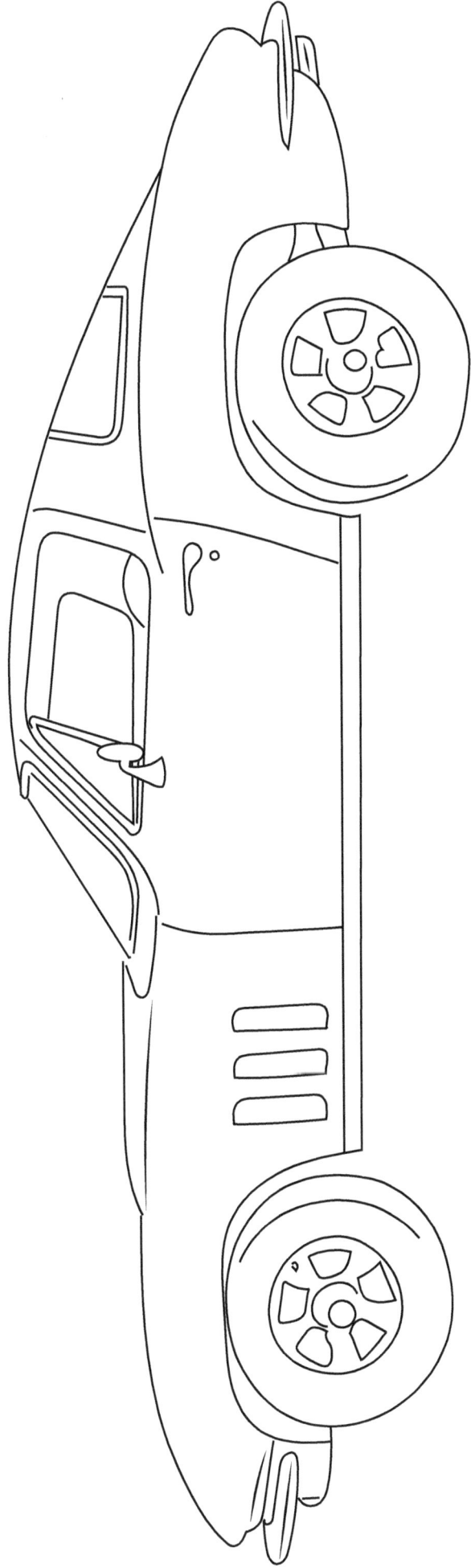

1966 Corvette

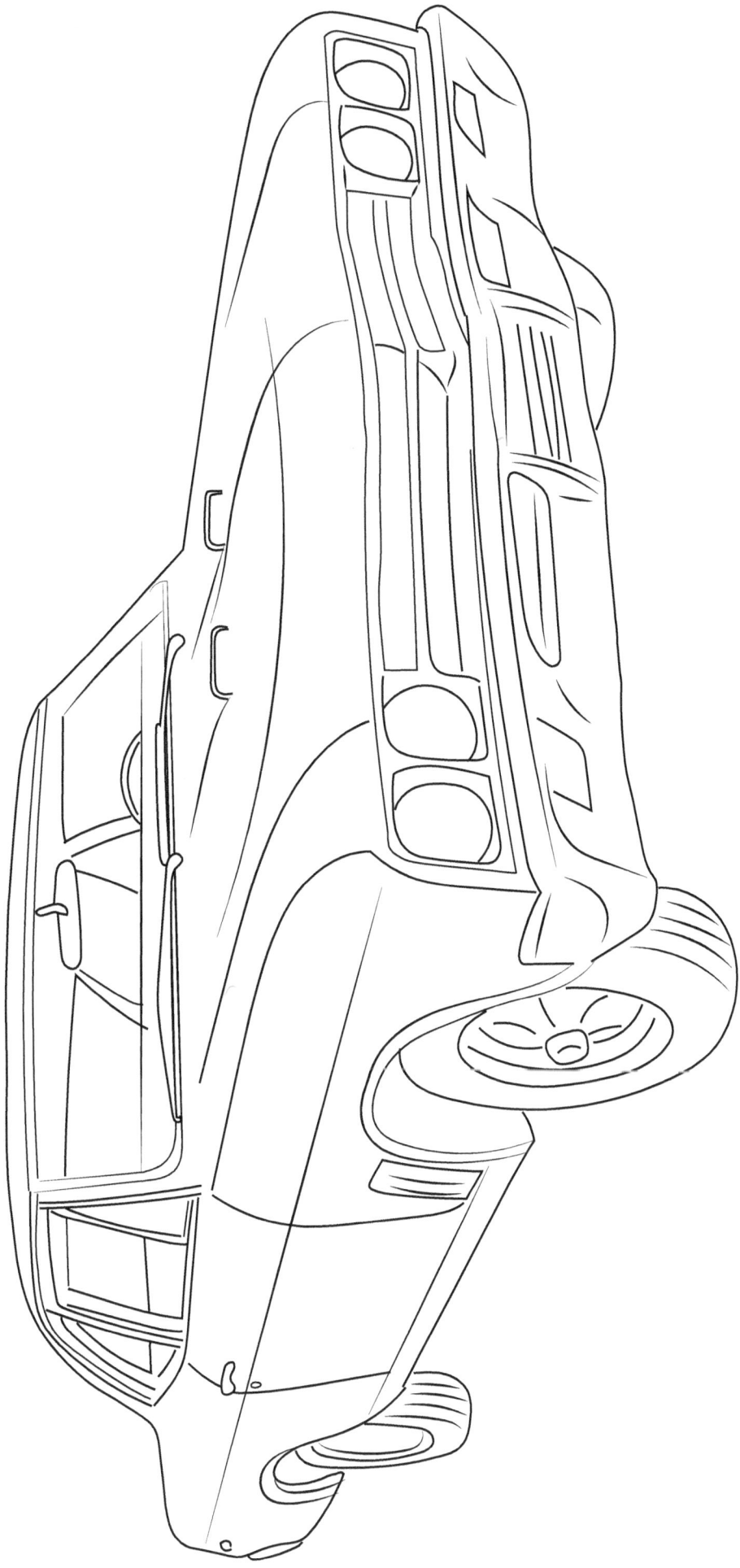

1967 Buick Gransport

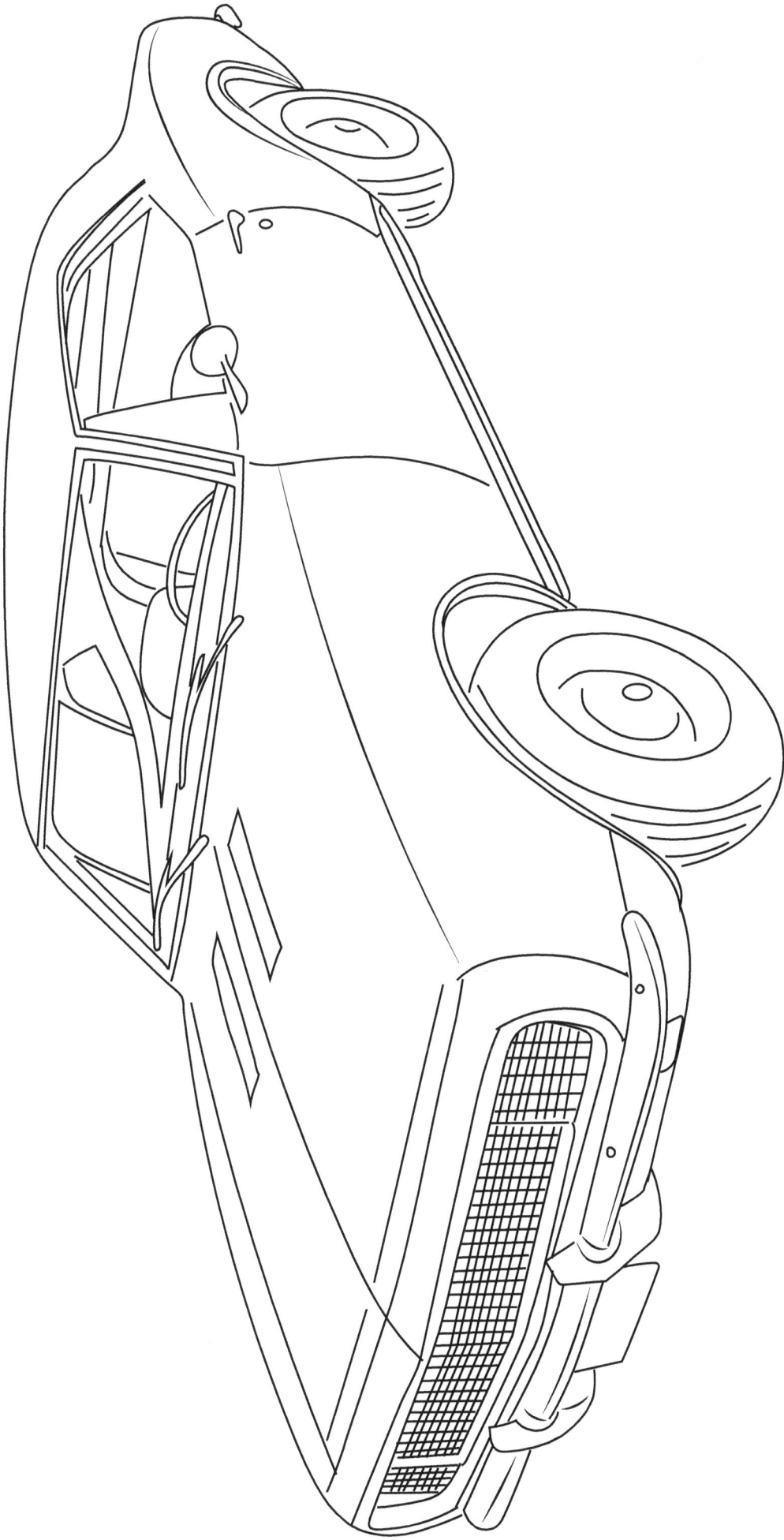

1967 Camaro SS

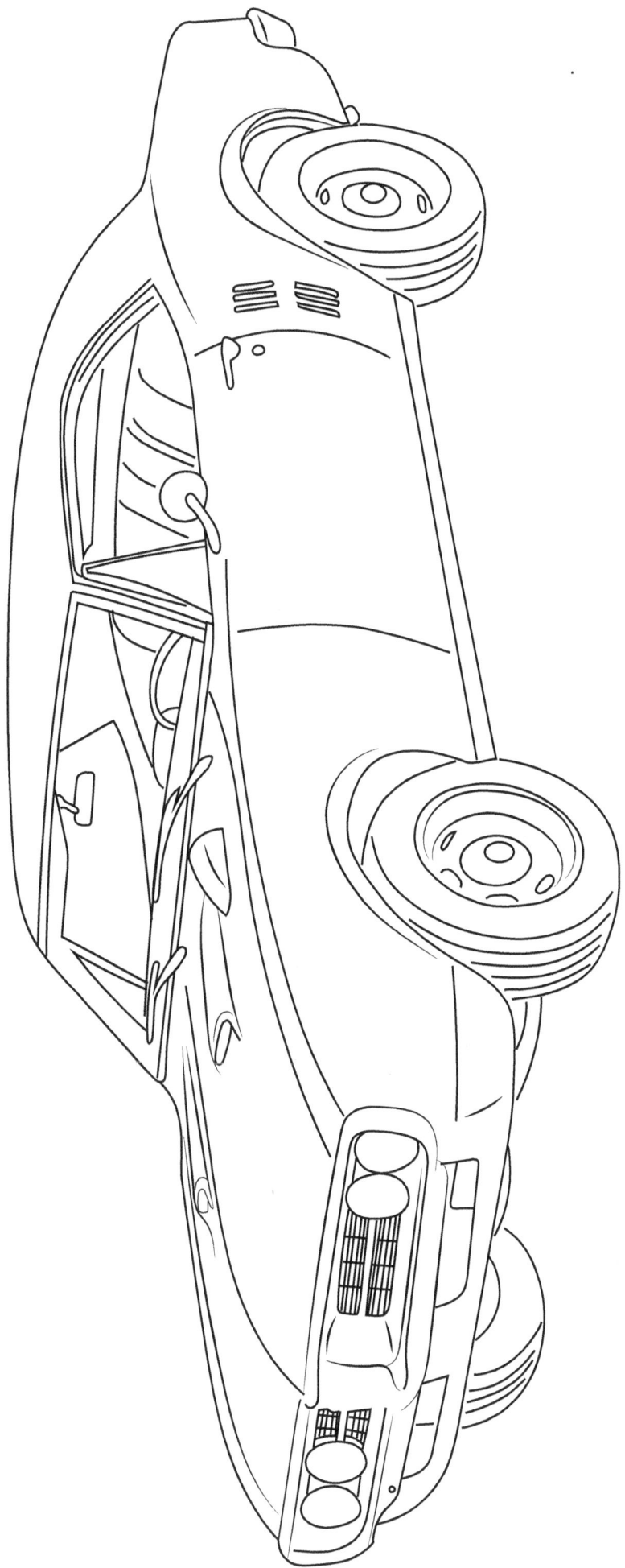

1967 Firebird

1967 Chevy Impala

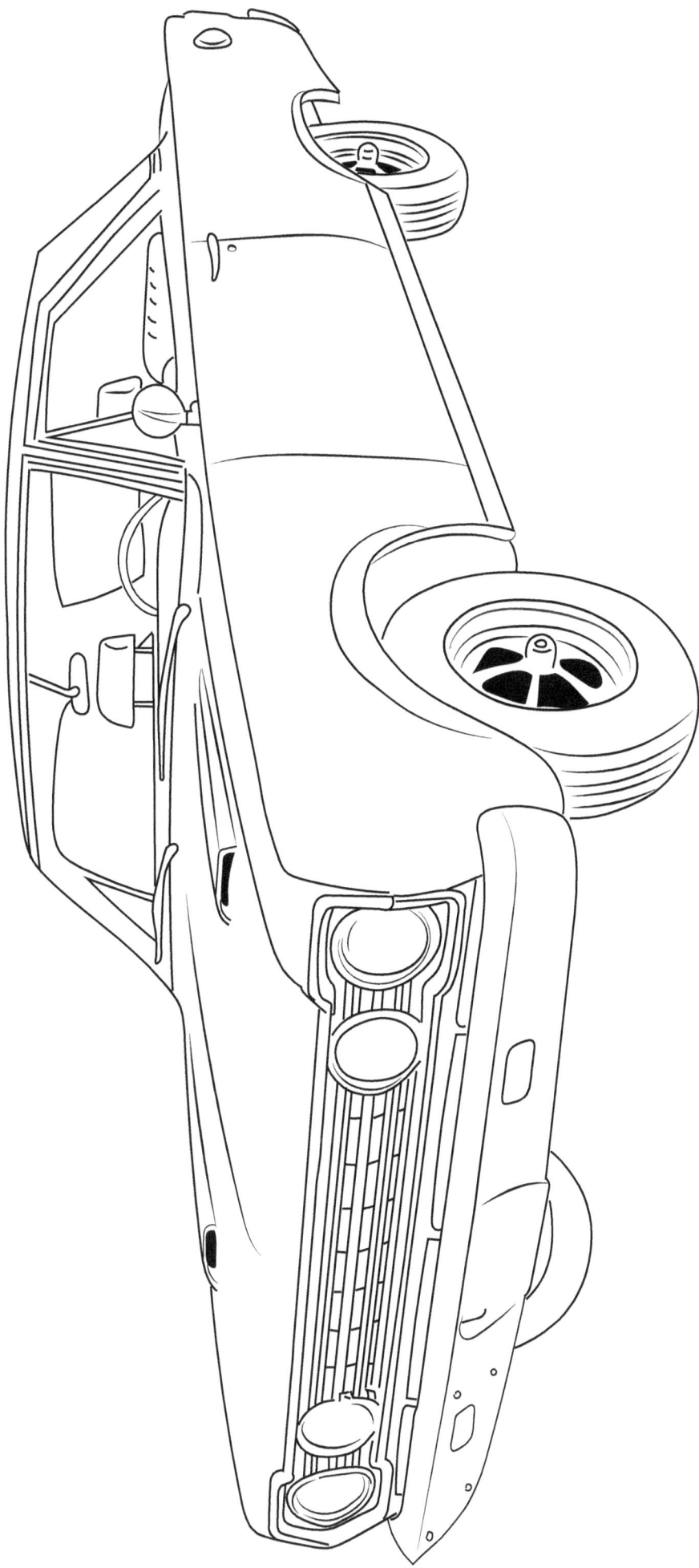

1967 Plymouth GTX

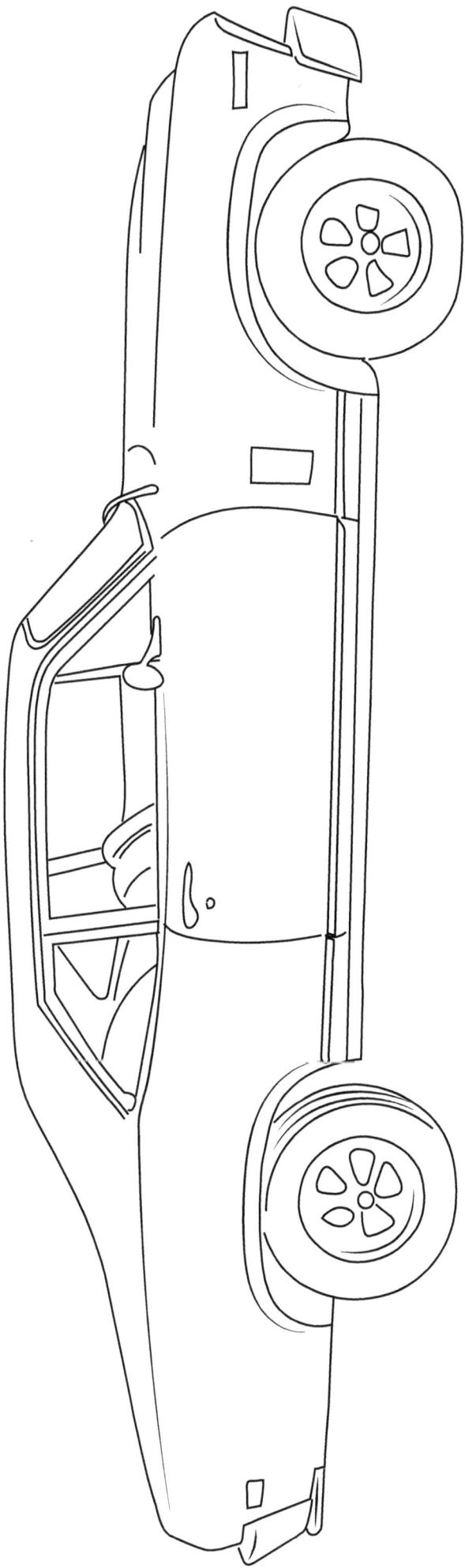

1968 Chevy Nova

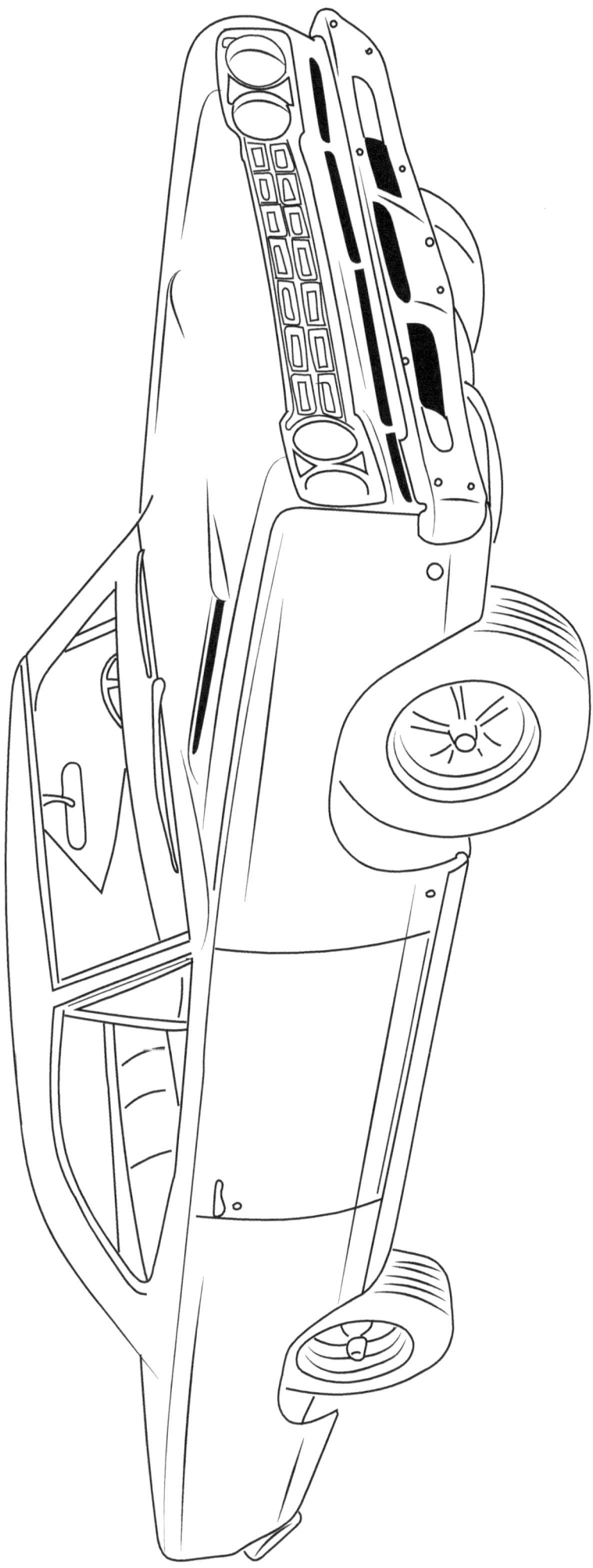

1968 Plymouth Roadrunner

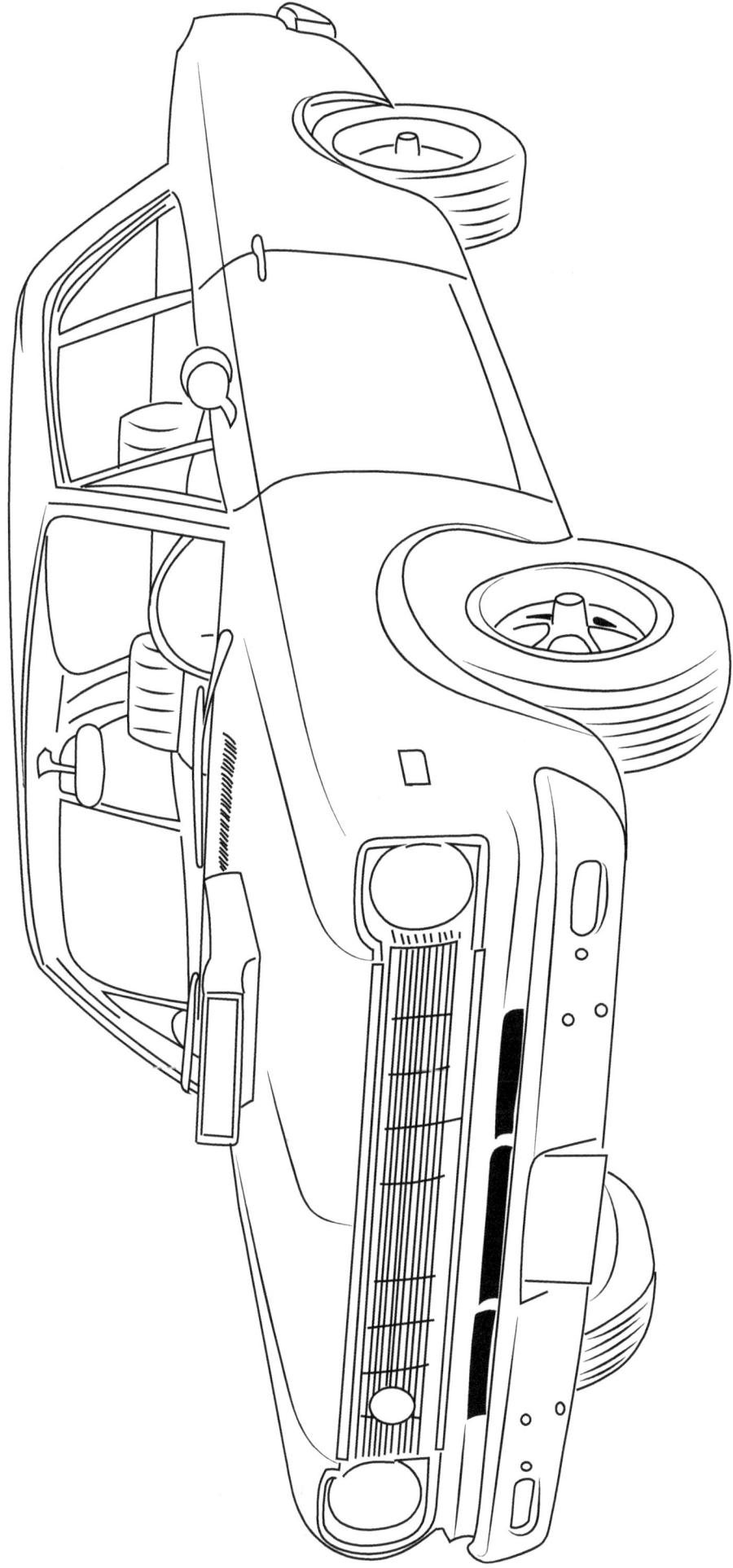

1969 AMC Scrambler

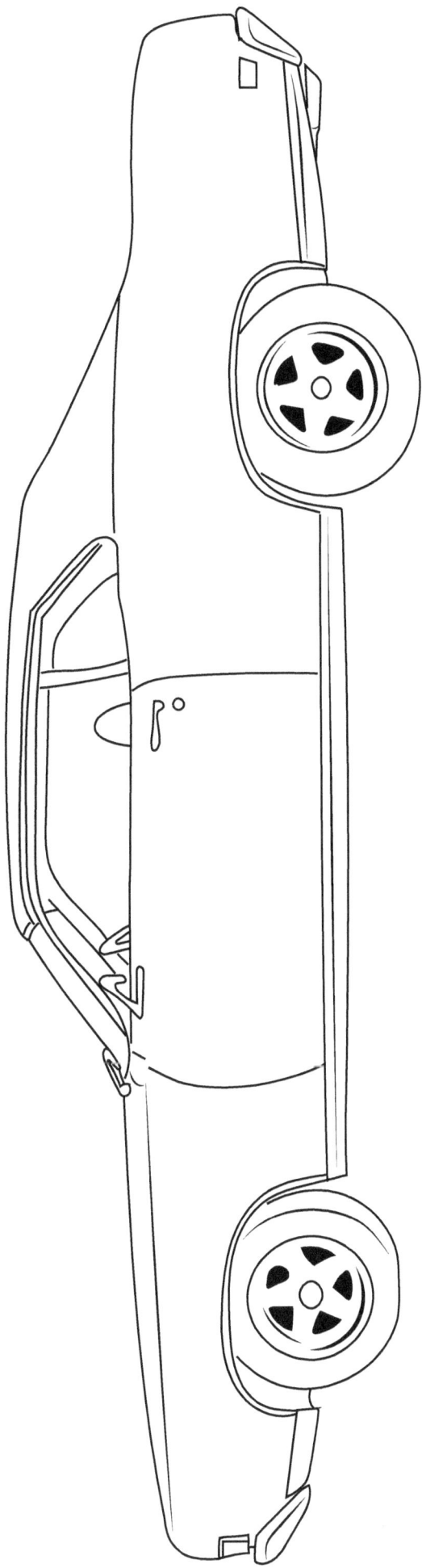

1969 Ford Torino

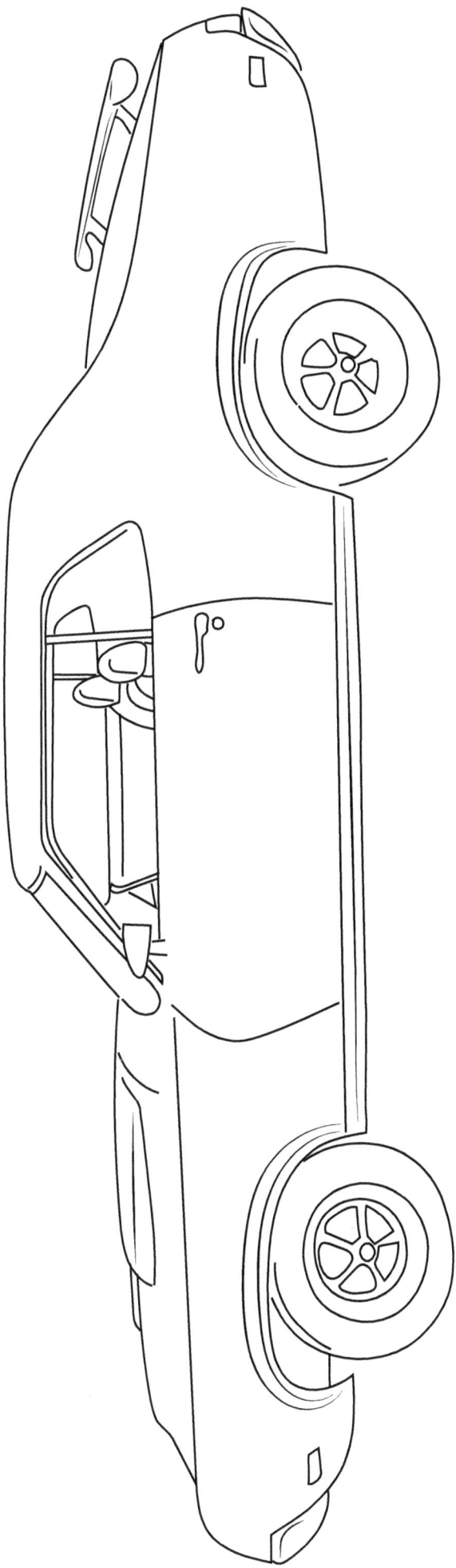

1969 Mercury Cougar

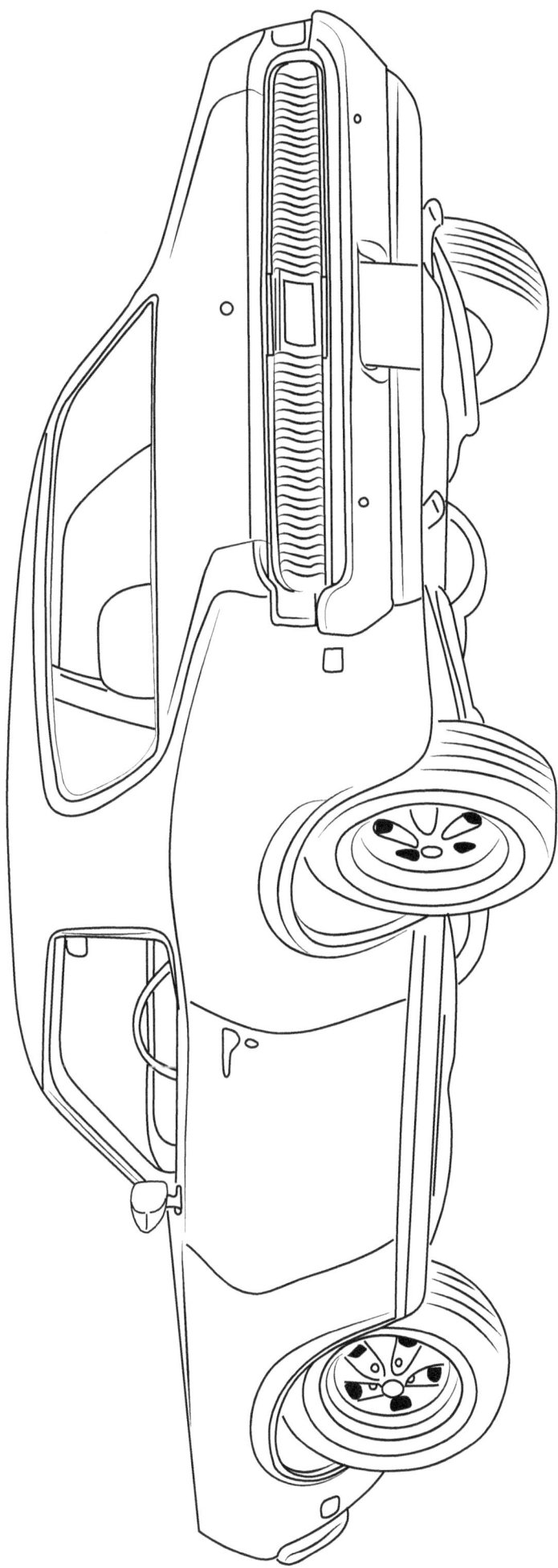

1969 Mercury Cougar

1964 Pontiac GTO

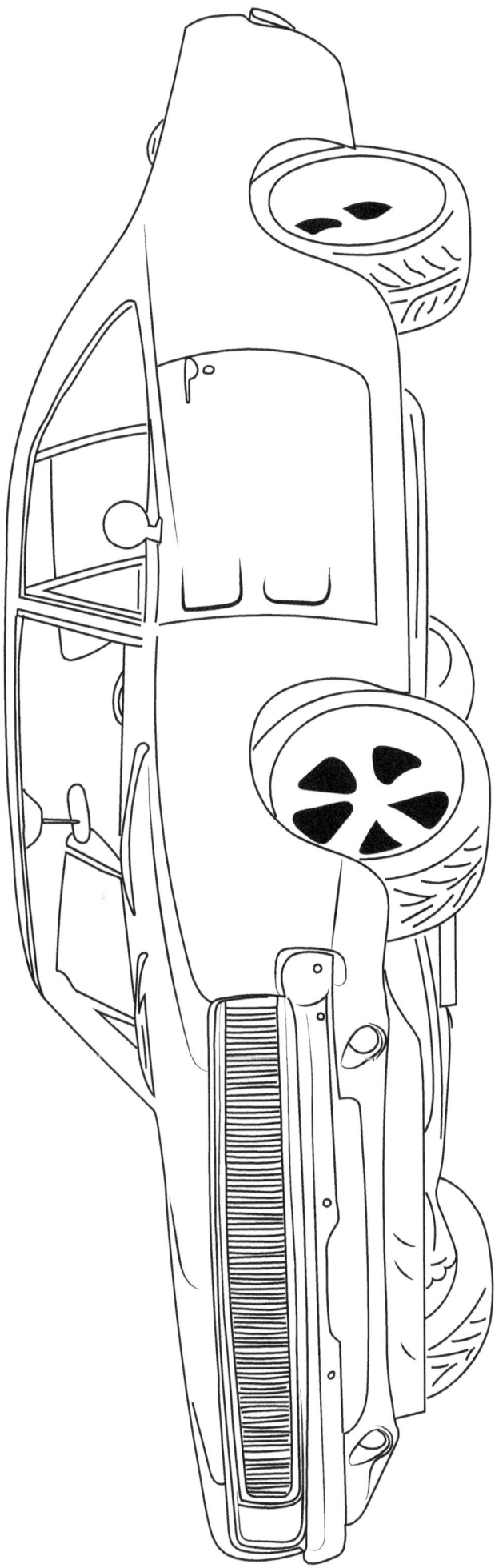

1968 Dodge Charger

1970 PLYMOUTH BARRACUDA

1970 AMC REBEL

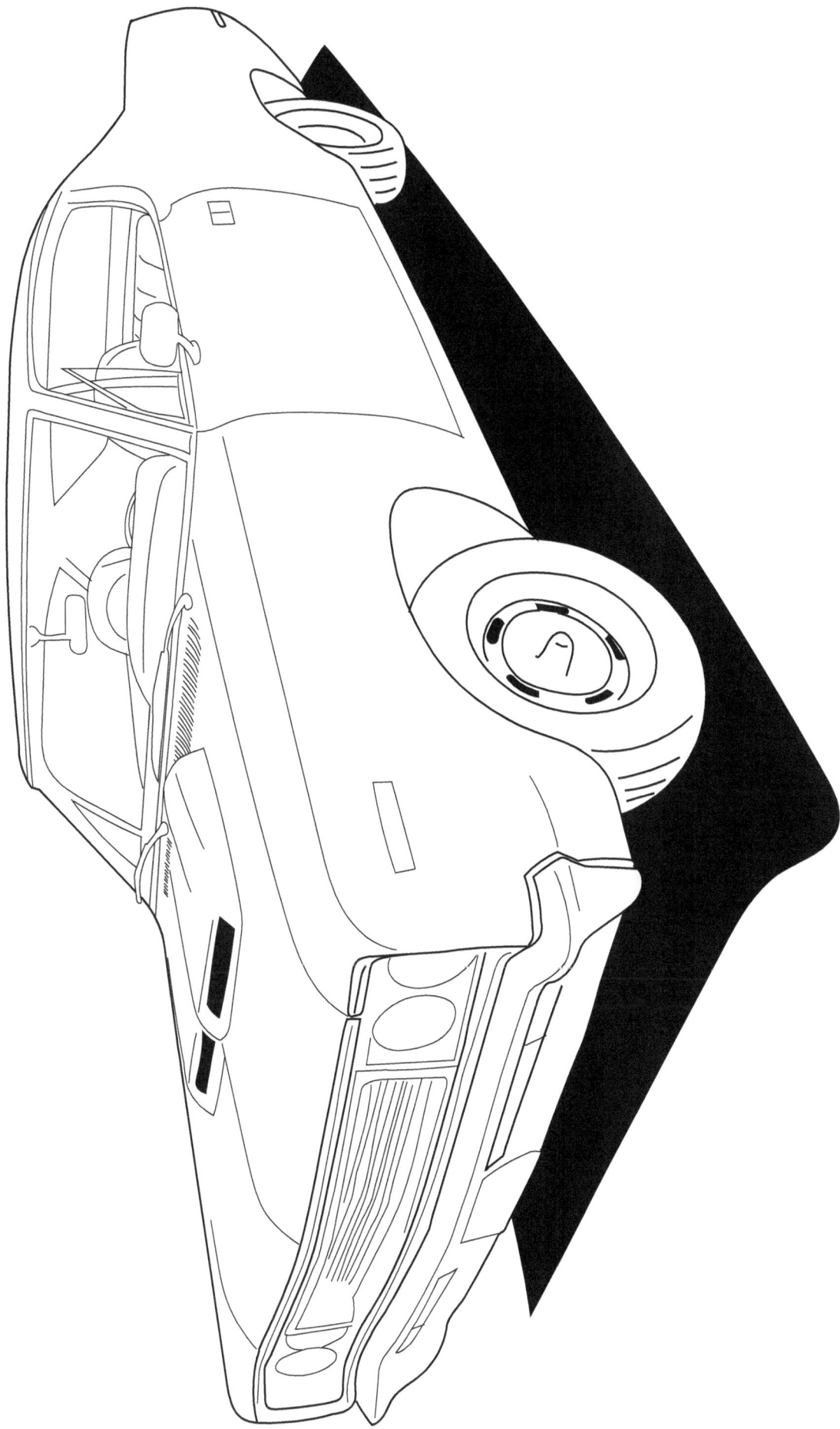

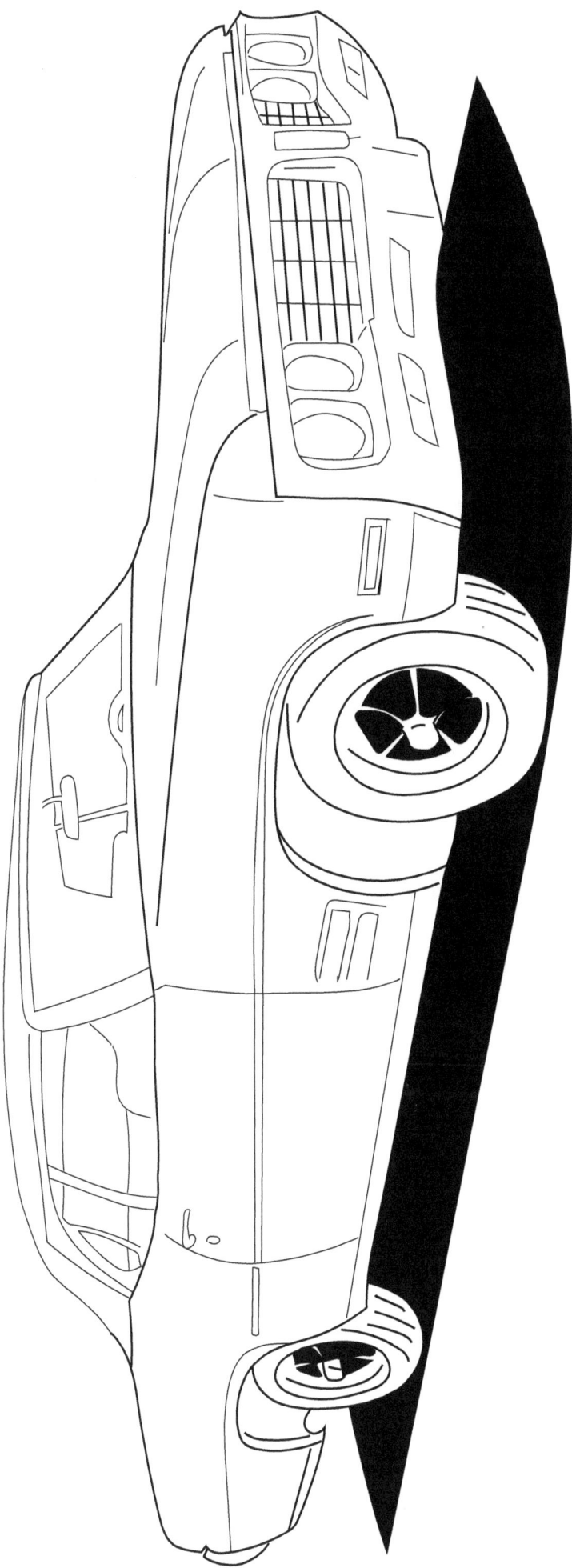

1970 BUICK WILDCAT

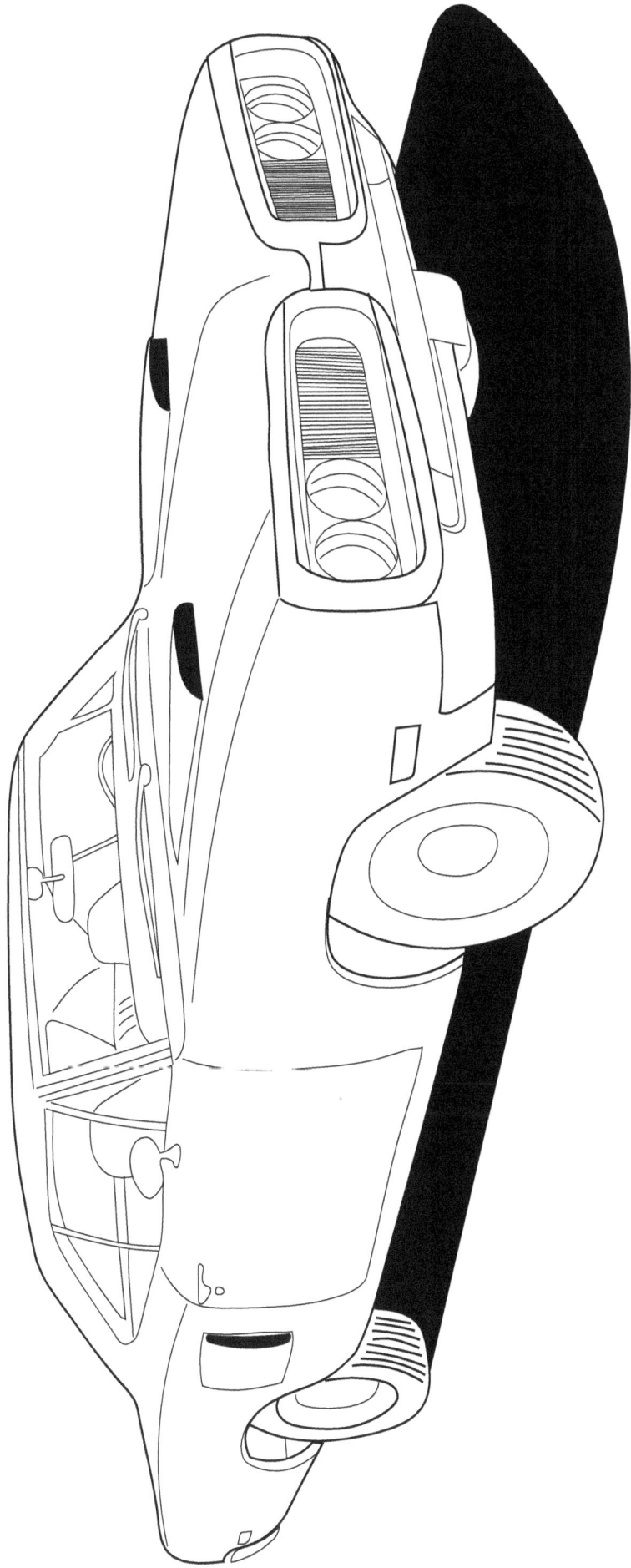

1970 DODGE CORONET

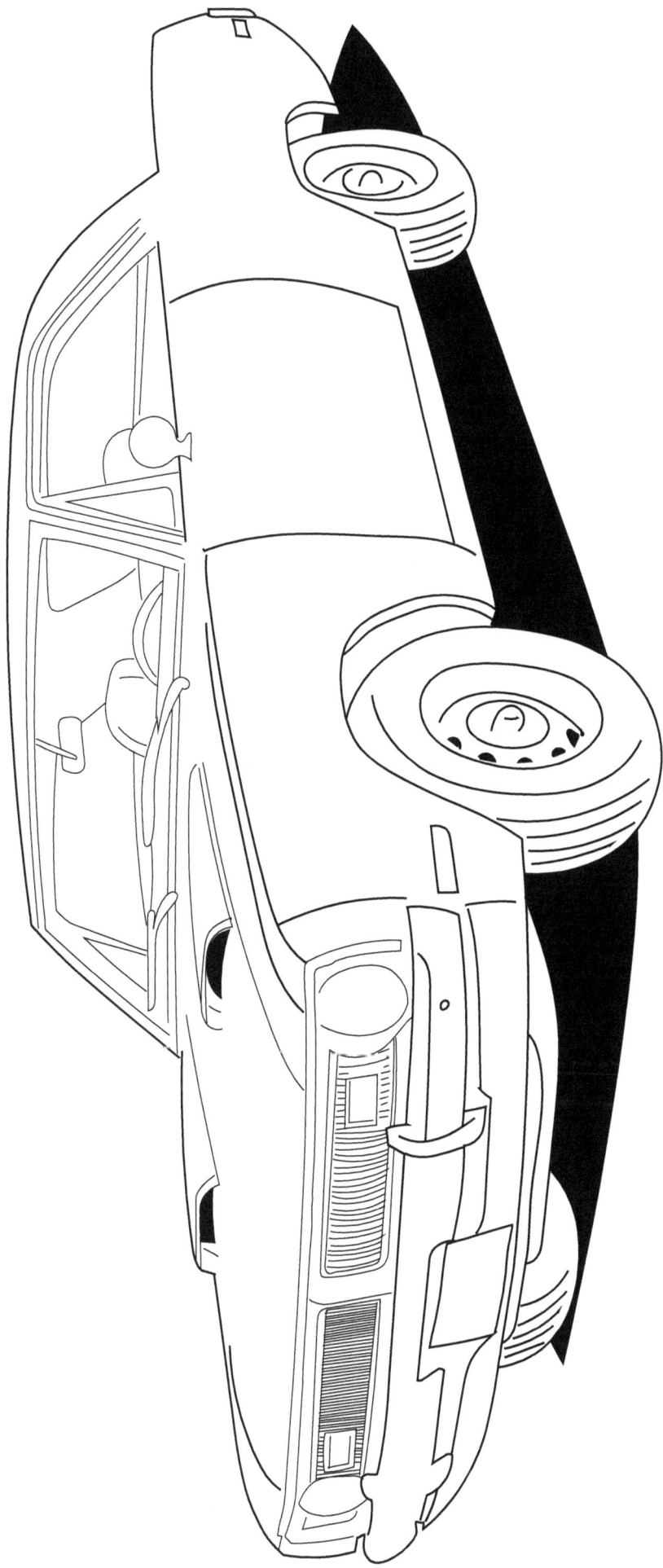

1970 DODGE DART

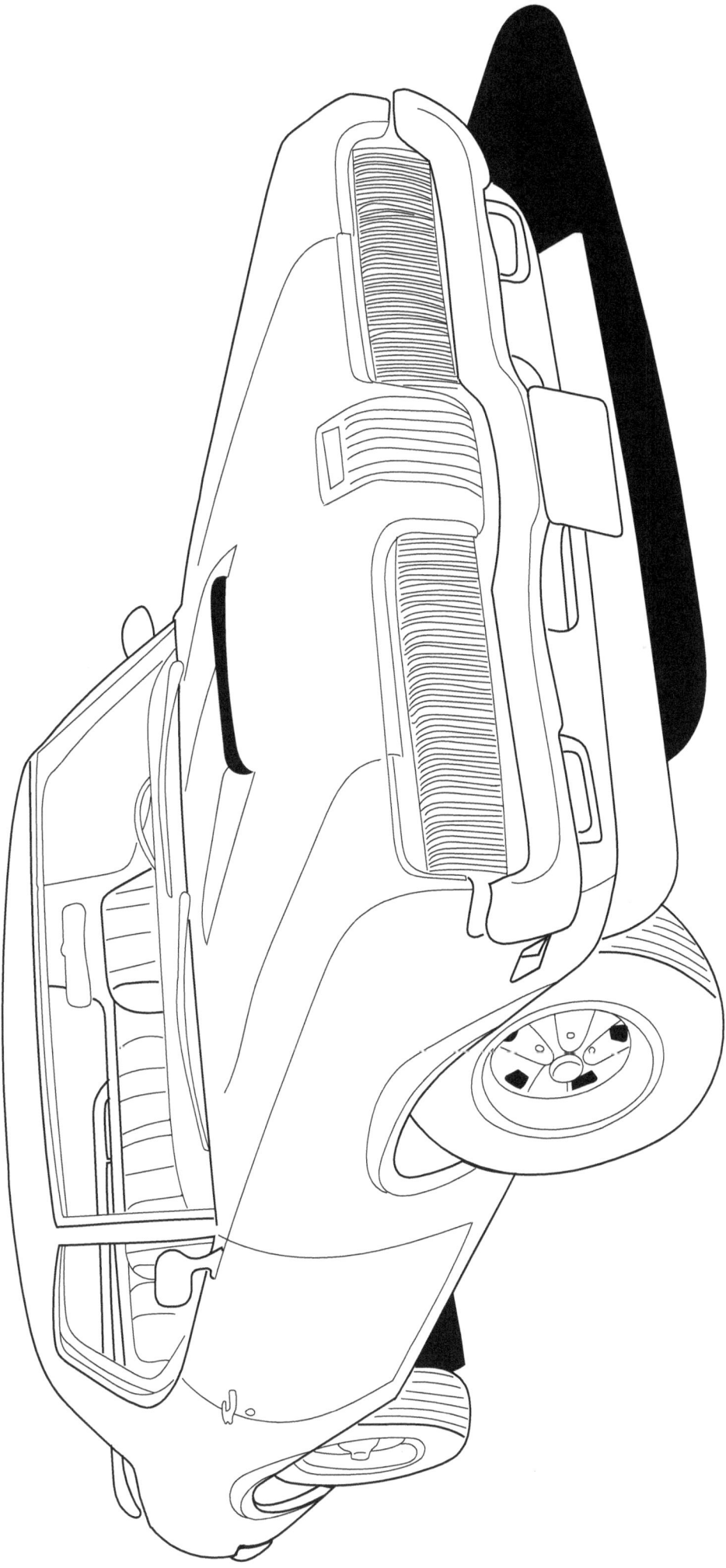

1970 MERCURY COUGAR

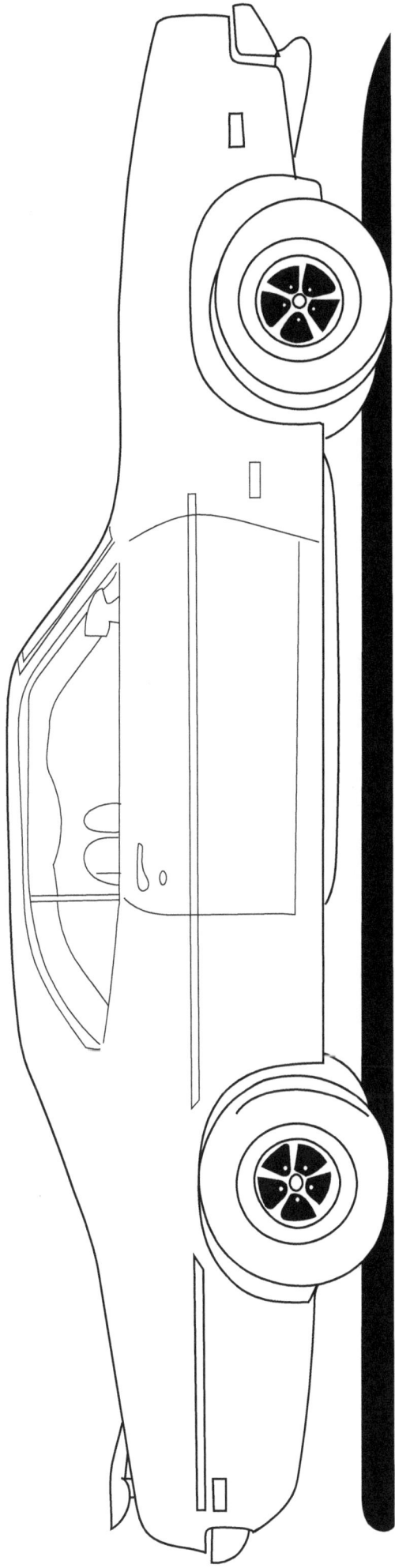

1970 MERCURY CYCLONE

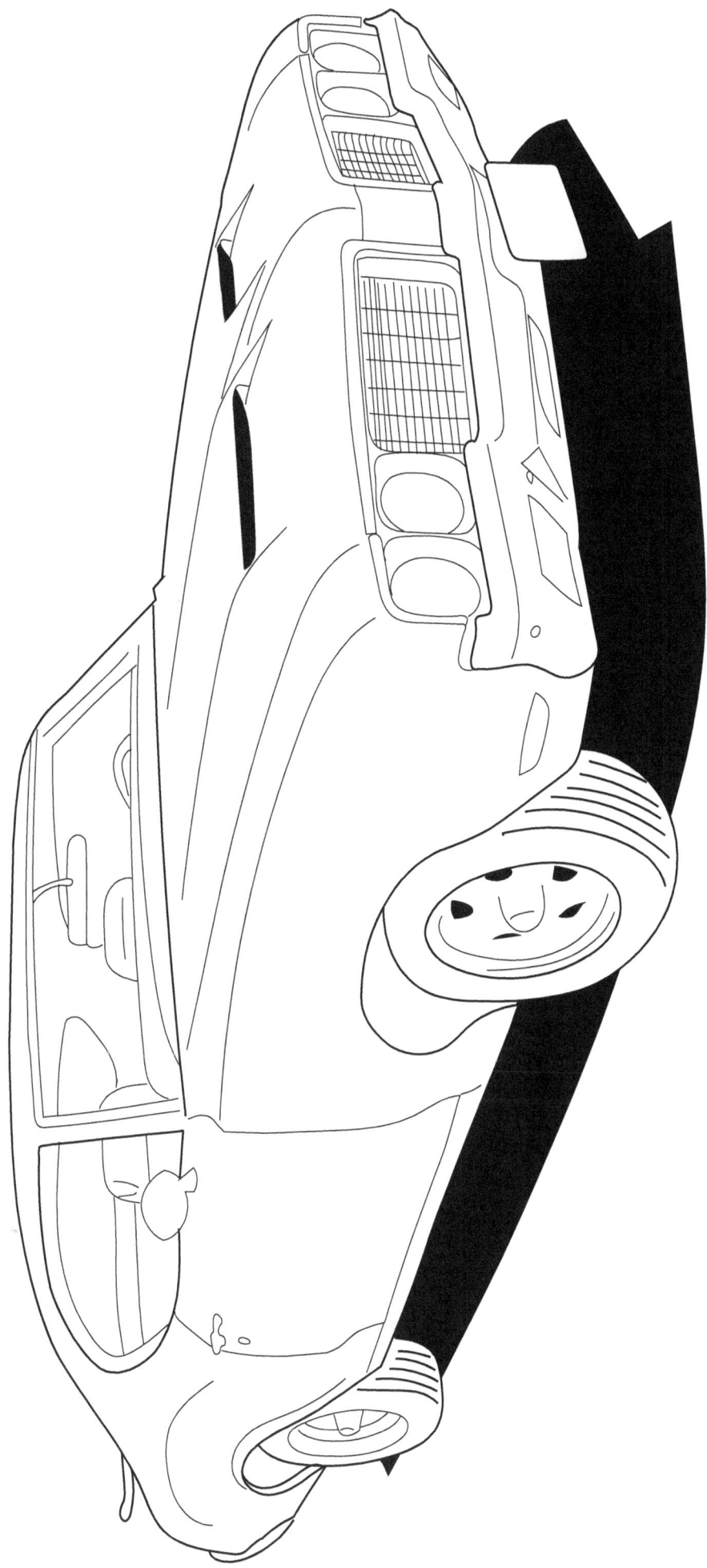

1970 OLDSMOBILE RALLYE 350

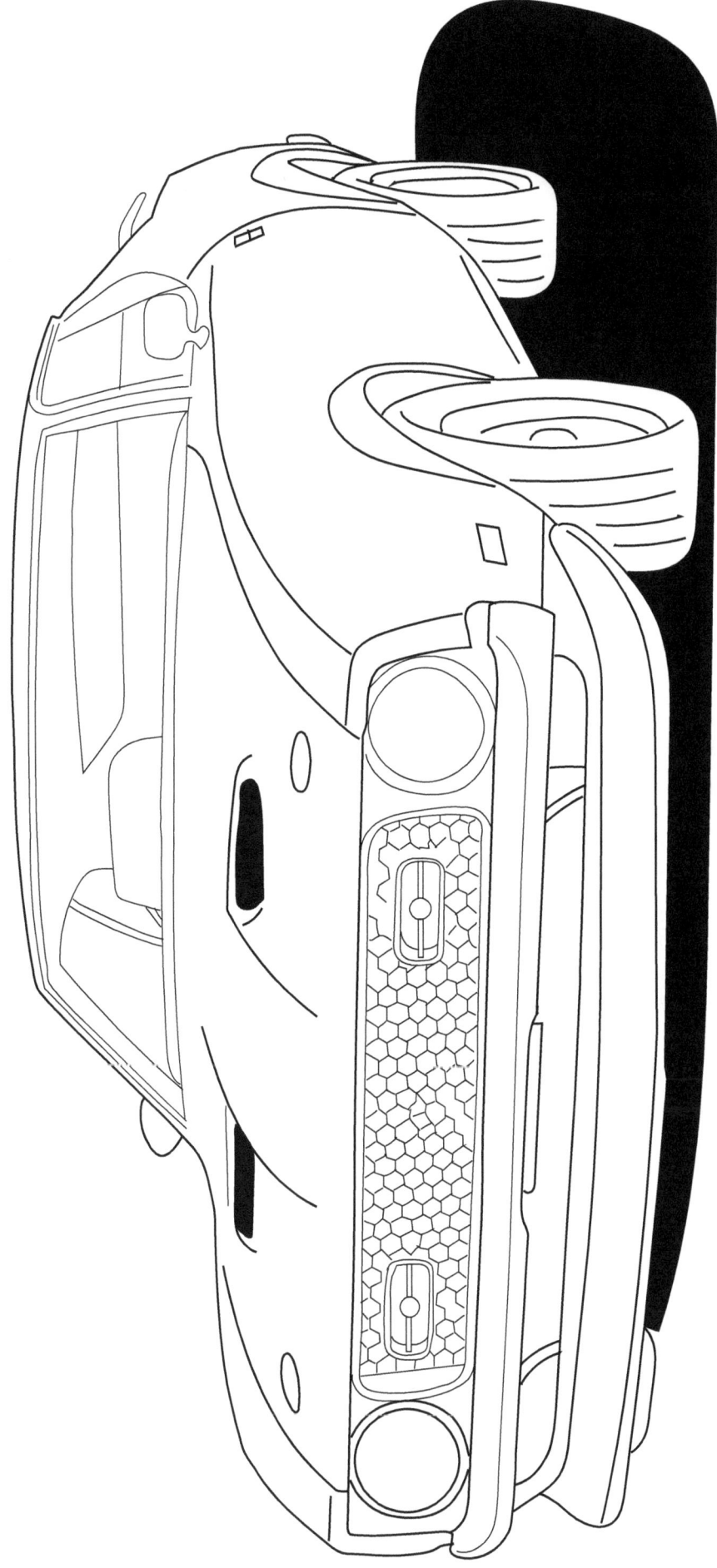

1970 SHLEBY MUSTANG GT 350

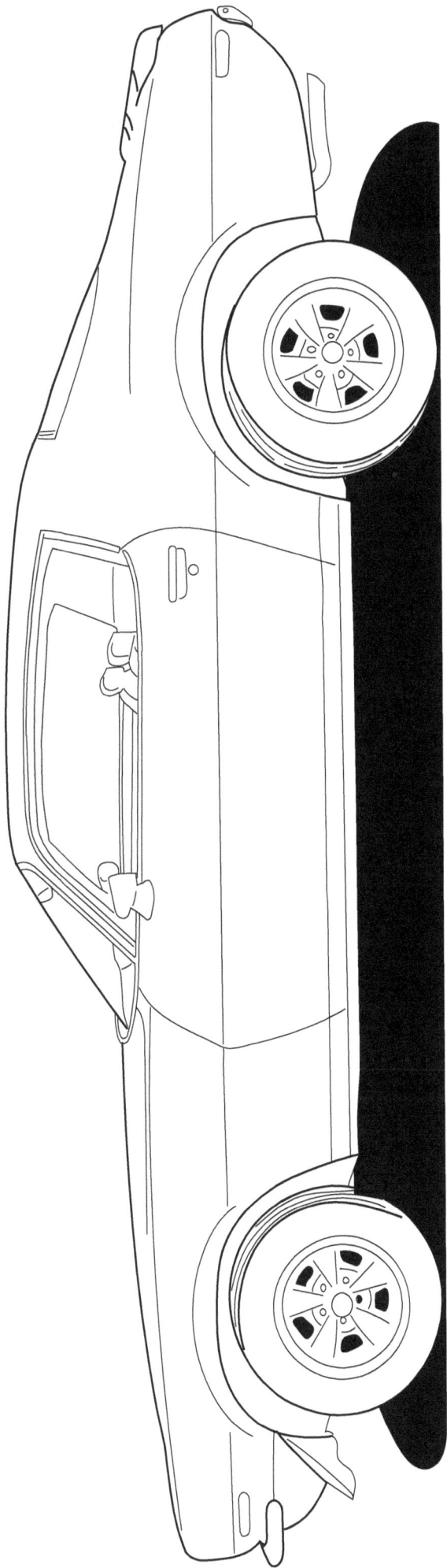

1970 CHEVY CAMARO Z28

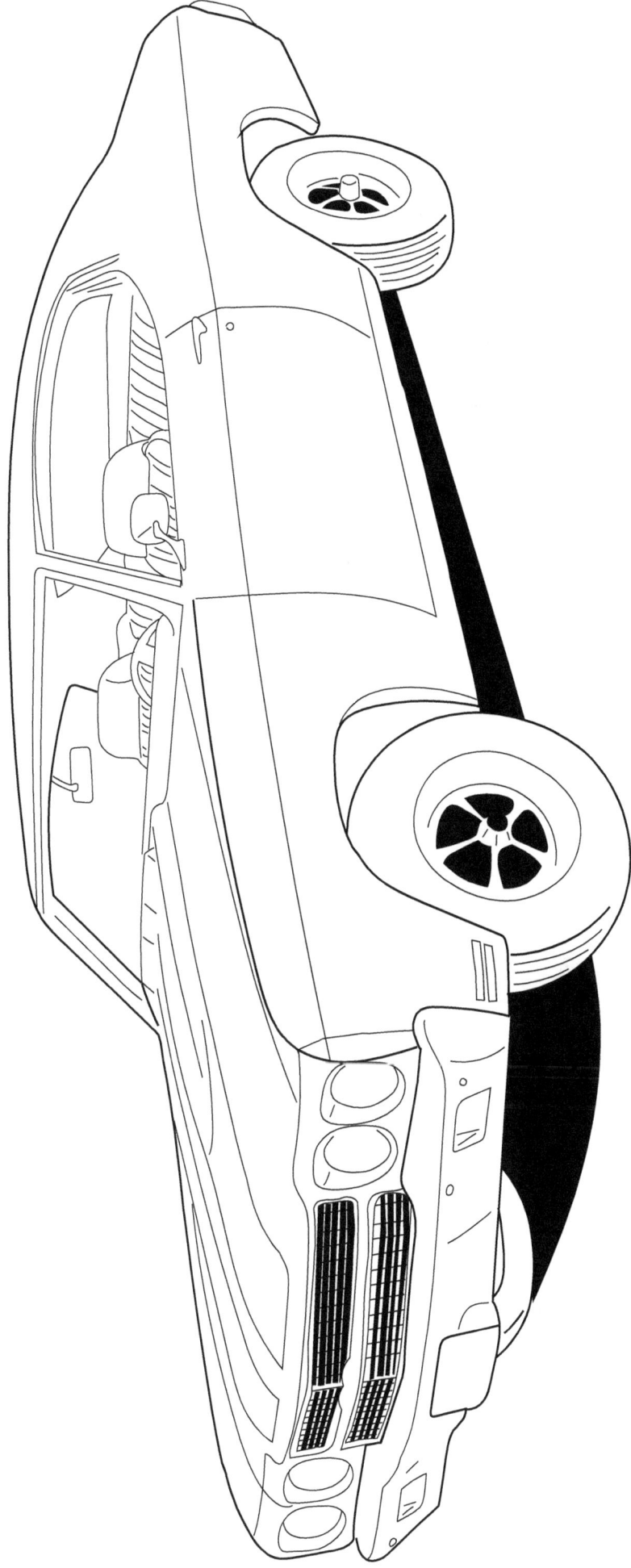

1970 CHEVY CHEVELLE SS

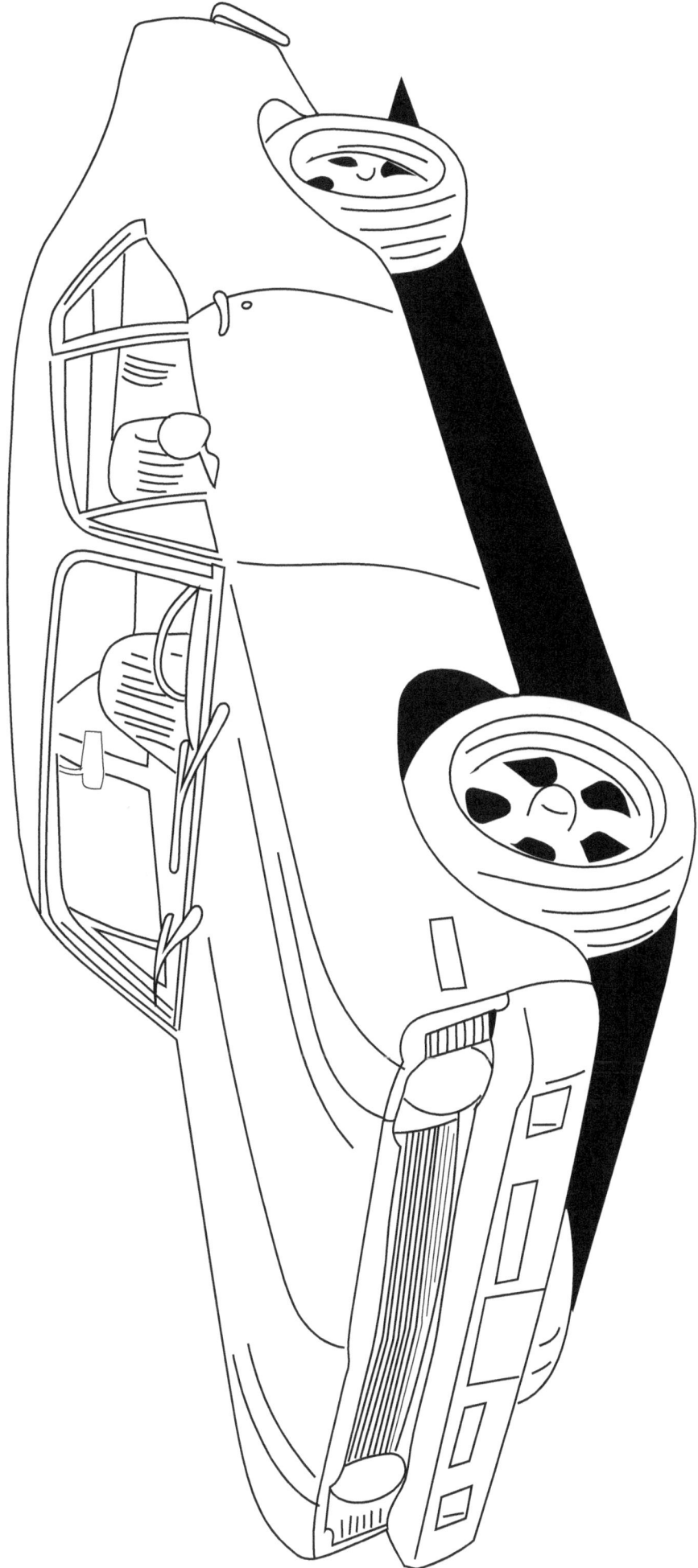

1970 CHEVY NOVA

1970 DODGE CHALLENGER

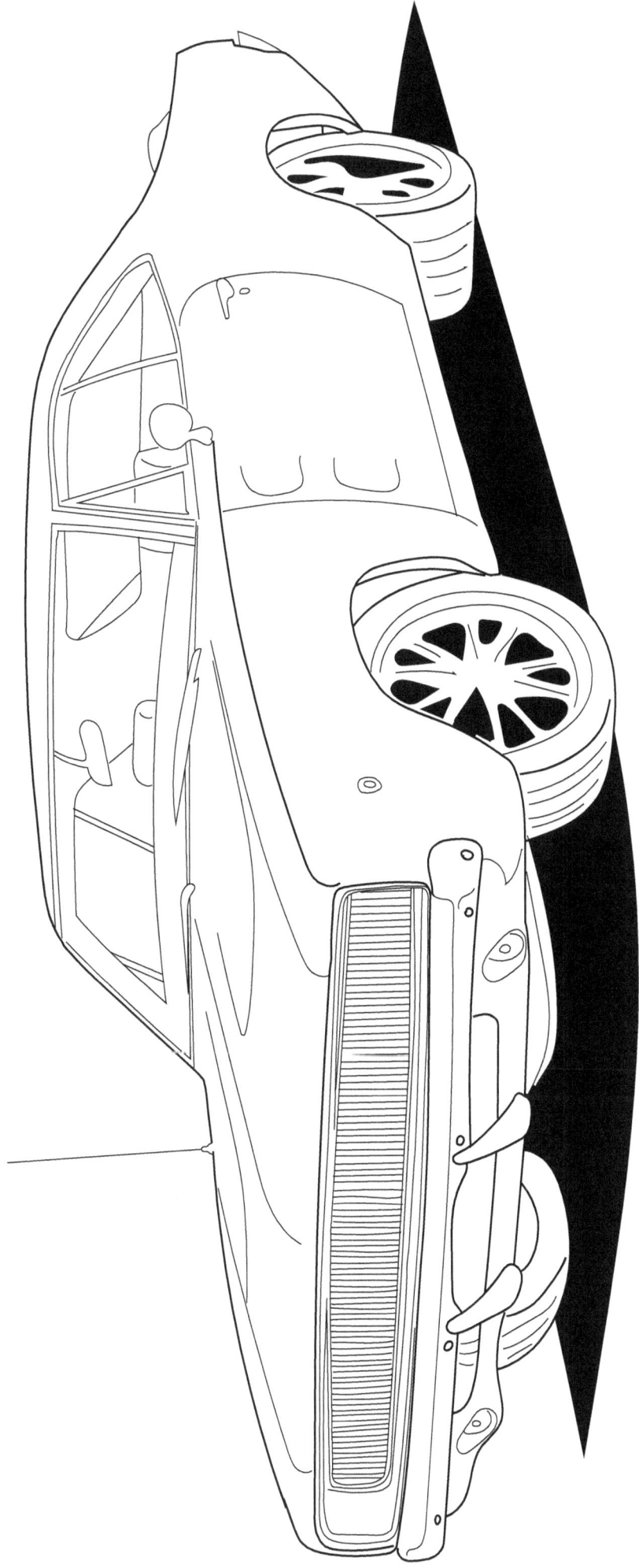

1970 DODGE CHARGER

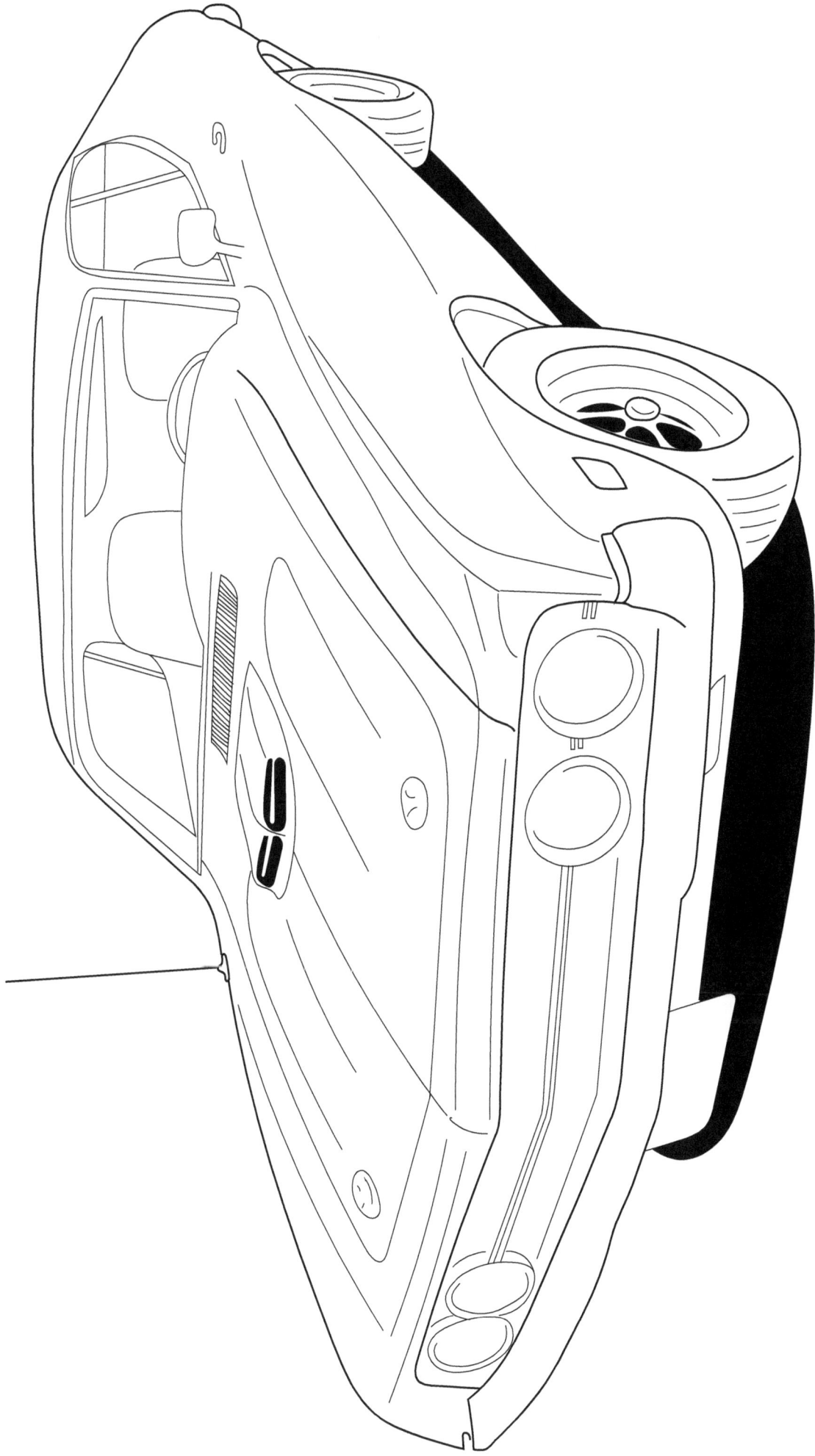

1970 FORD TORINO

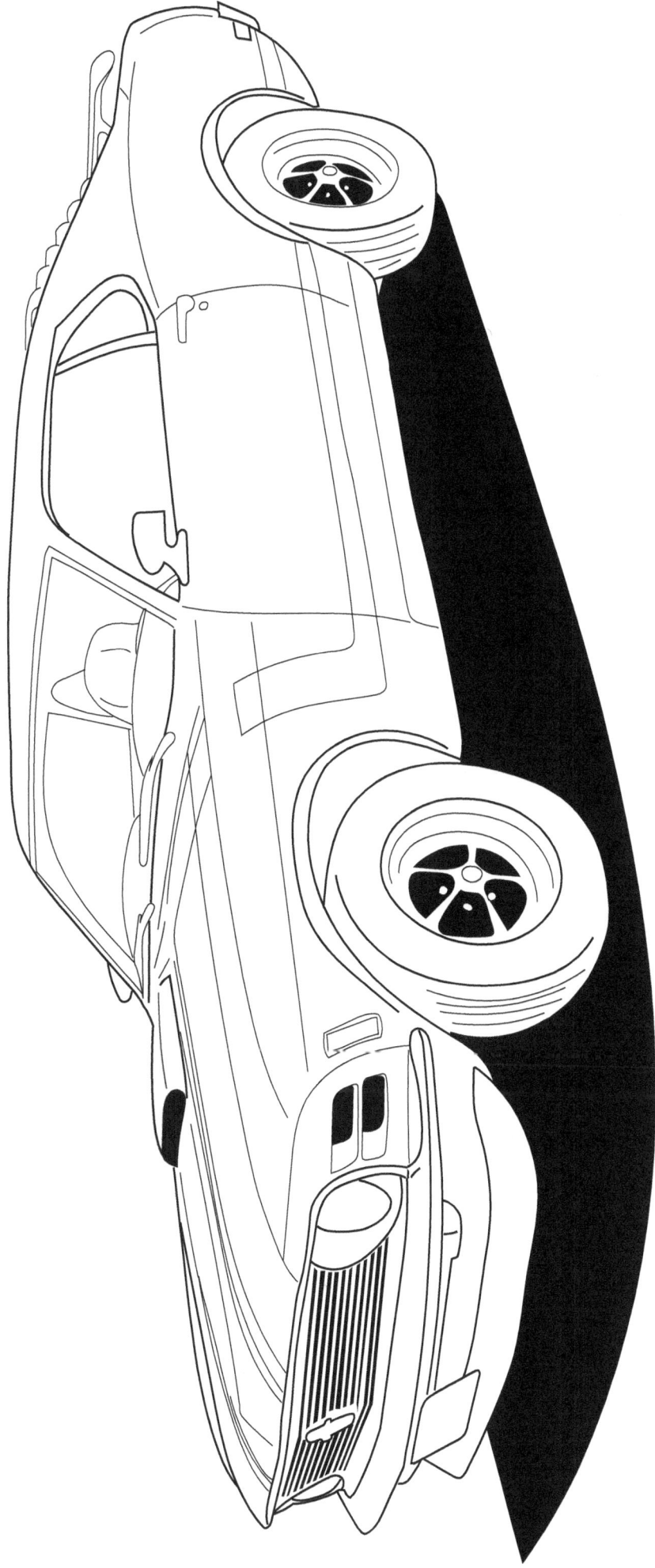

1970 FORD MUSTANG BOSS 302

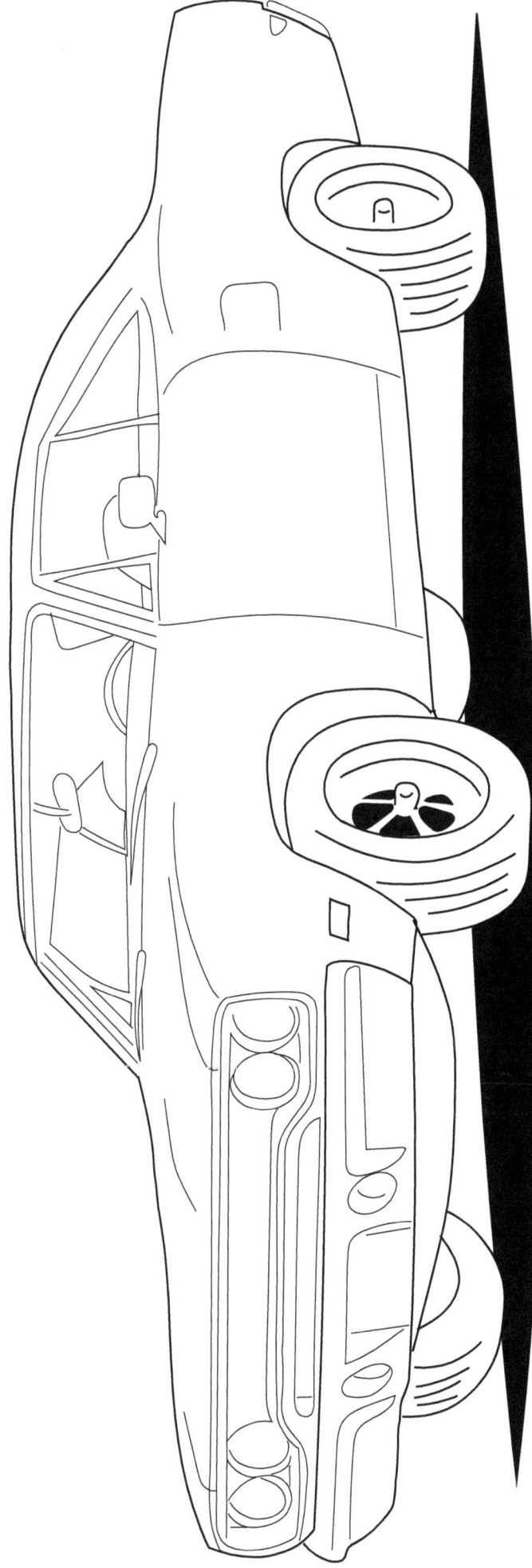

1970 PLYMOUTH GTX440 6 PACK

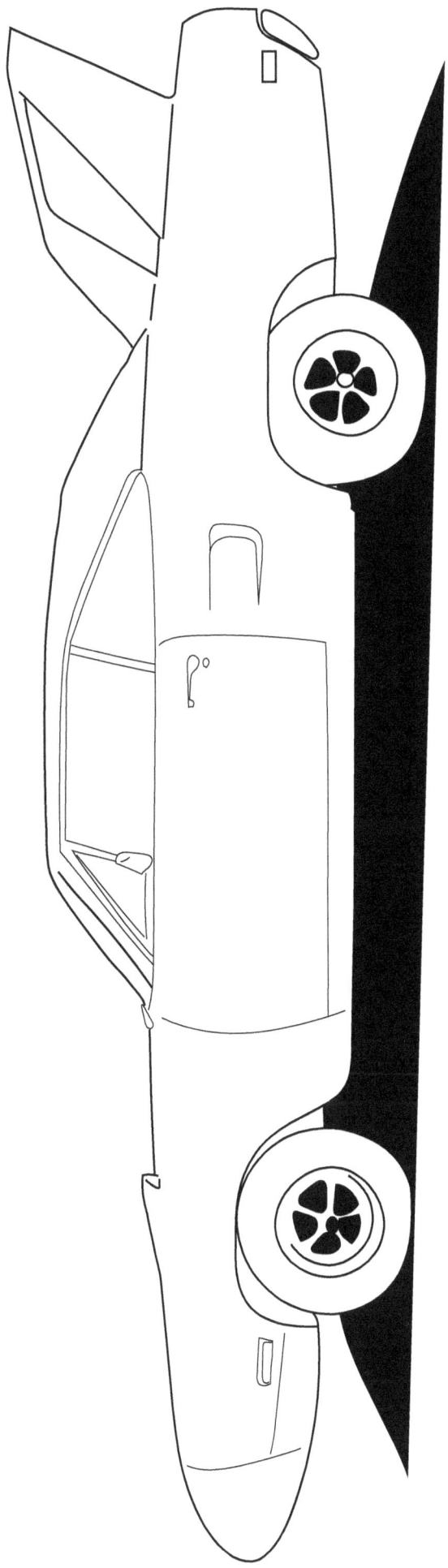

1970 PLYMOUTH HEMI SUPERBIRD

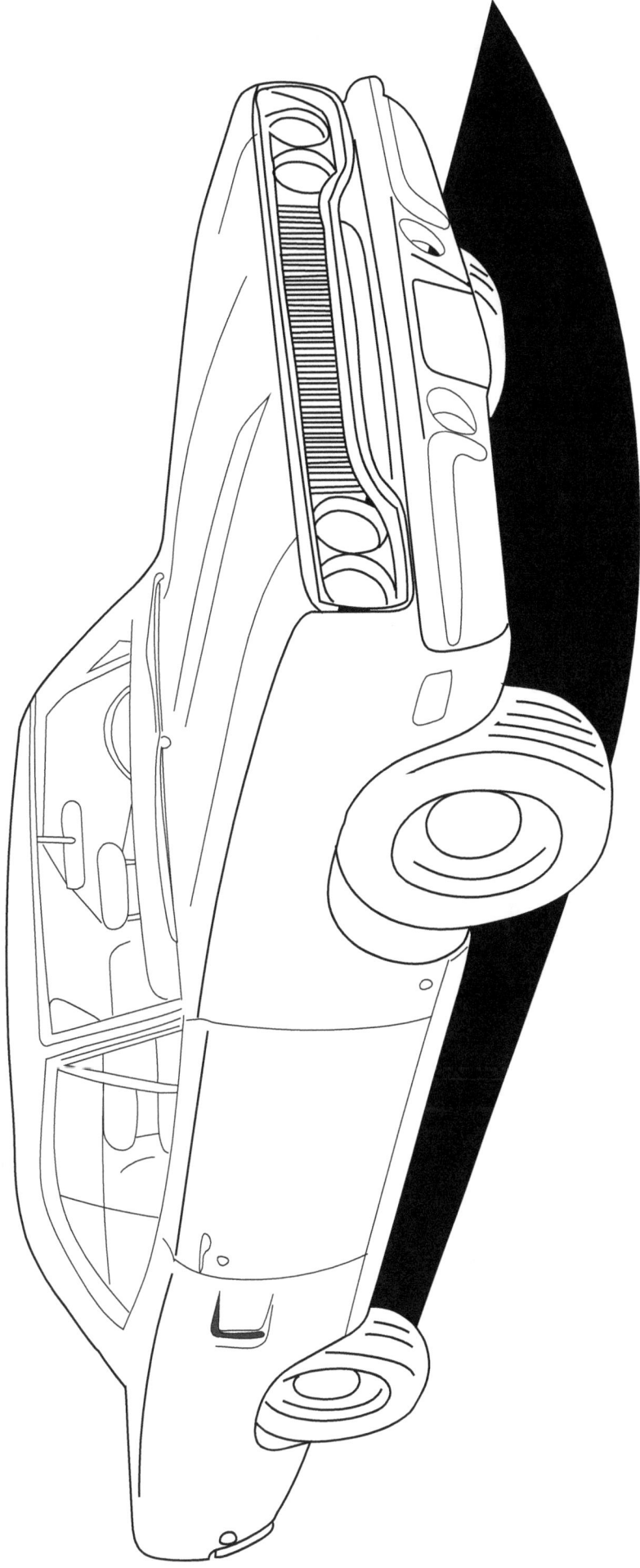

1970 PLYMOUTH ROADRUNNER

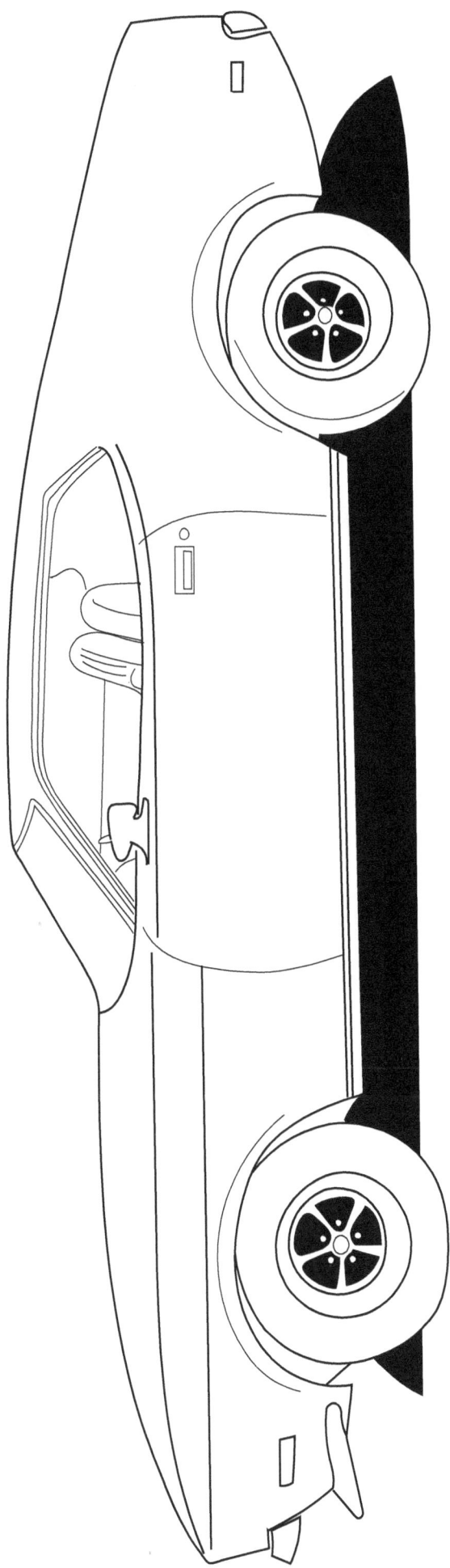

1971 FORD MUSTANG COBRA JET

1971 PONTIAC GTO JUDGE

1971 BUICK GSX

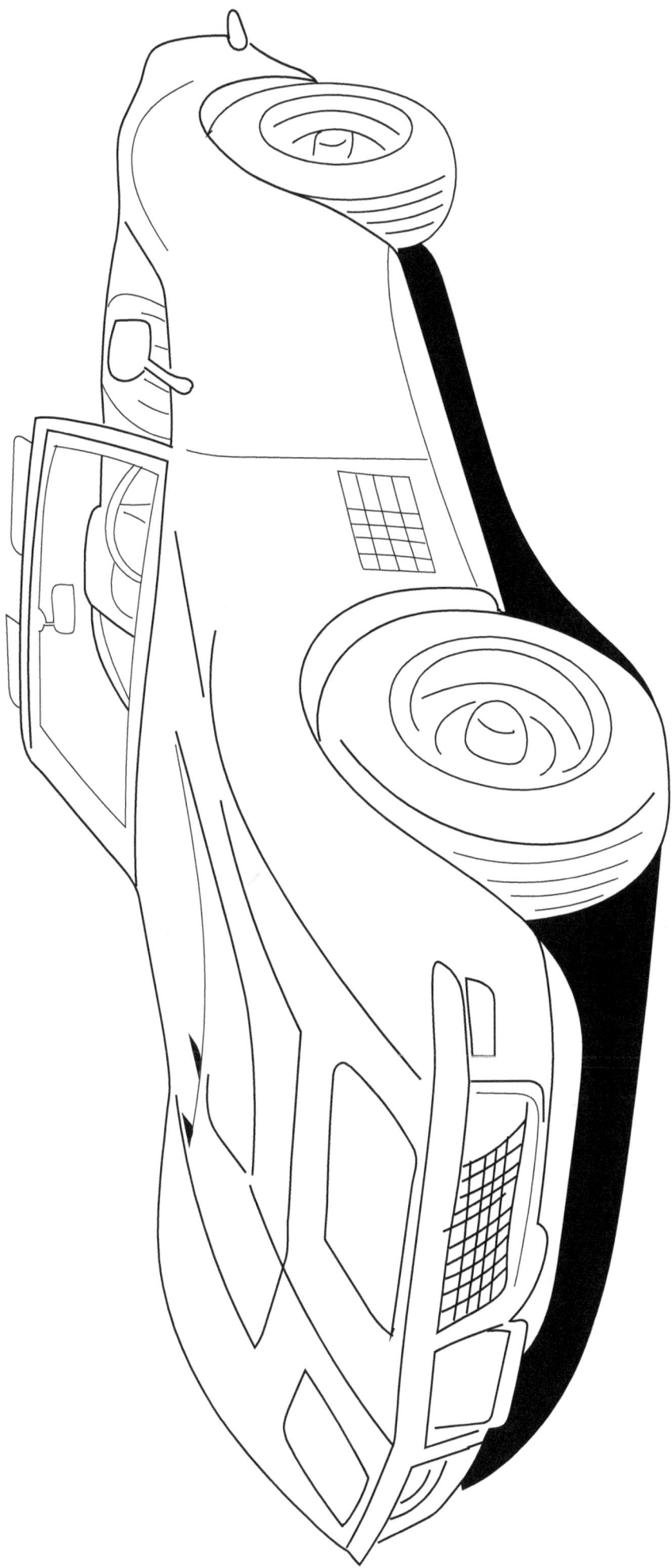

1971 CHEVY CORVETTE LS6

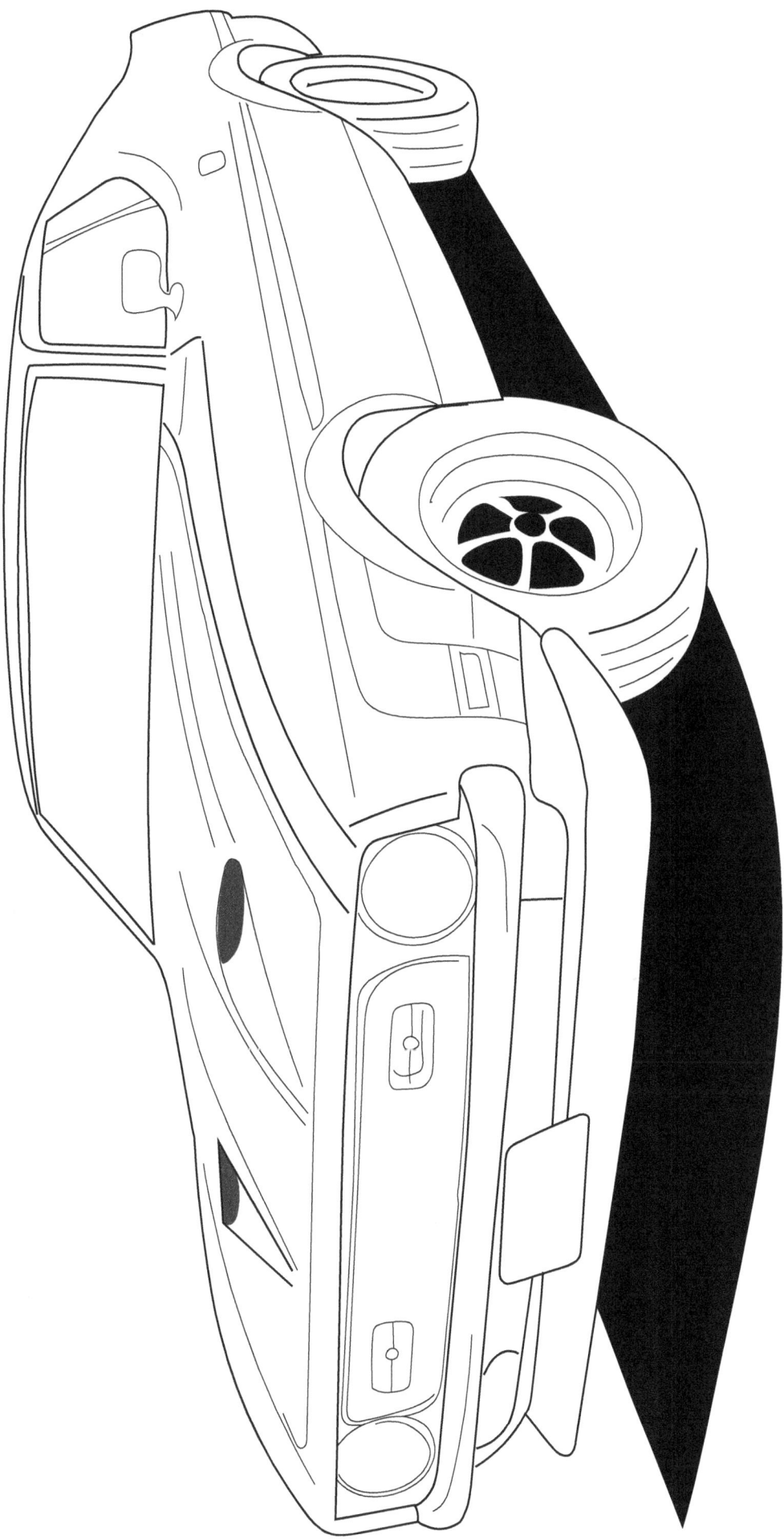

1971 FORD MUSTANG BOSS 351

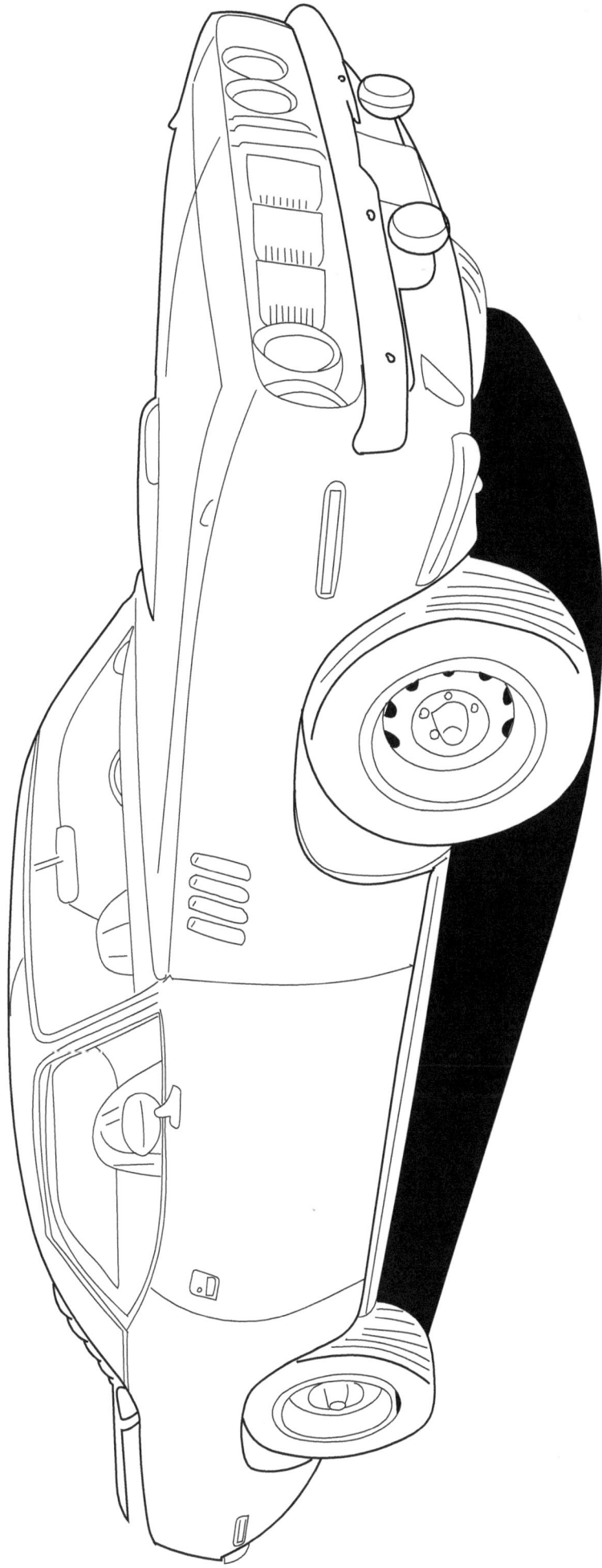

1971 PLYMOUTH HEMI CUDA

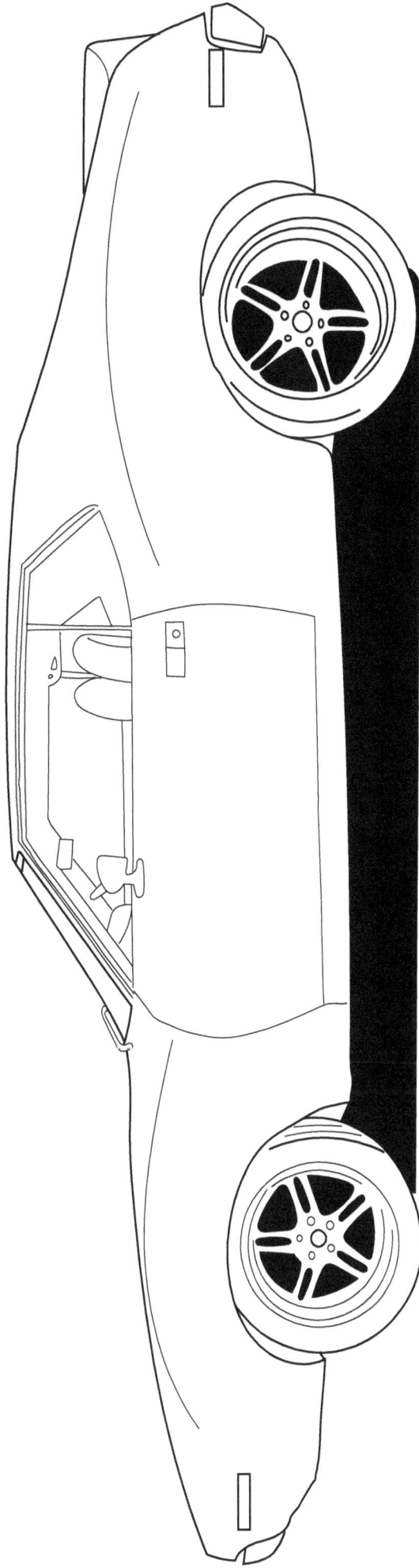

1972 AMC JAVELIN

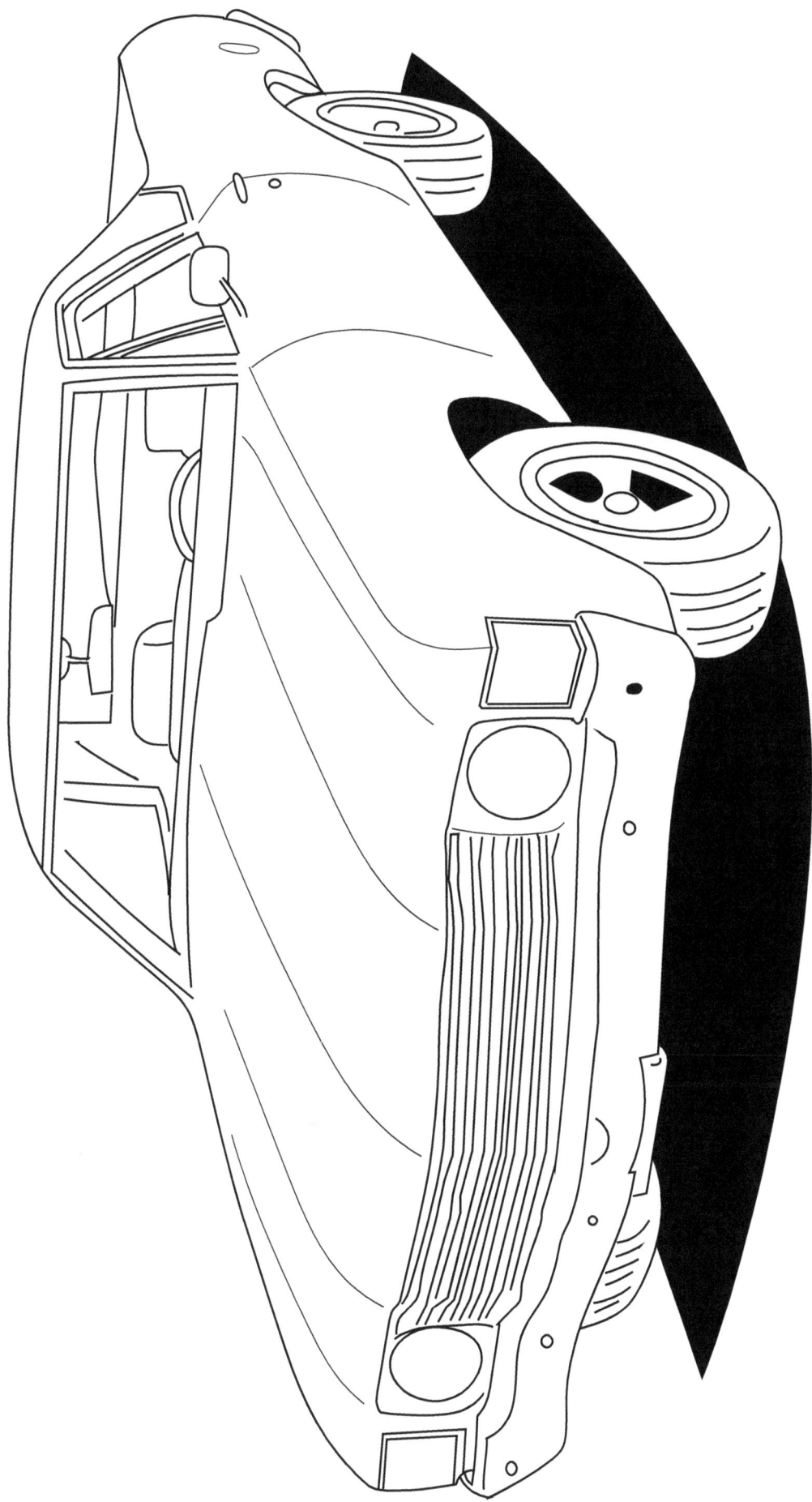

1972 FORD EL CAMINO

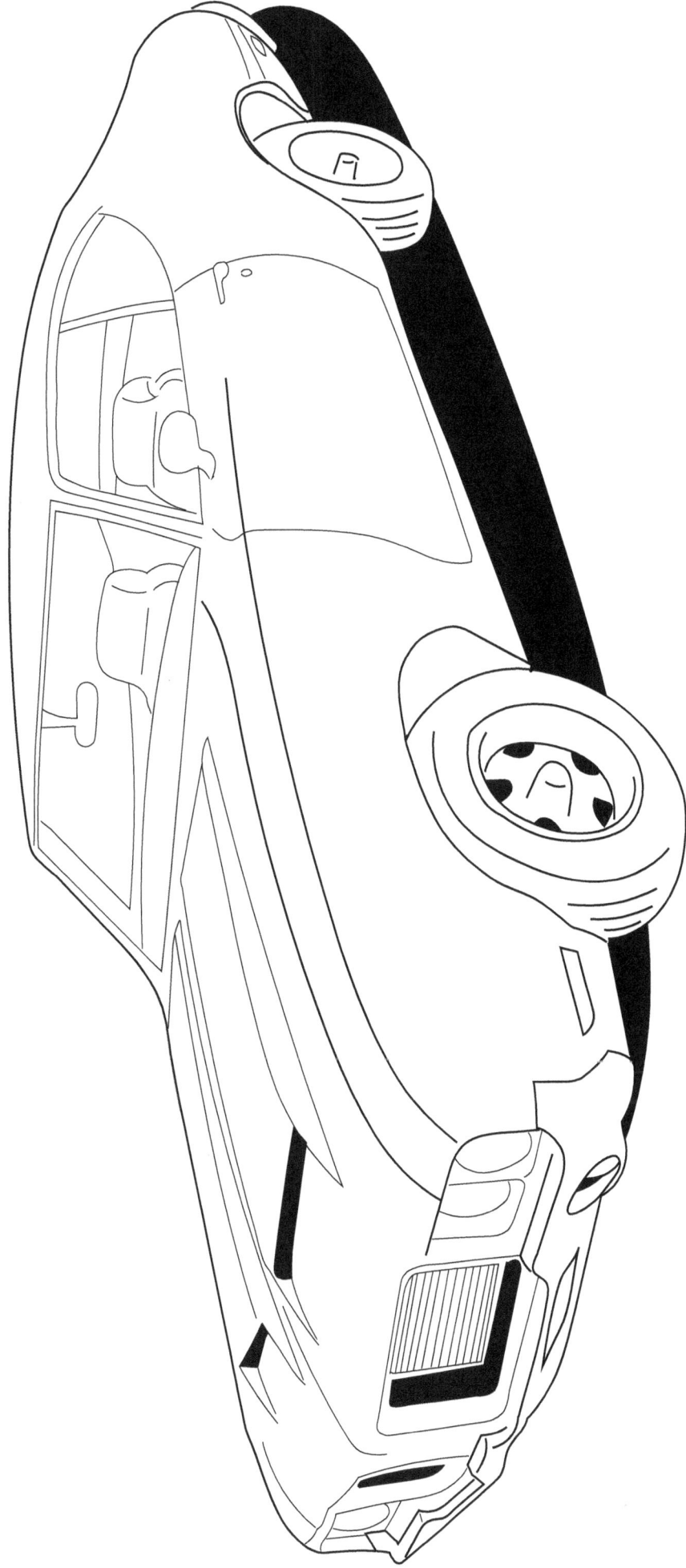

1972 OLDSMOBILE 442

1972 BUICK RIVERIA

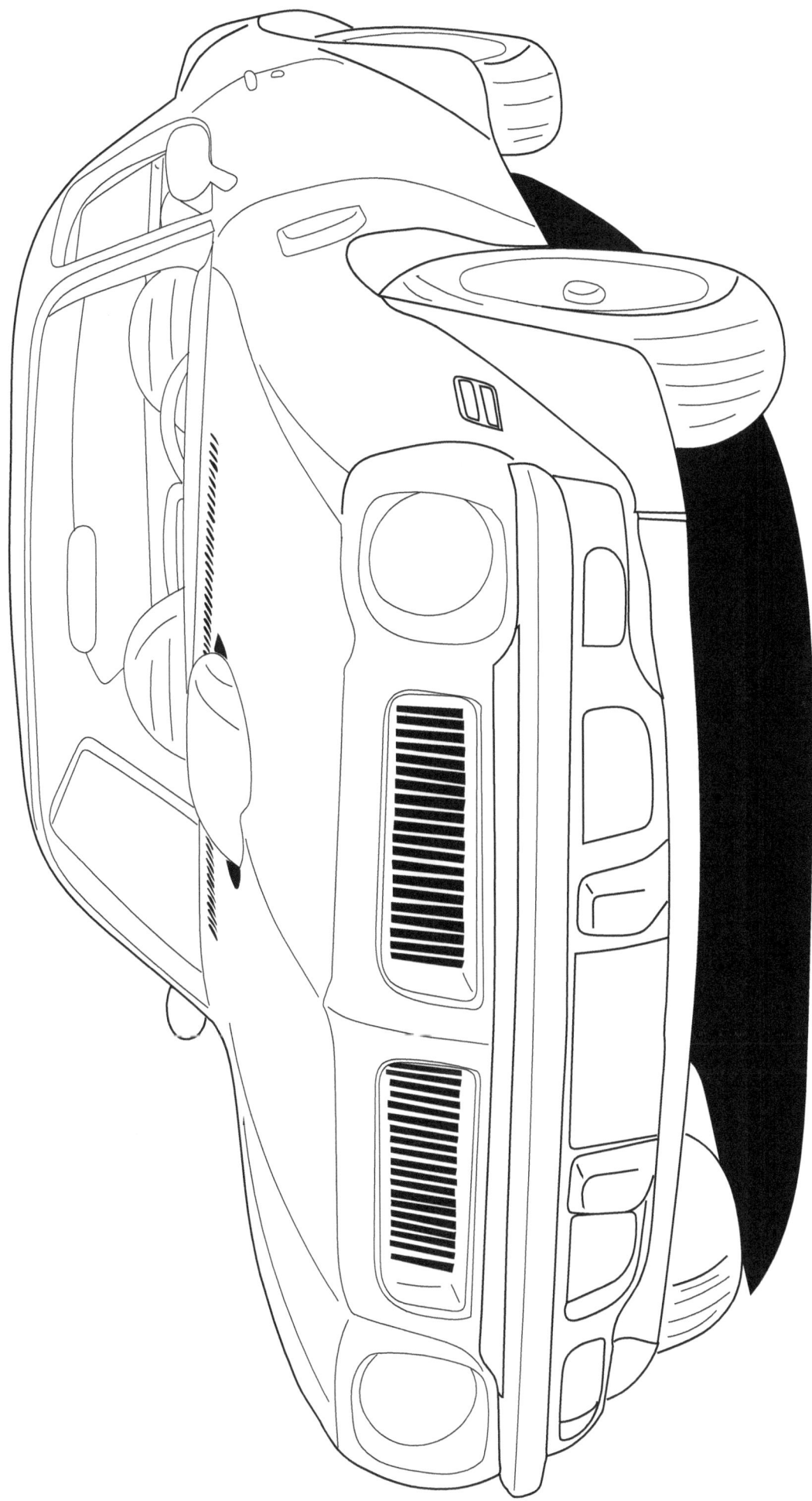

1974 PONTIAC
TRANS-AM FIREBIRD

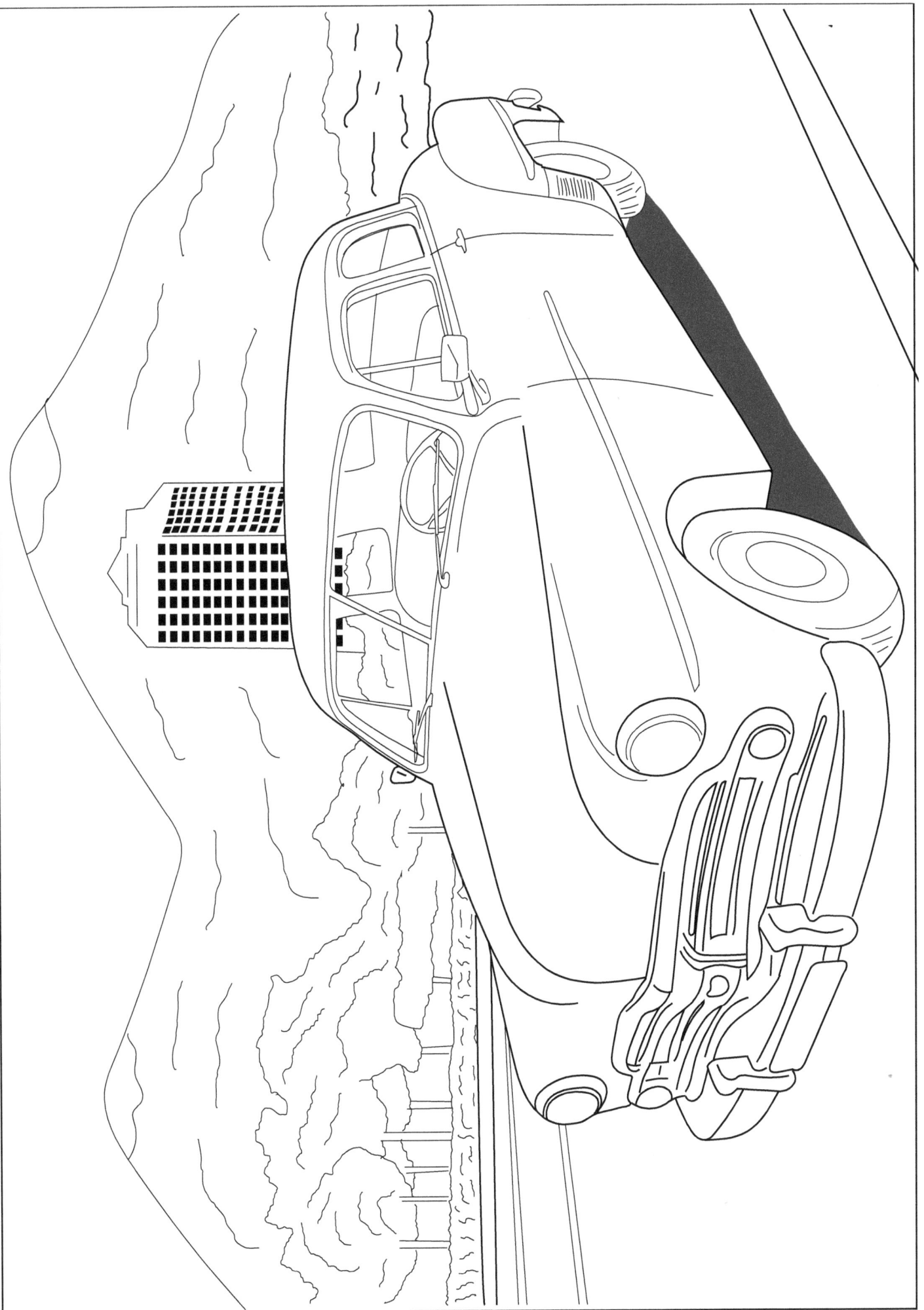

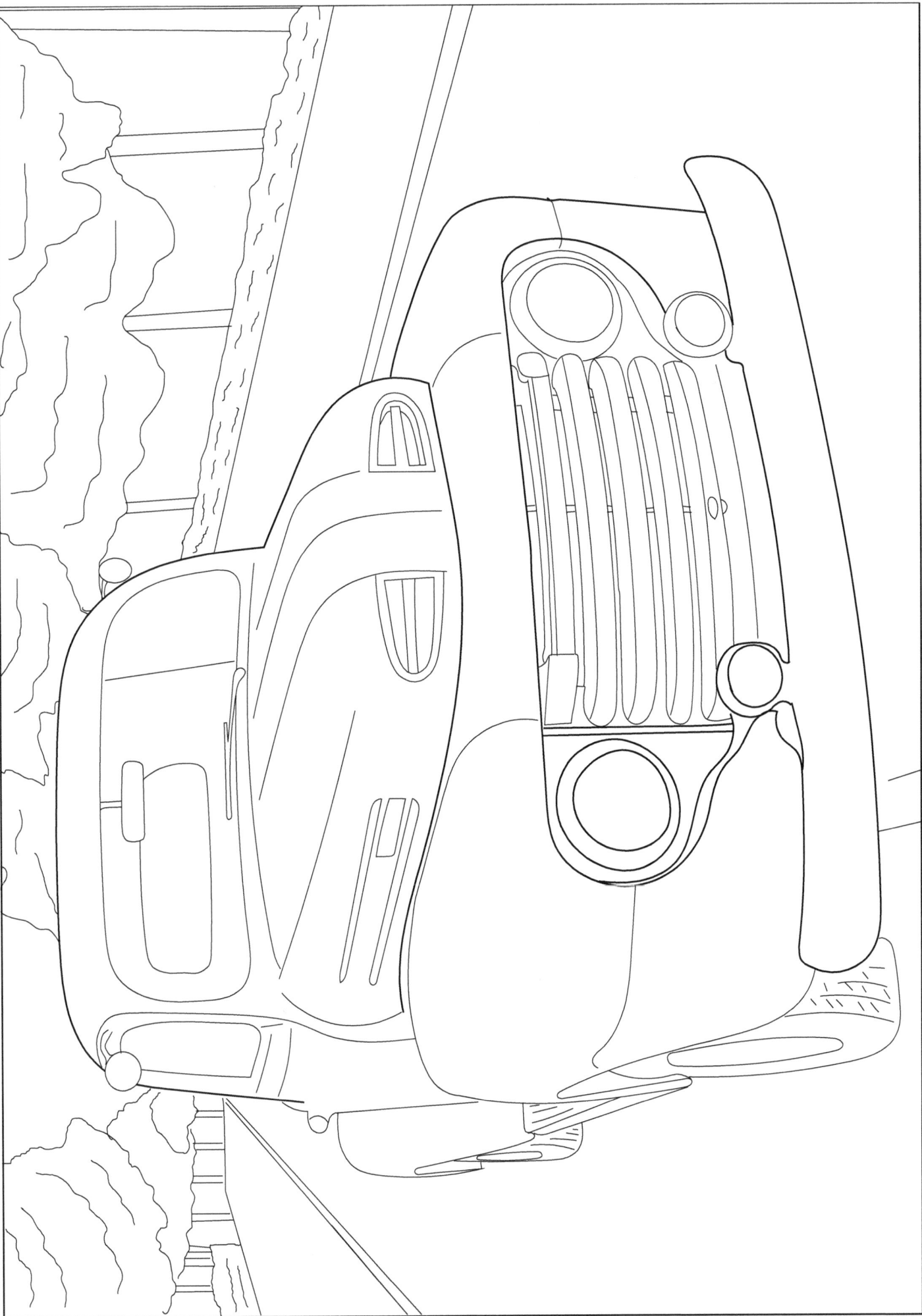

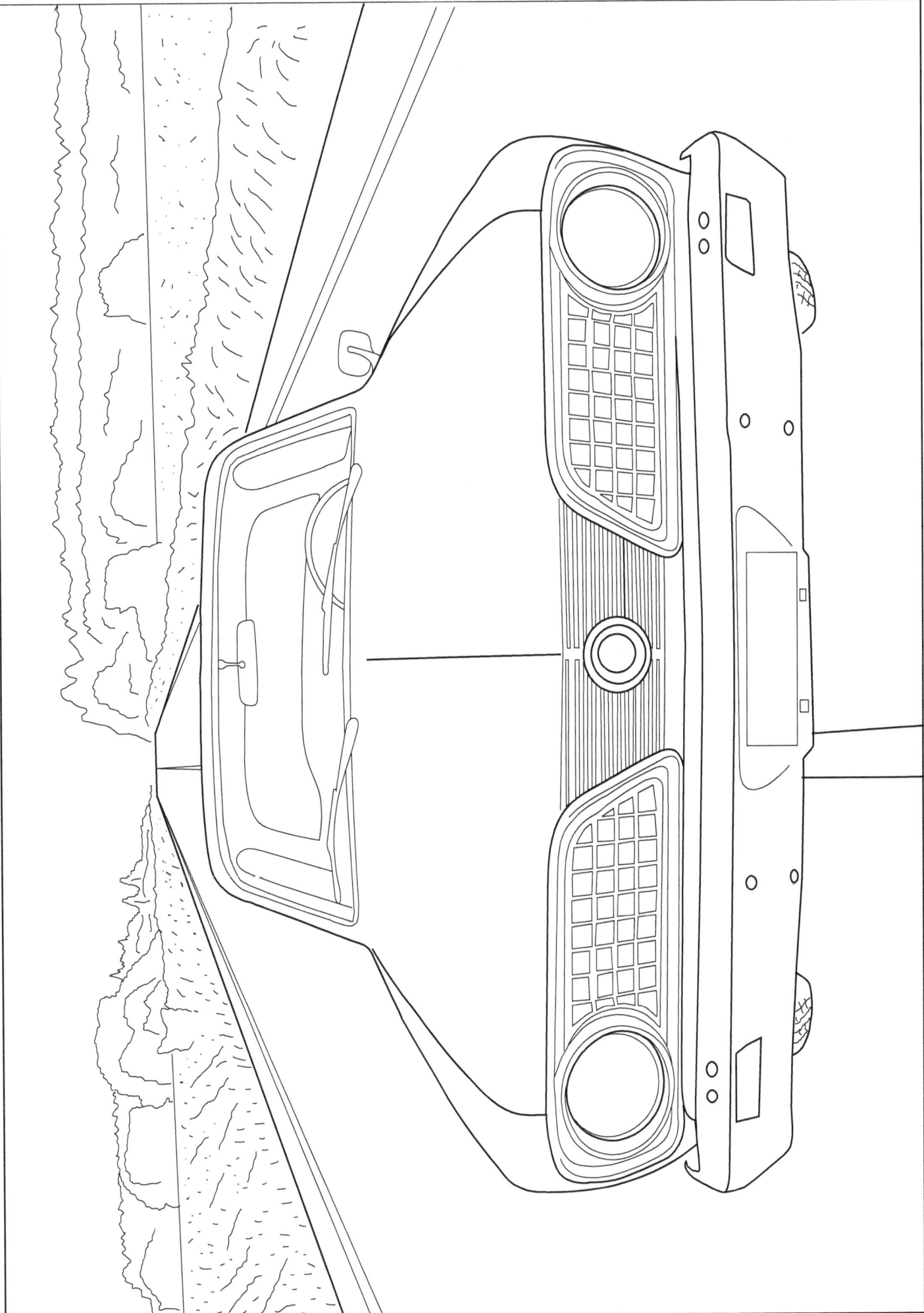

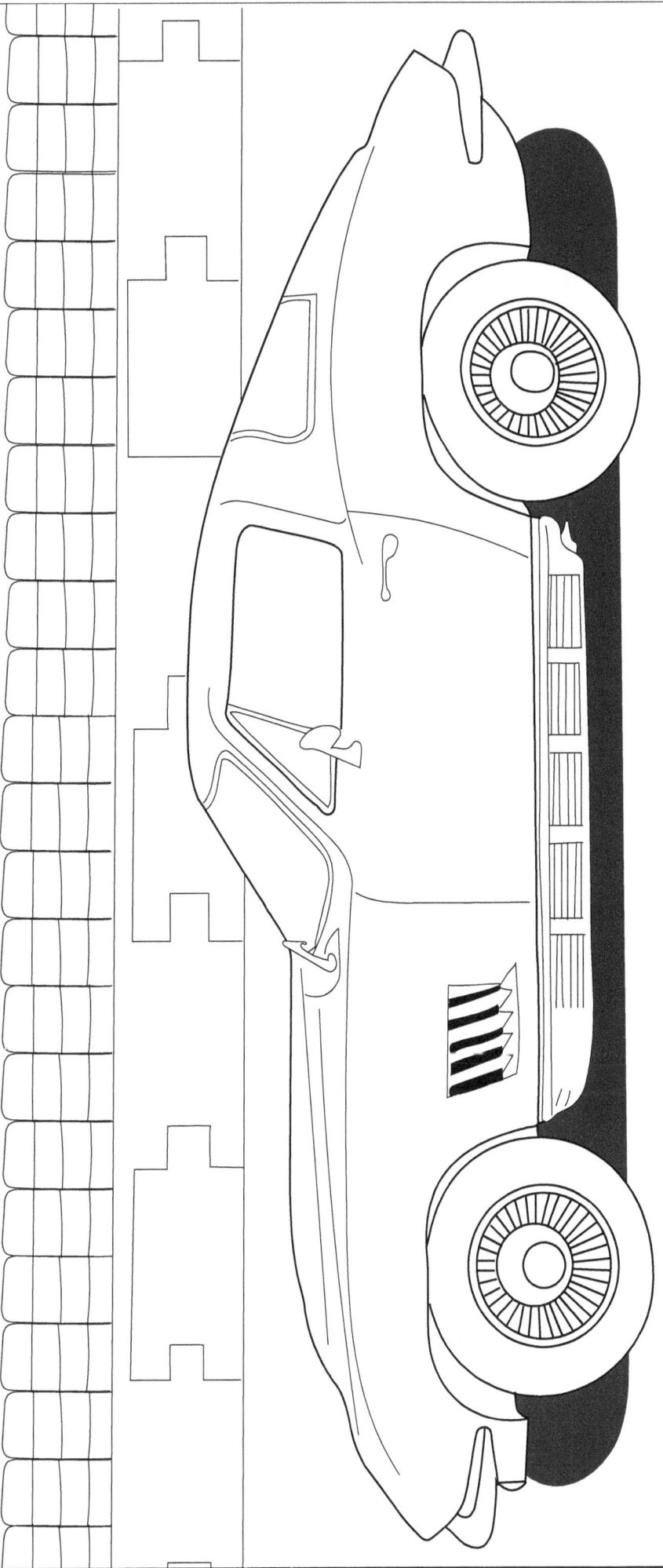

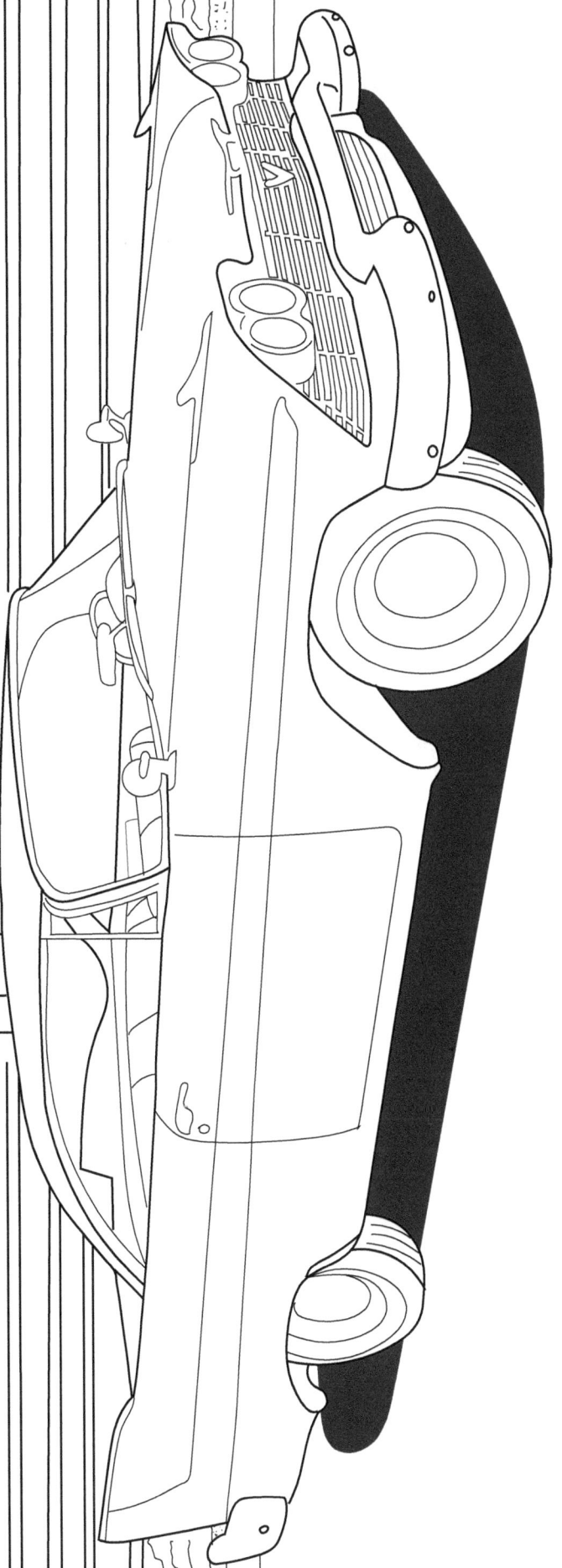

DINER

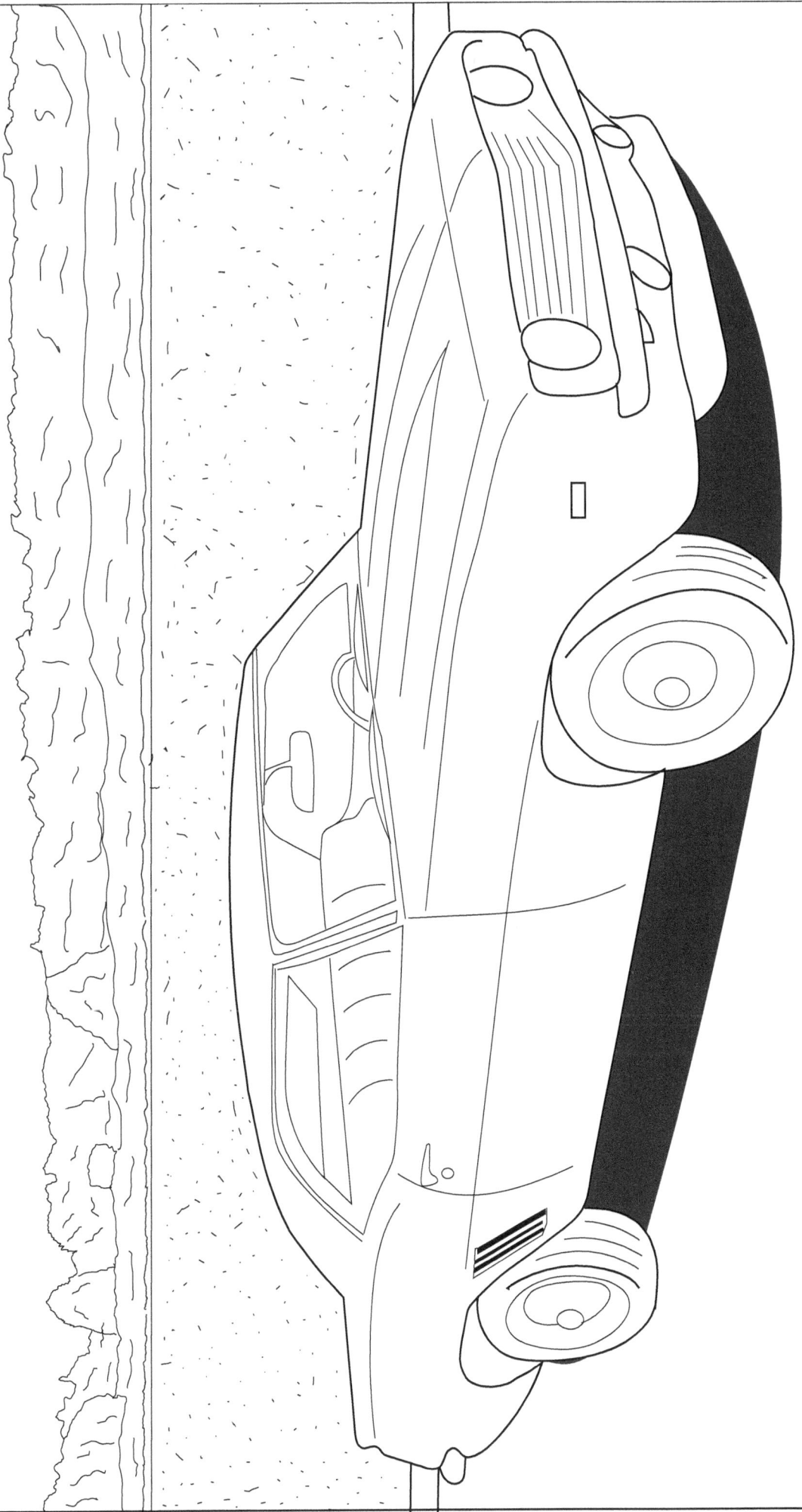

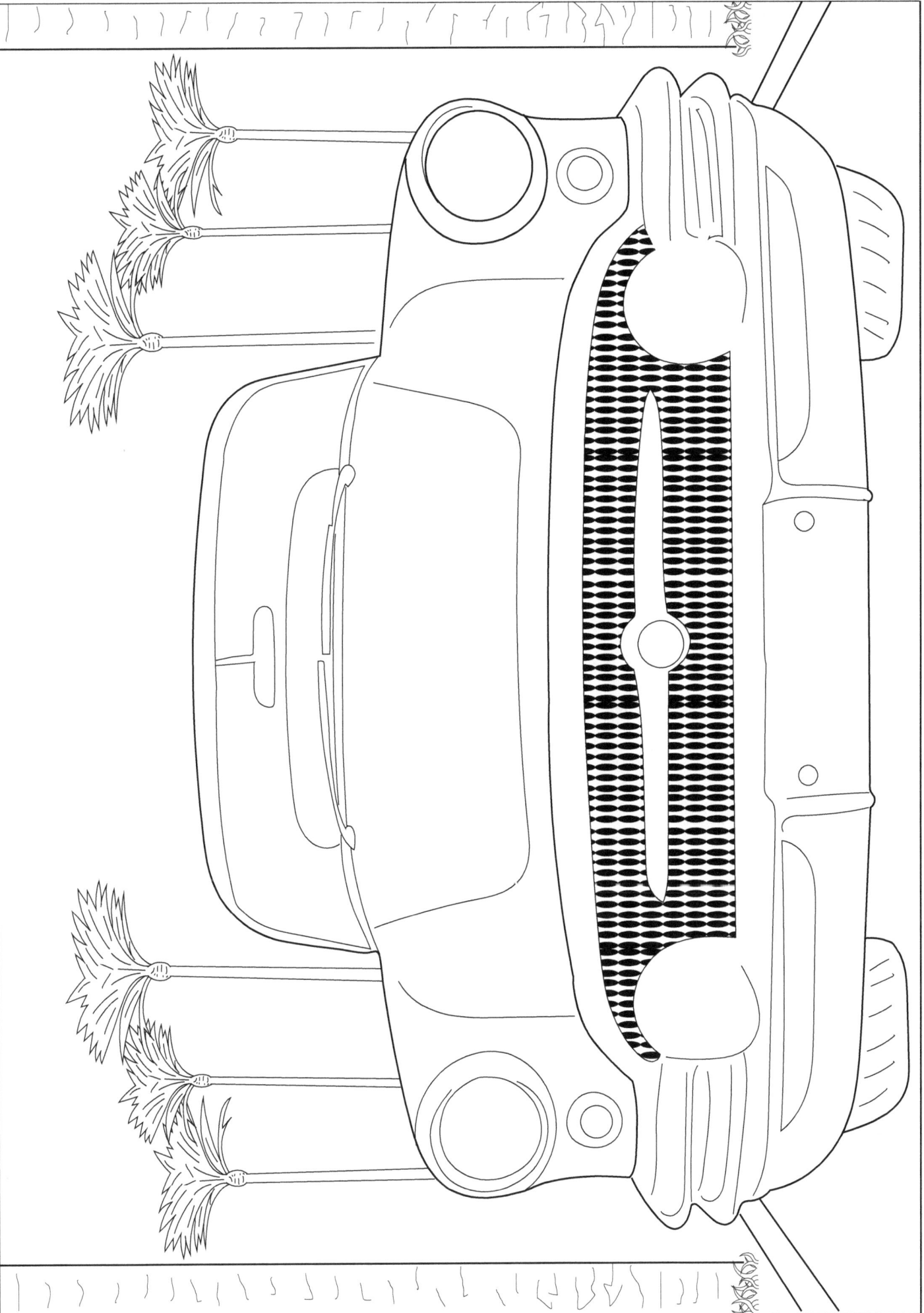

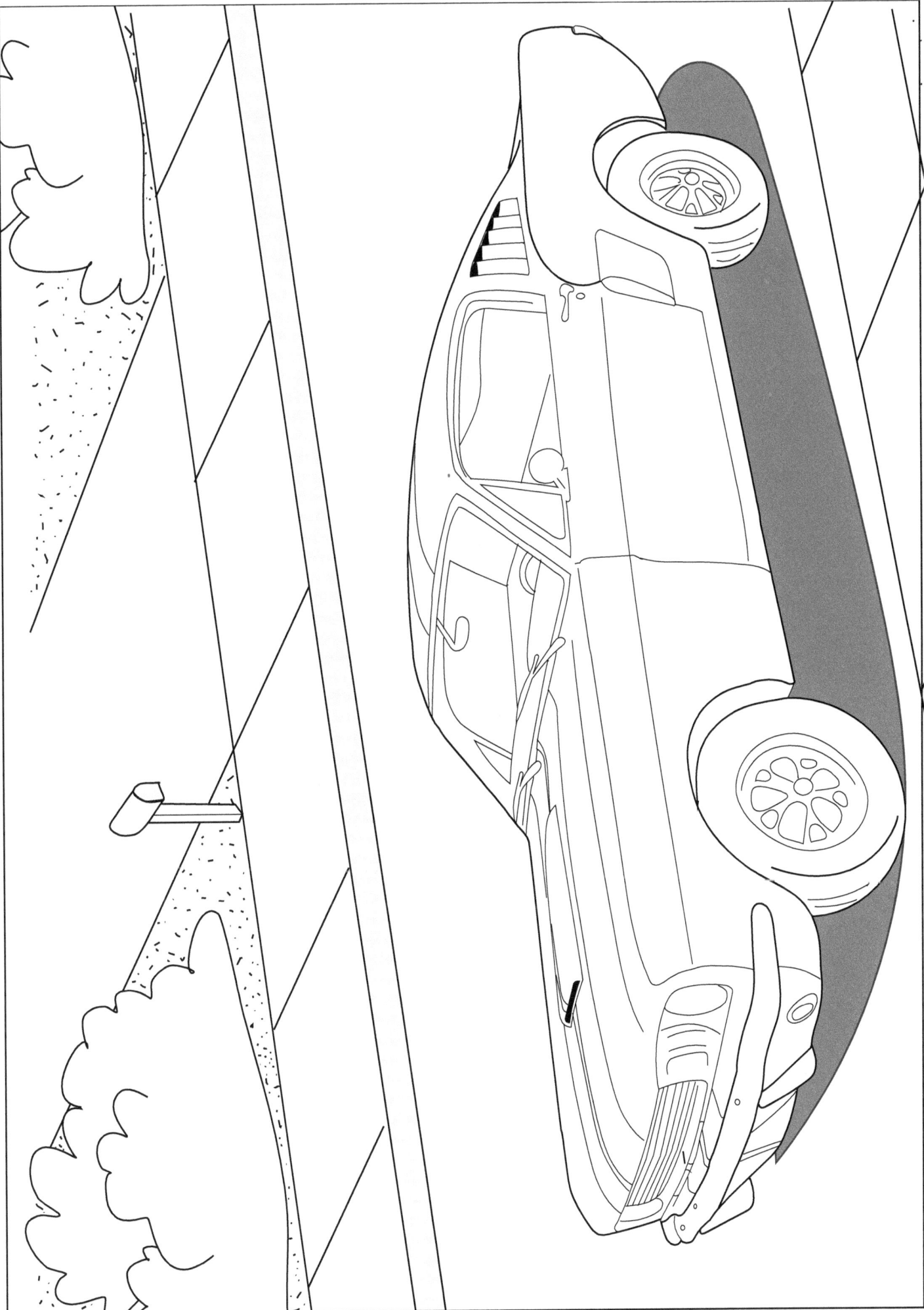

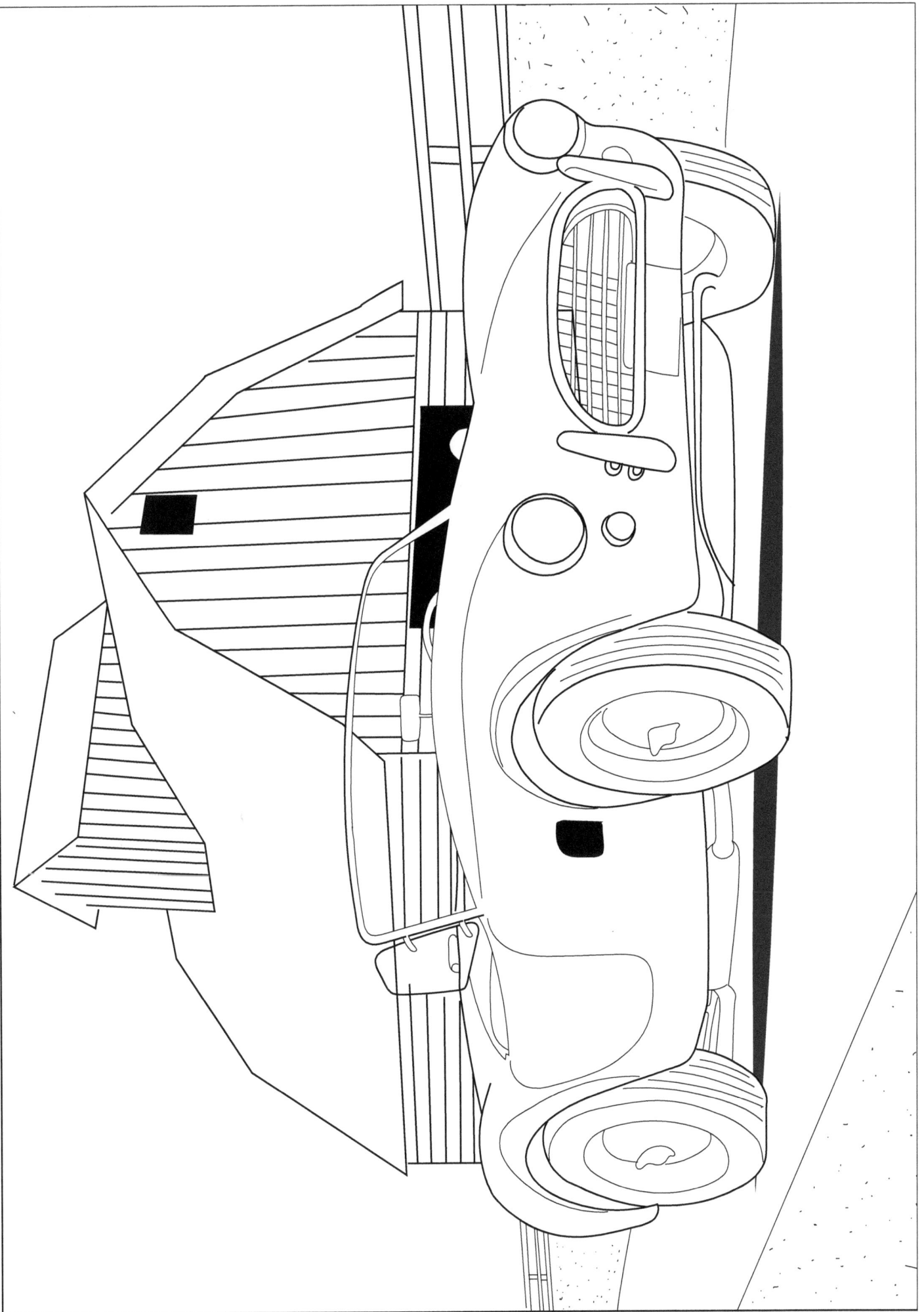

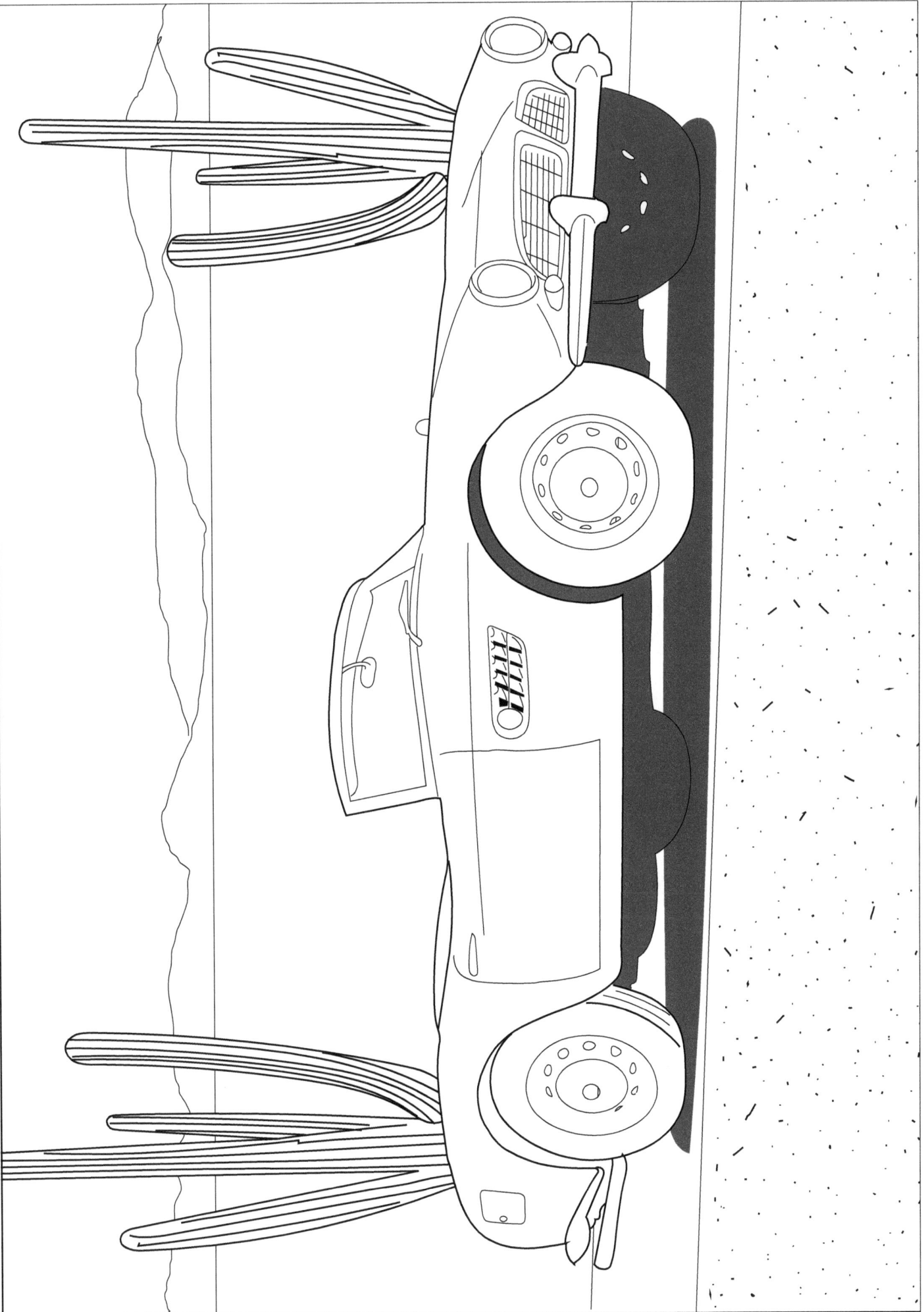

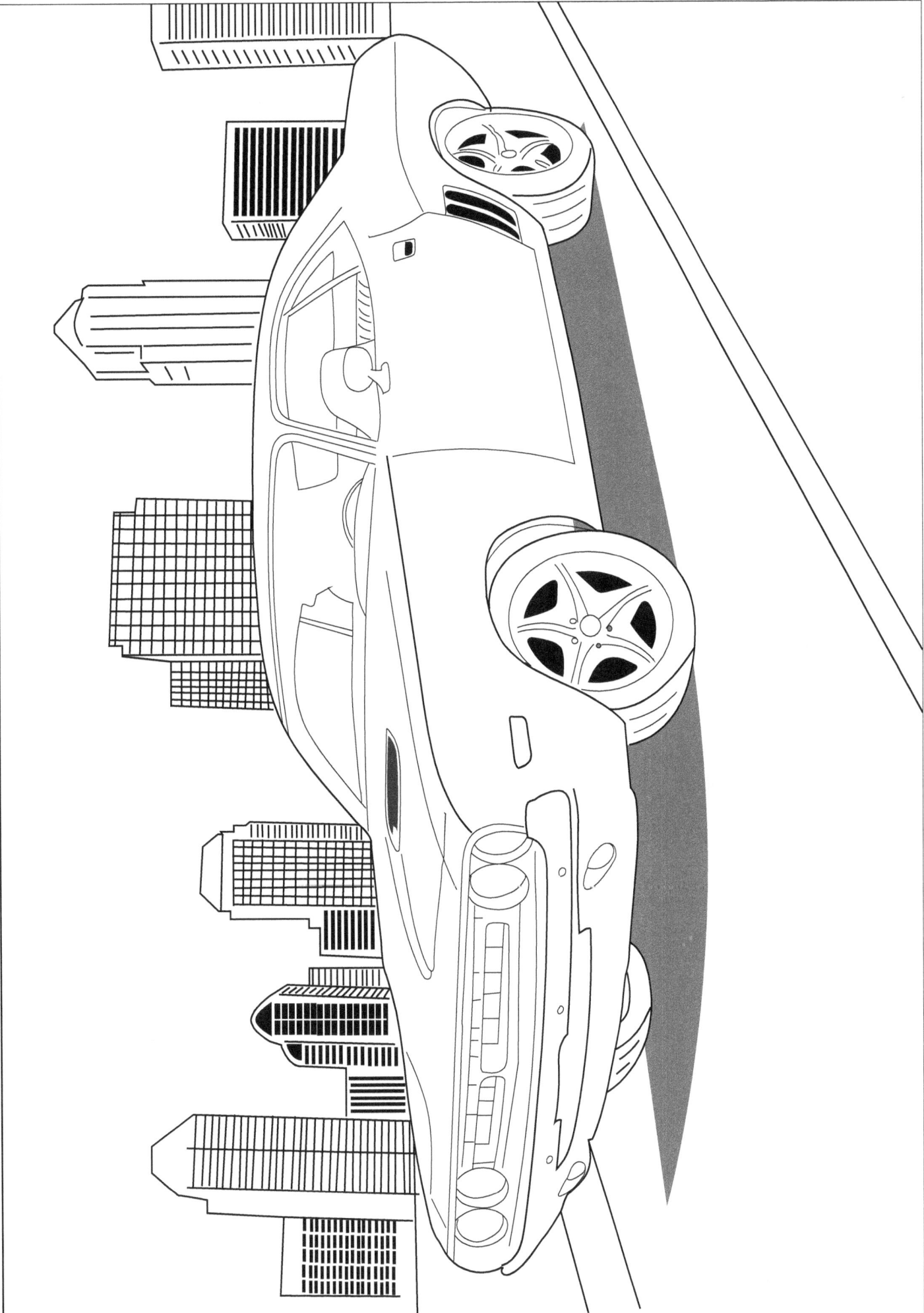

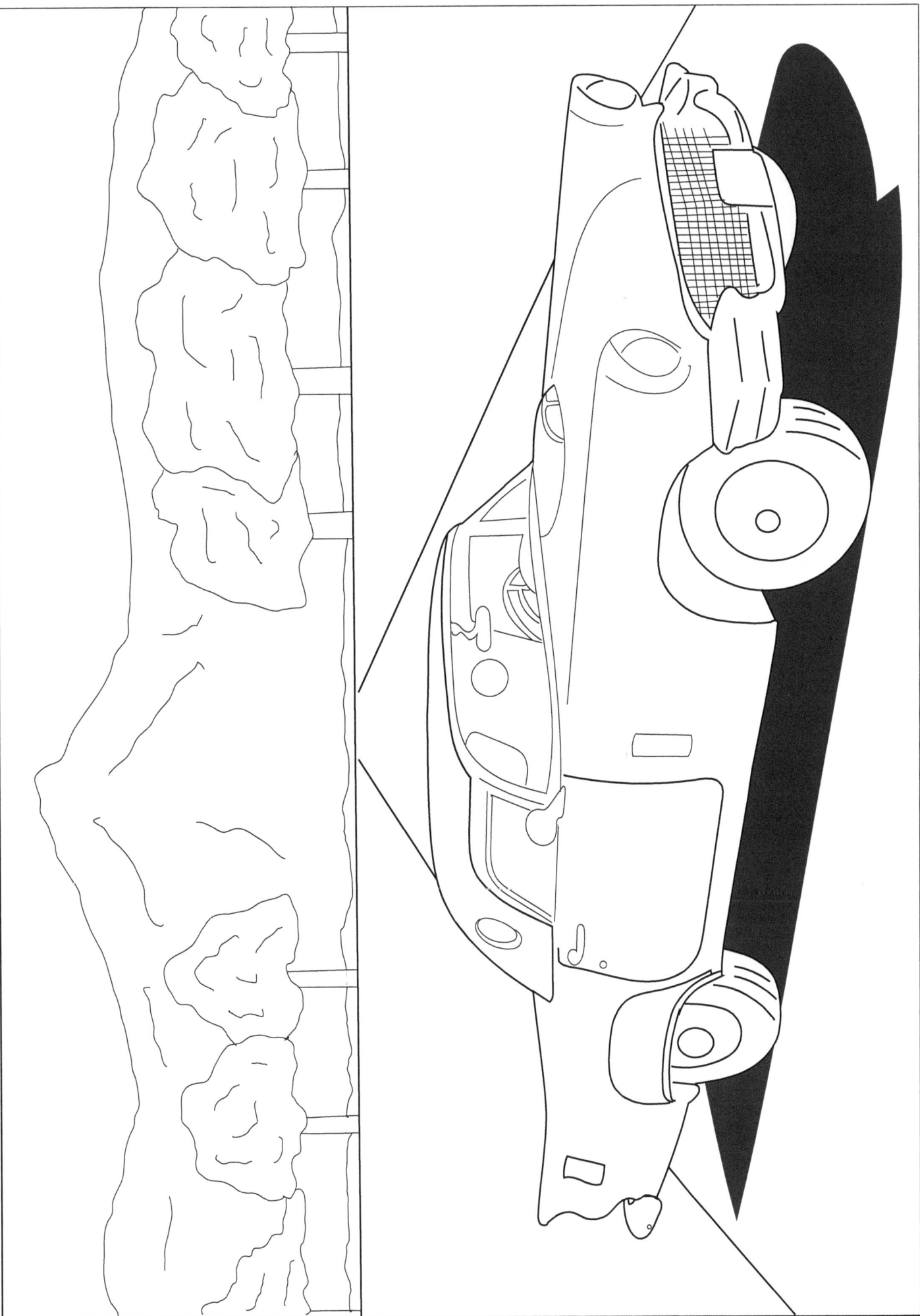

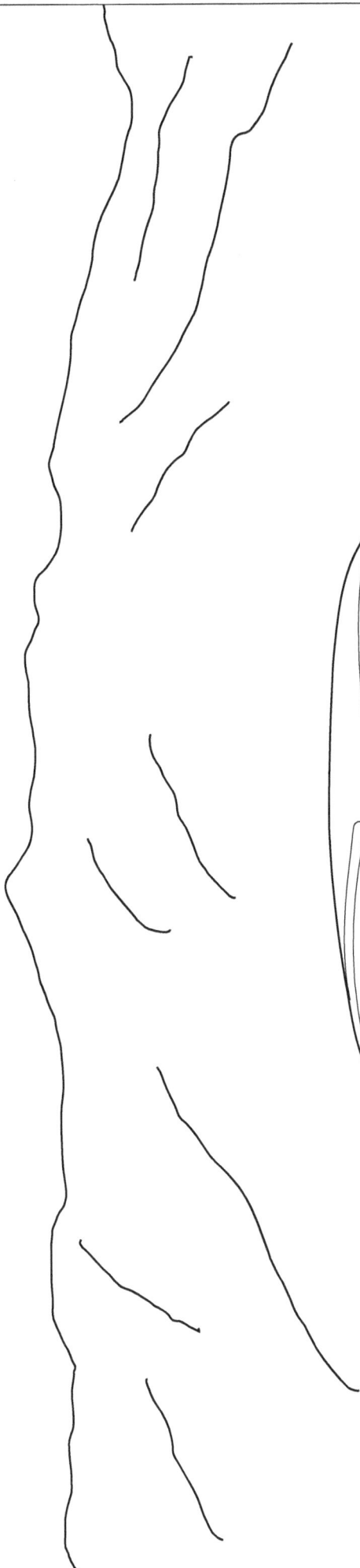

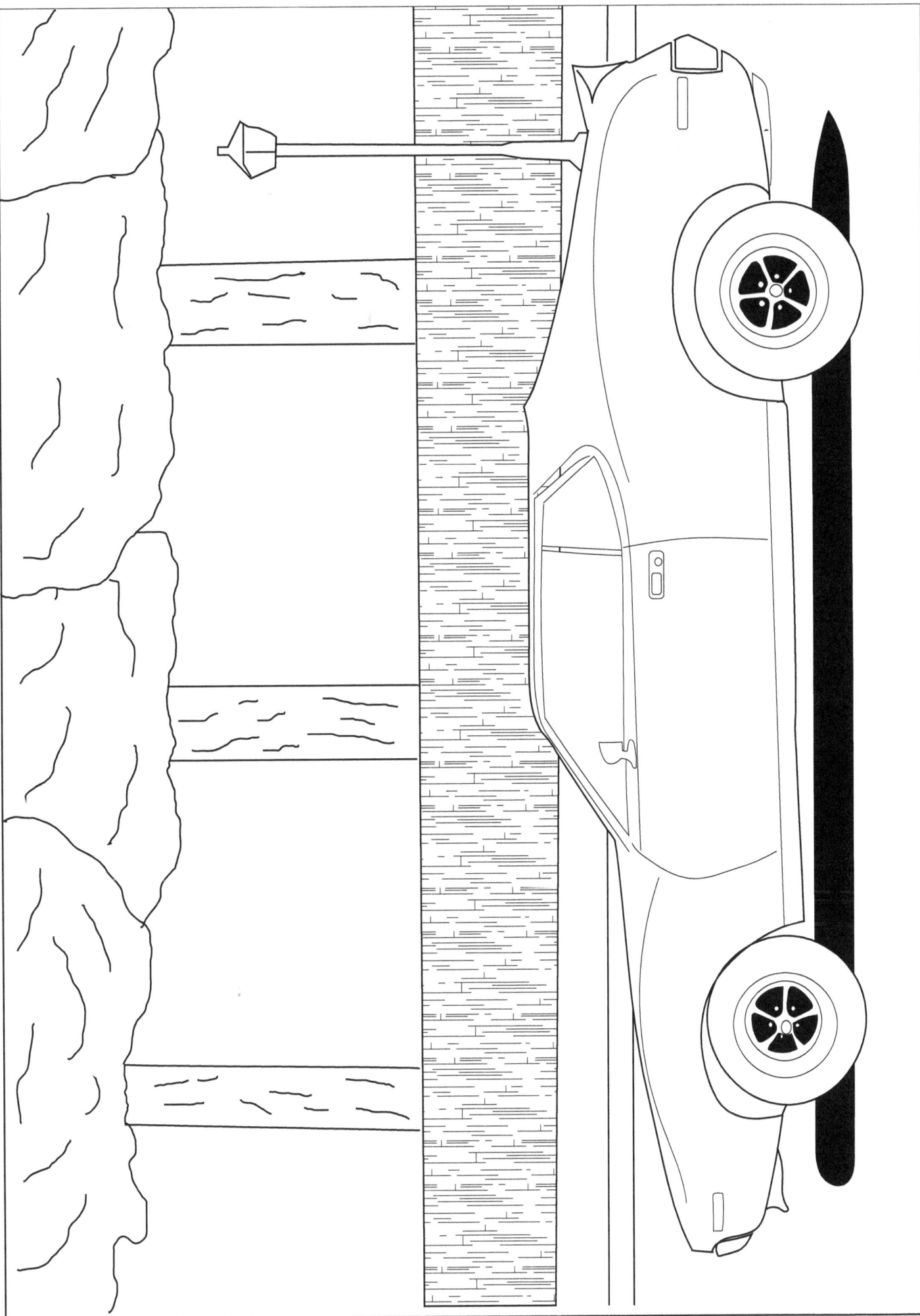

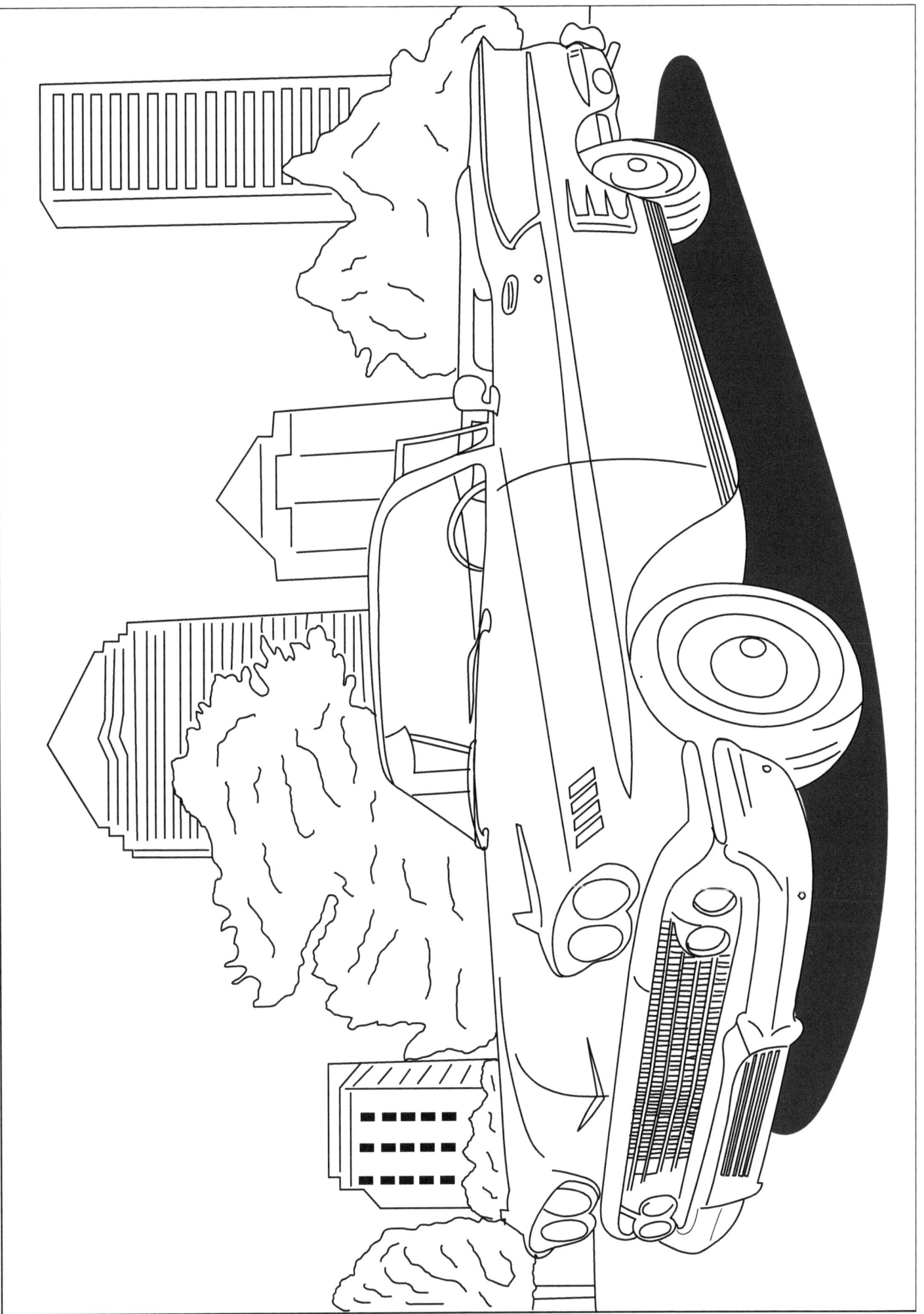

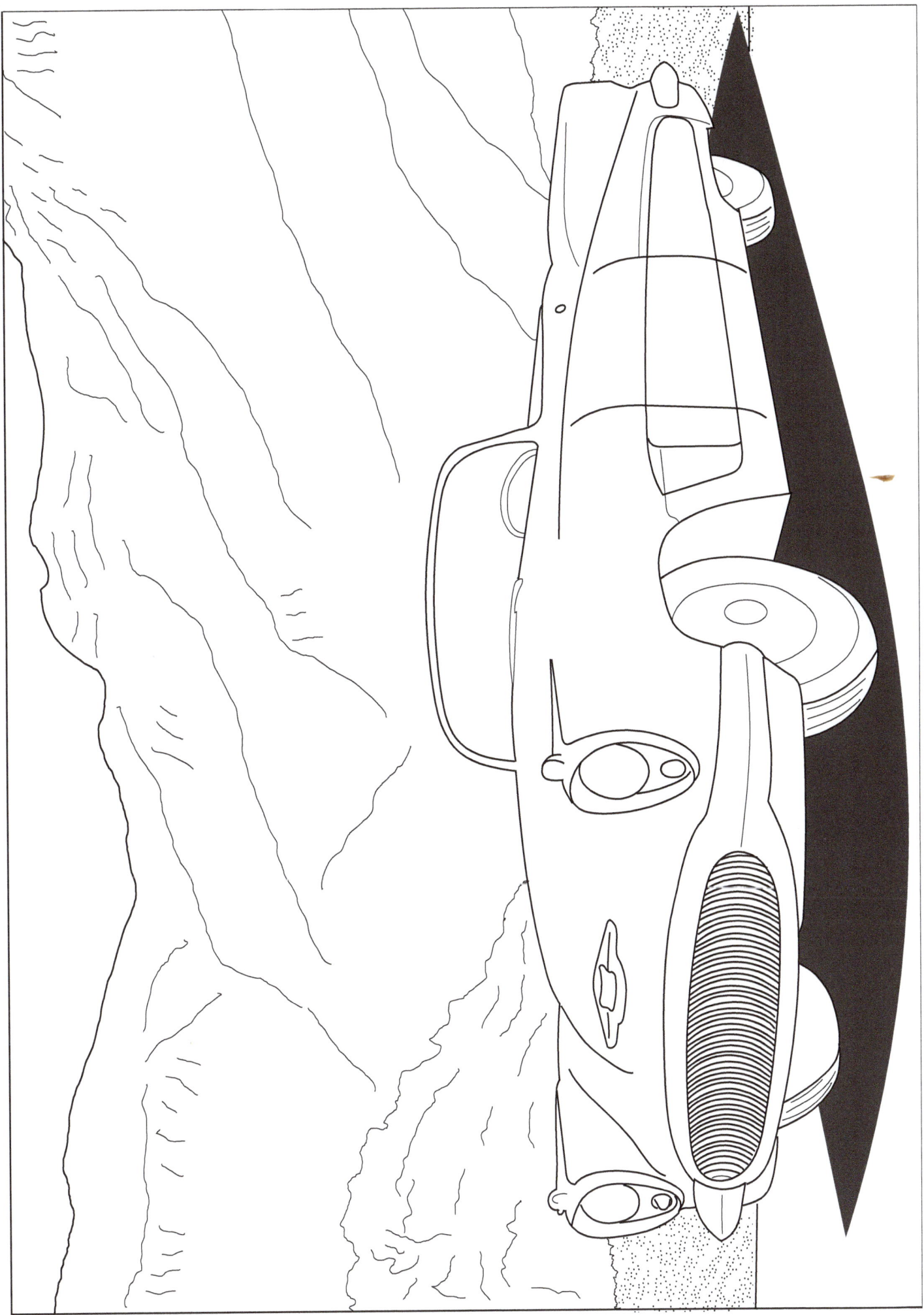

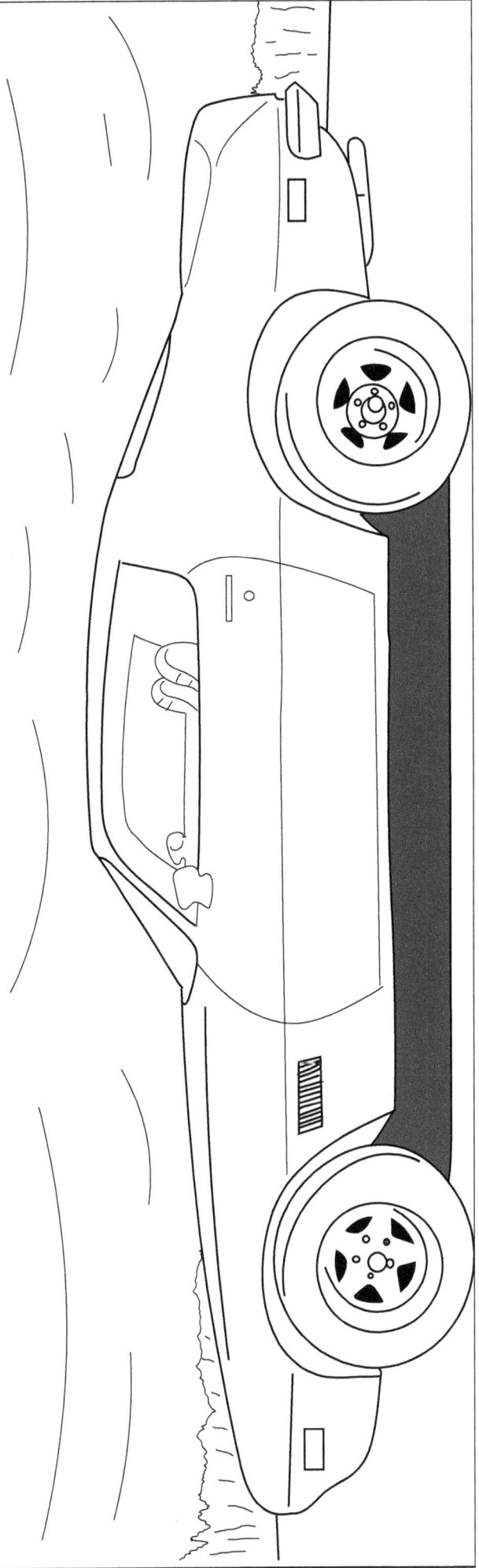

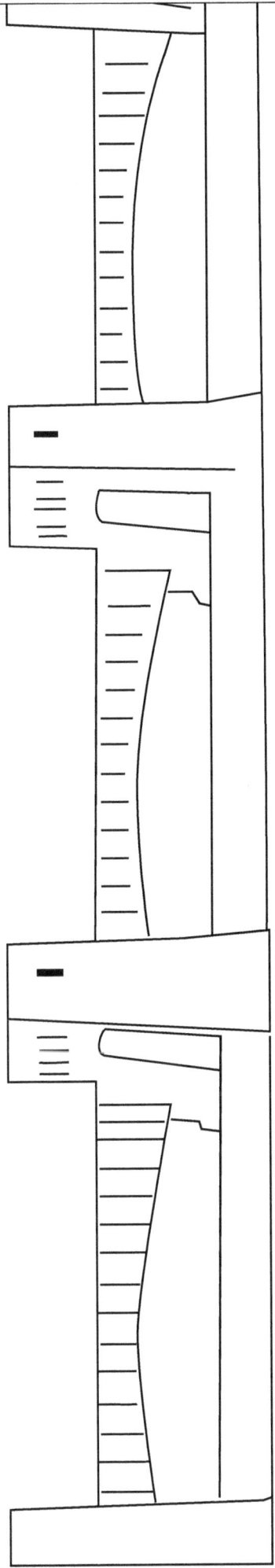

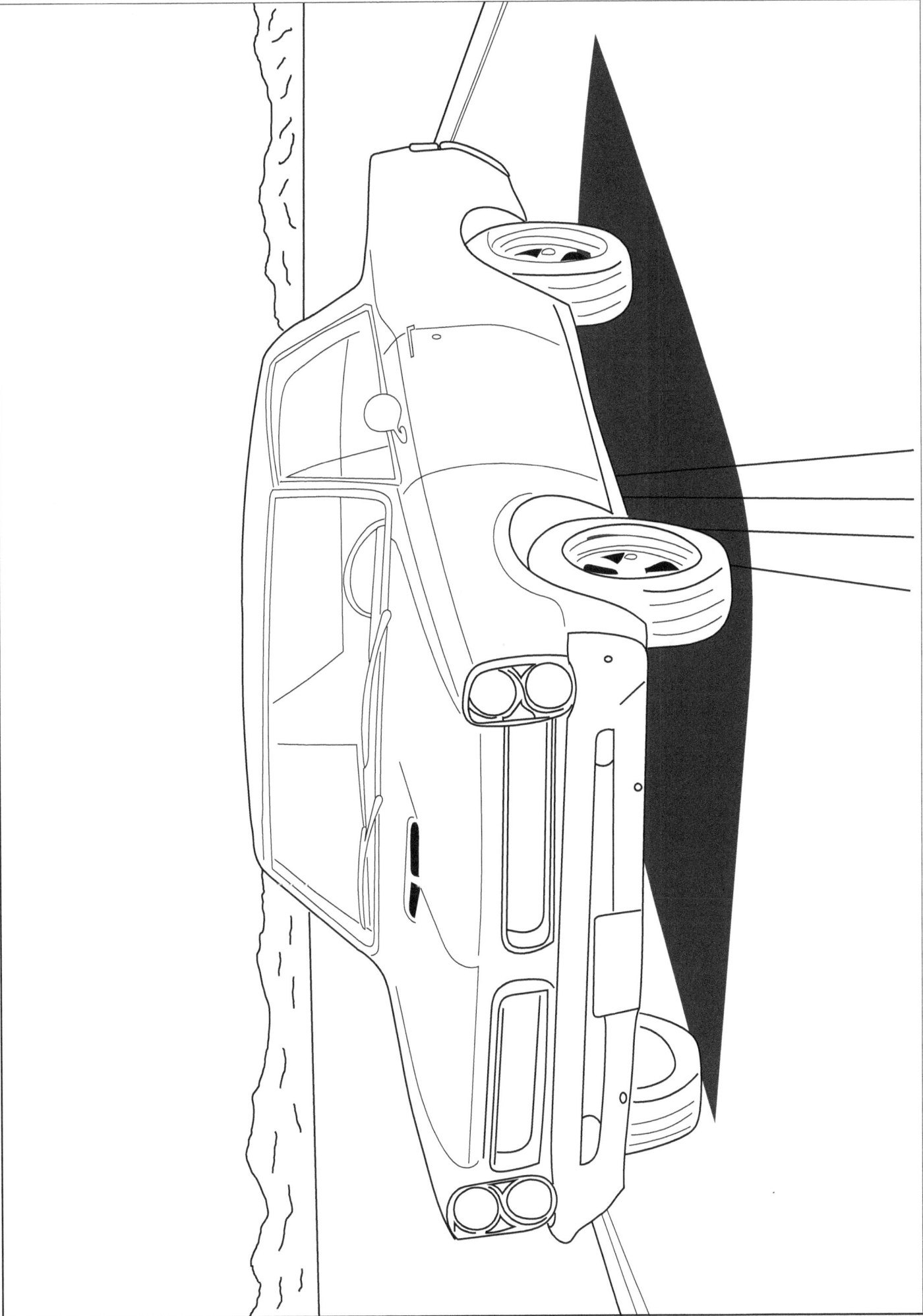

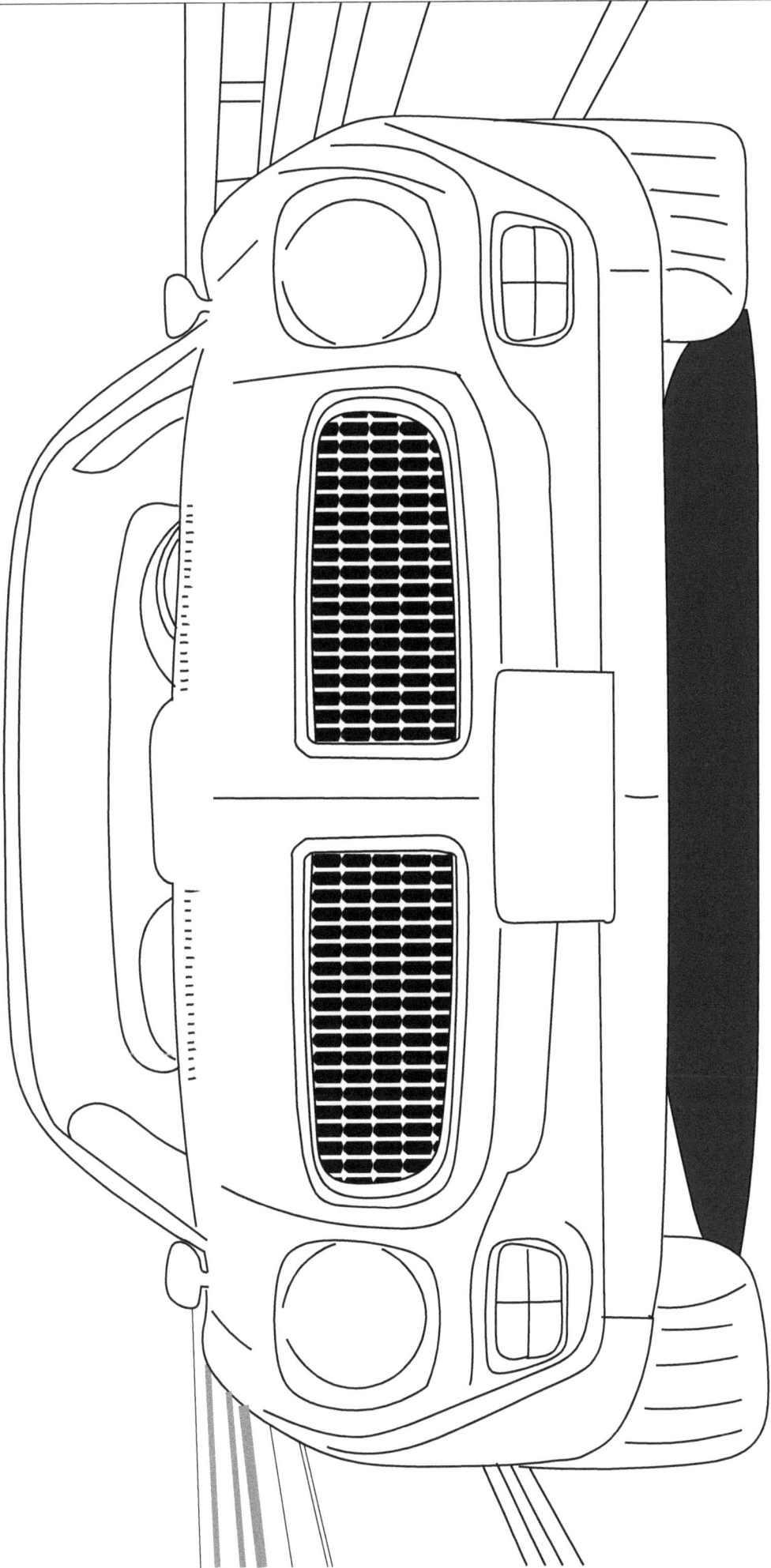

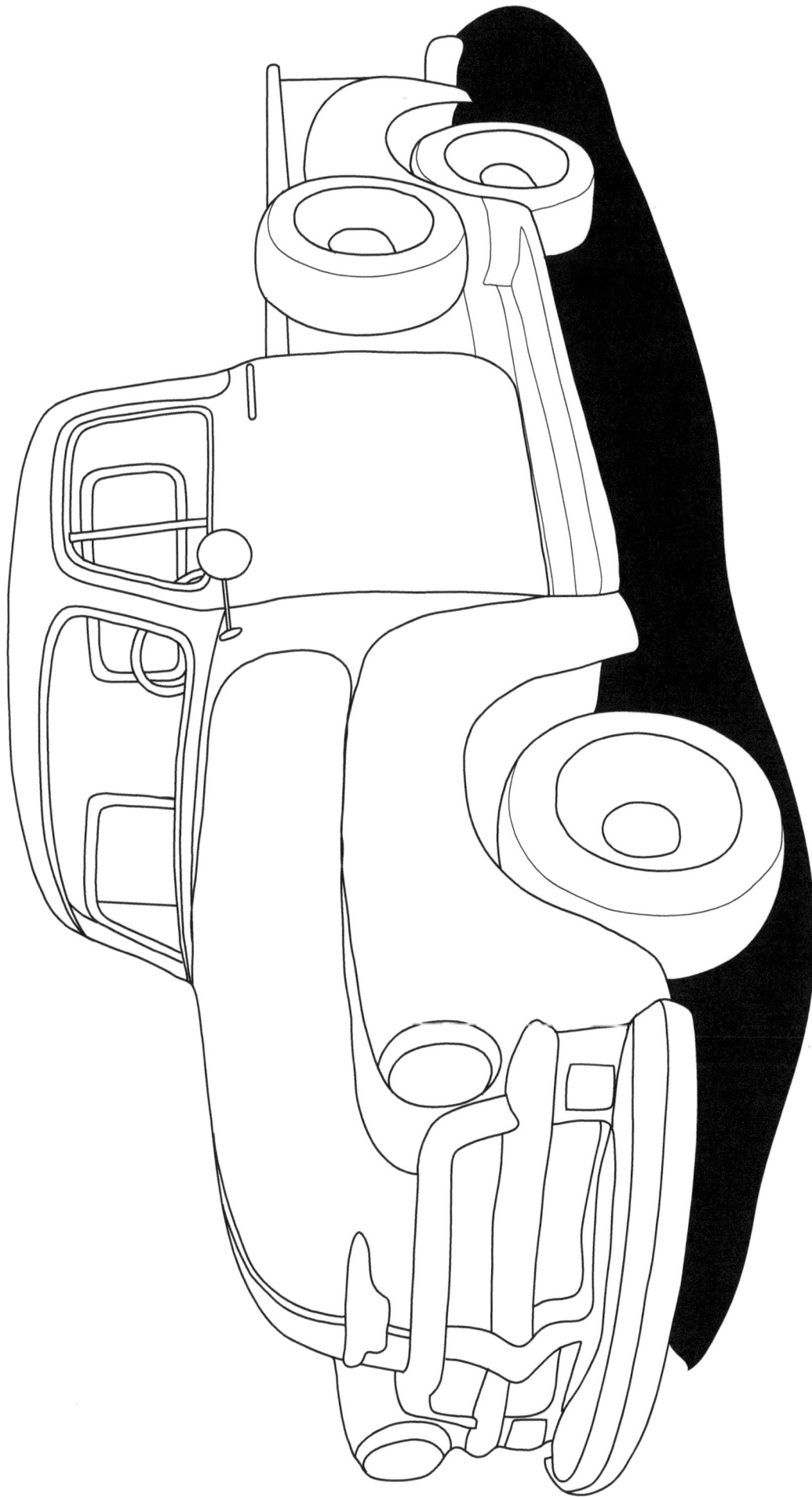

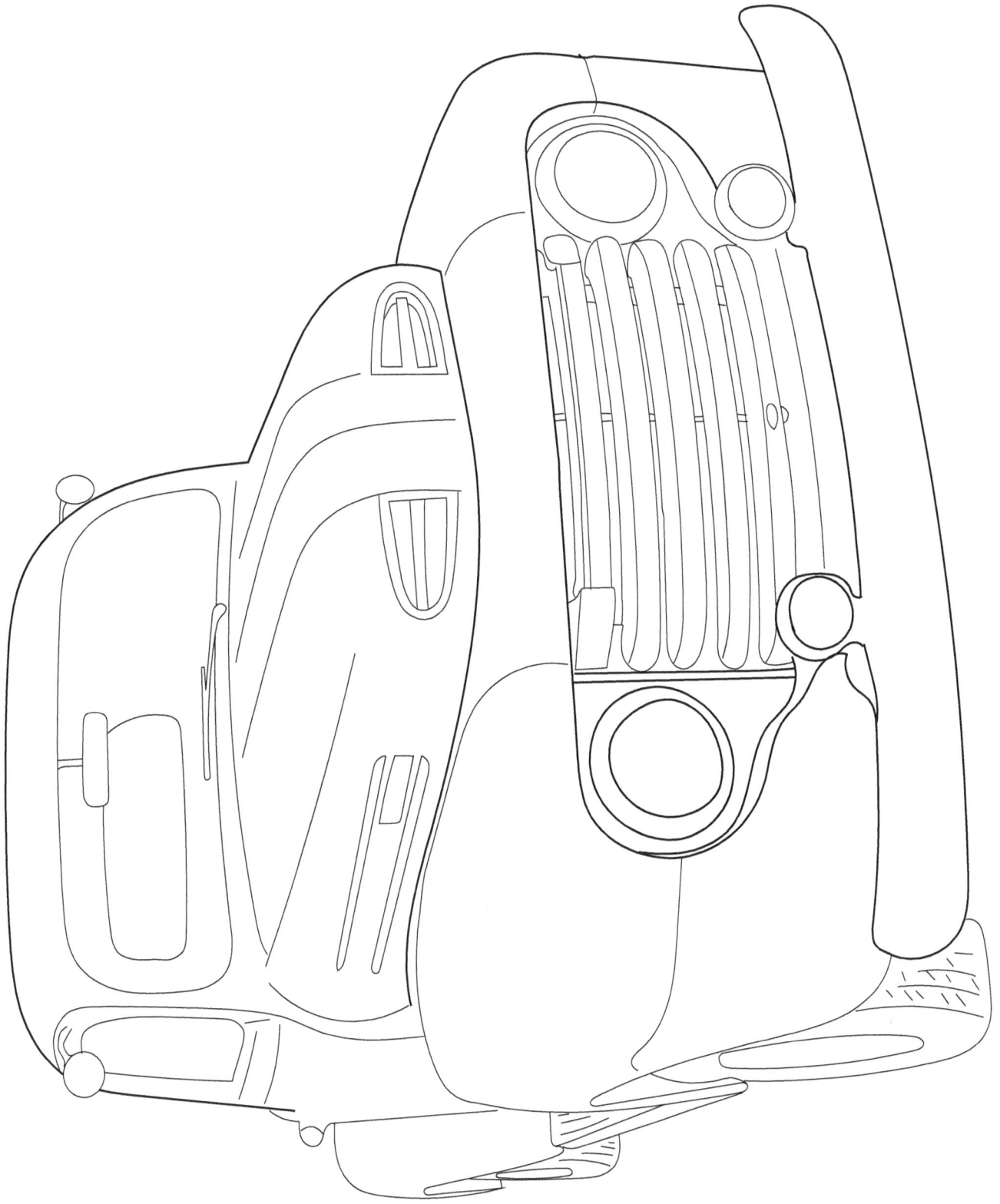

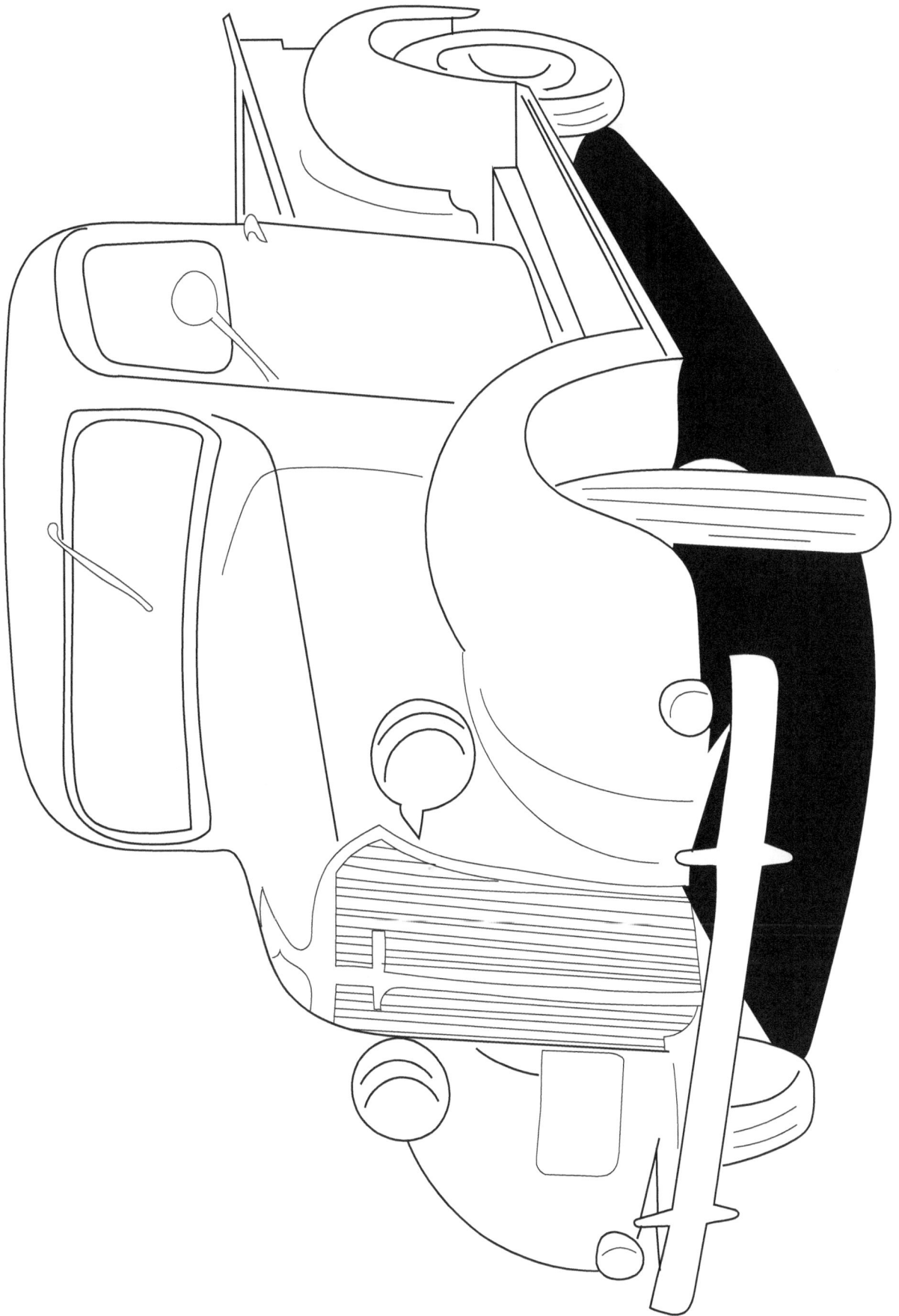

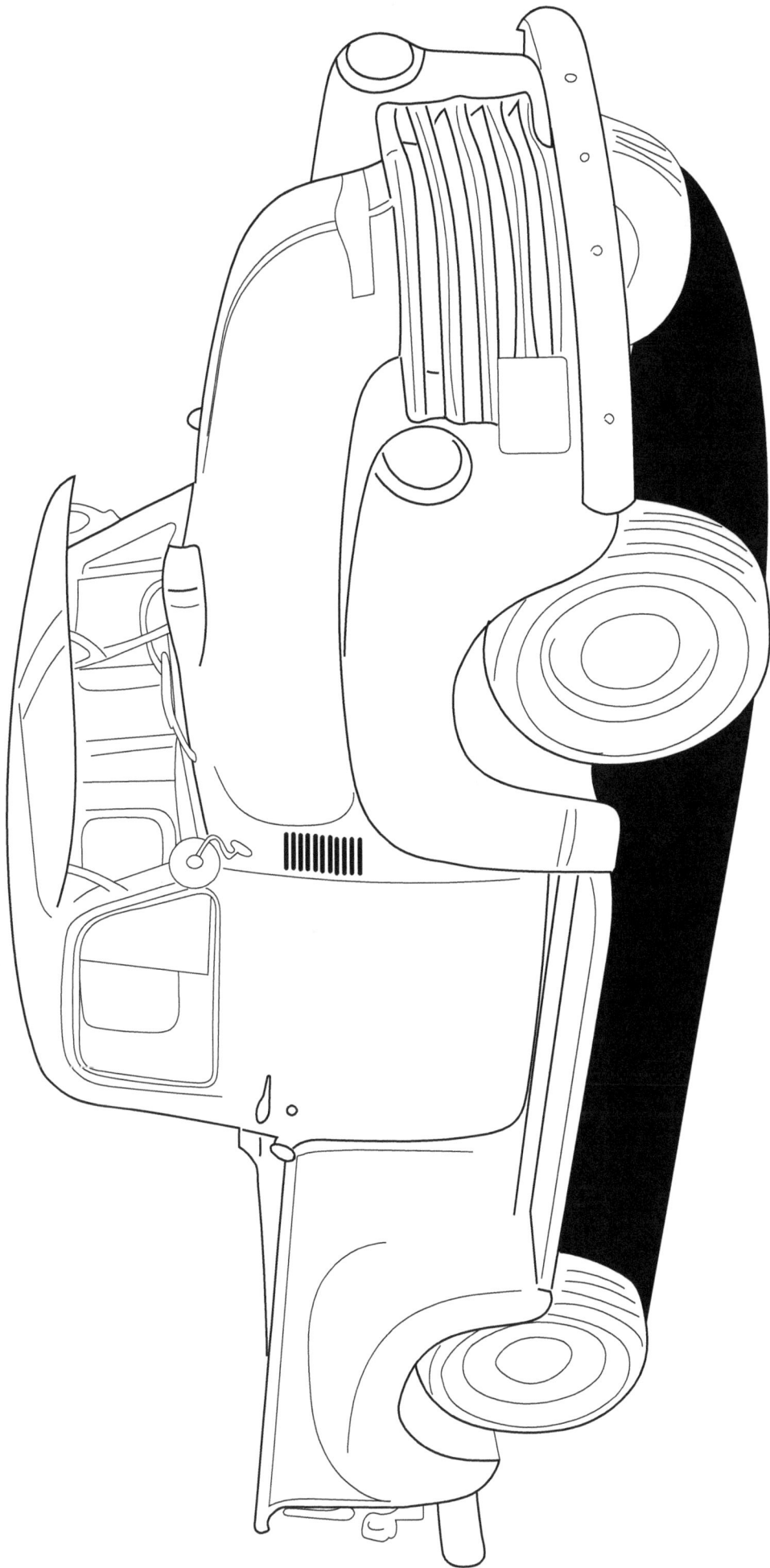

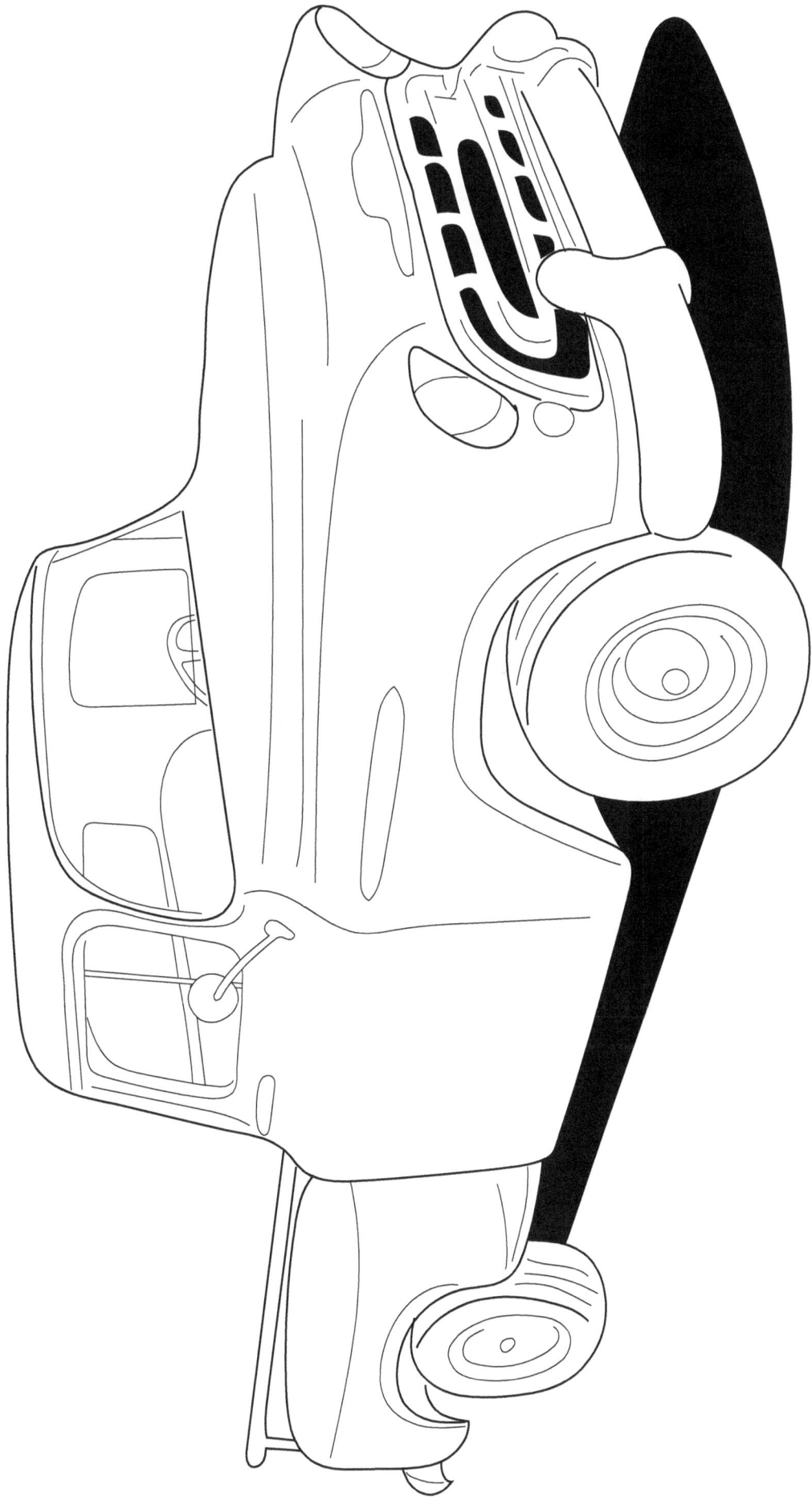

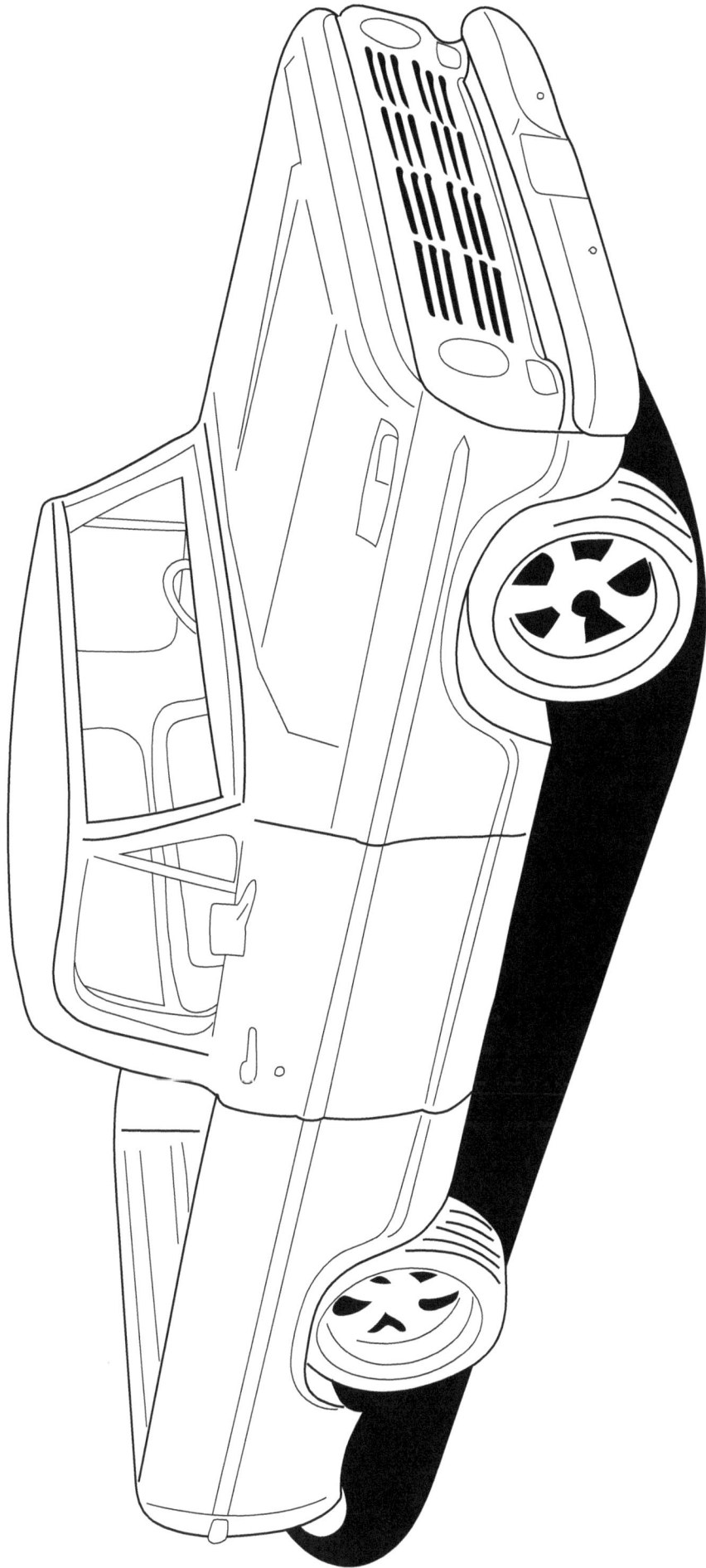

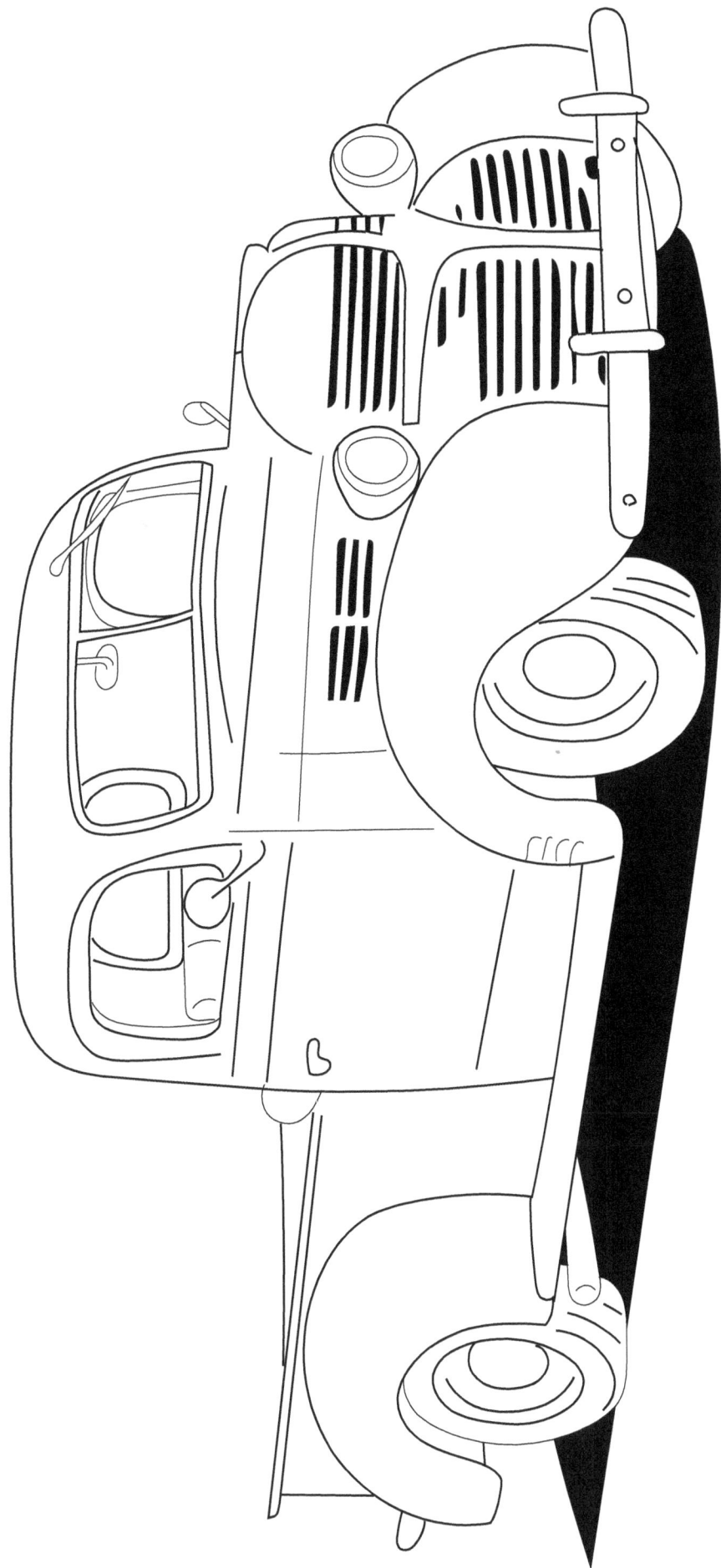

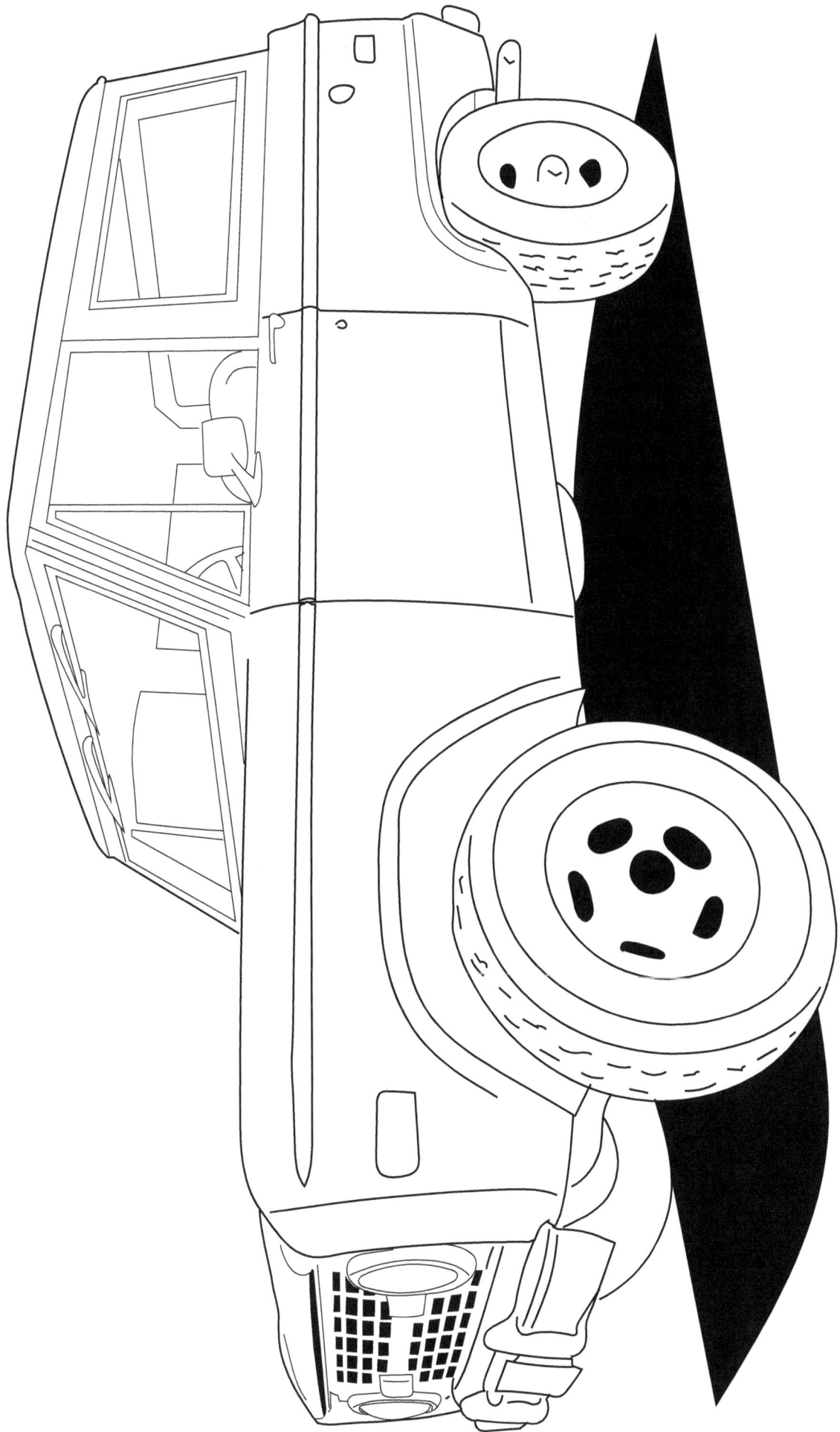

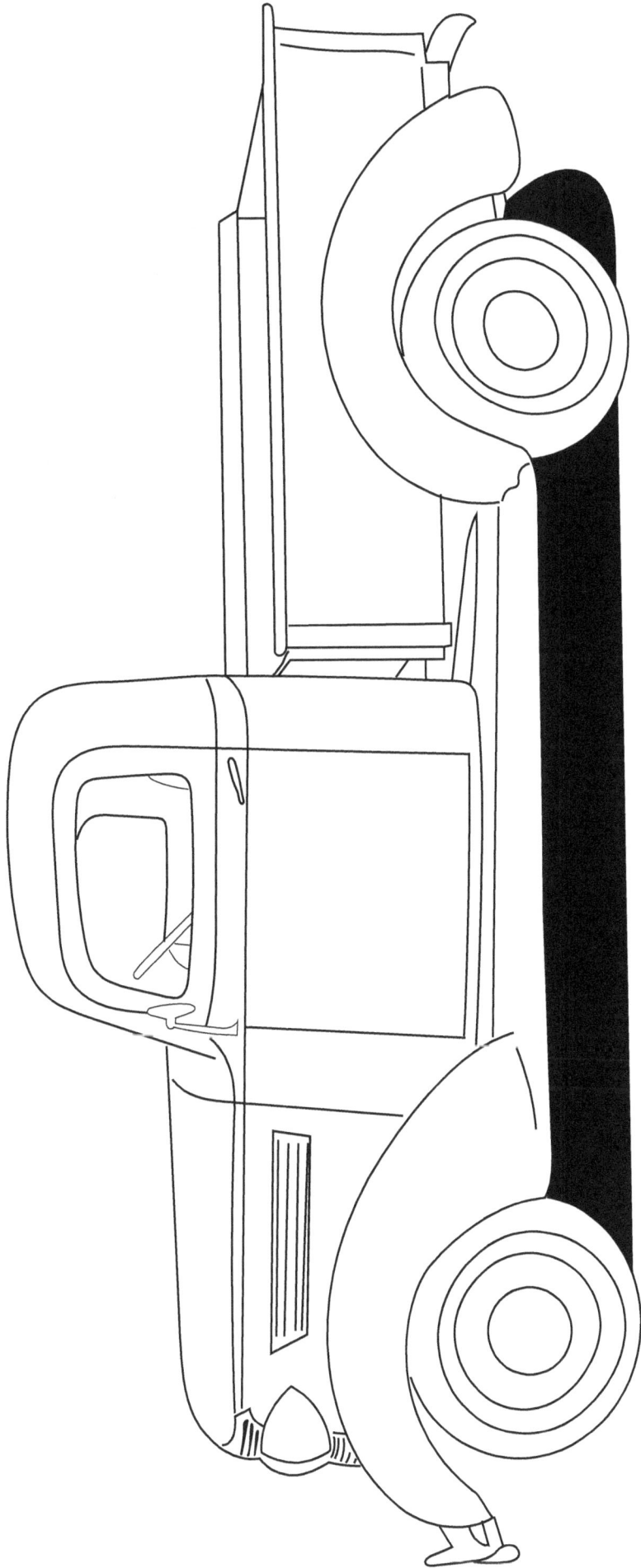

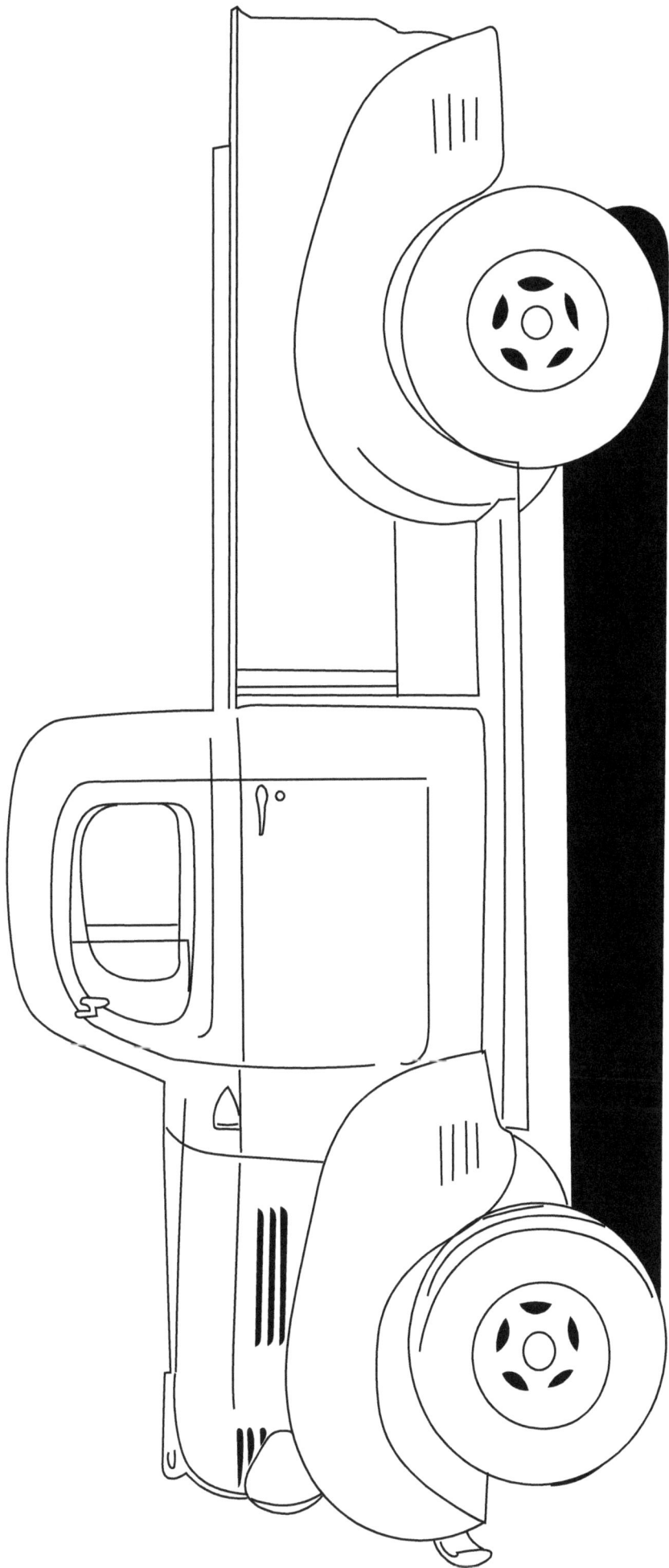

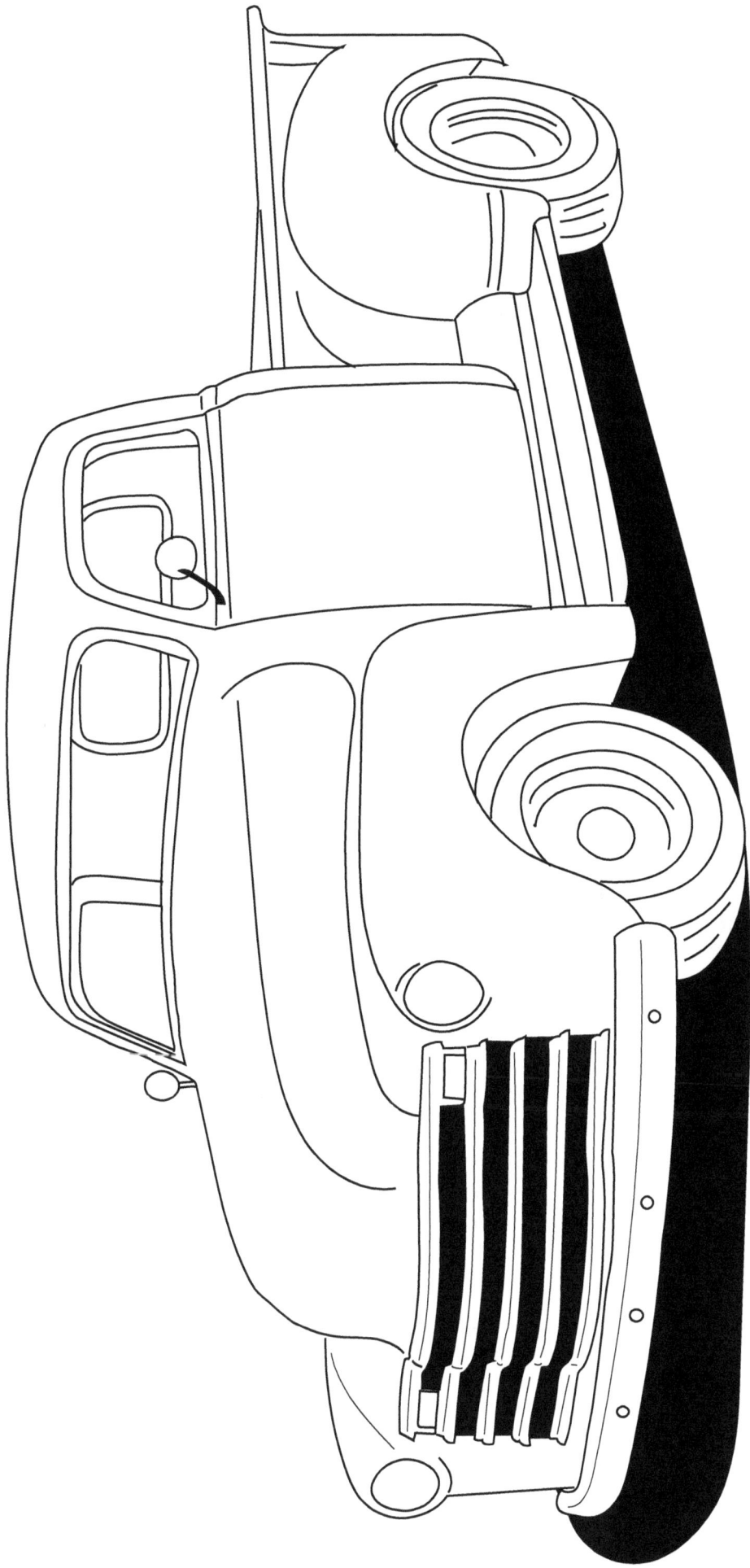

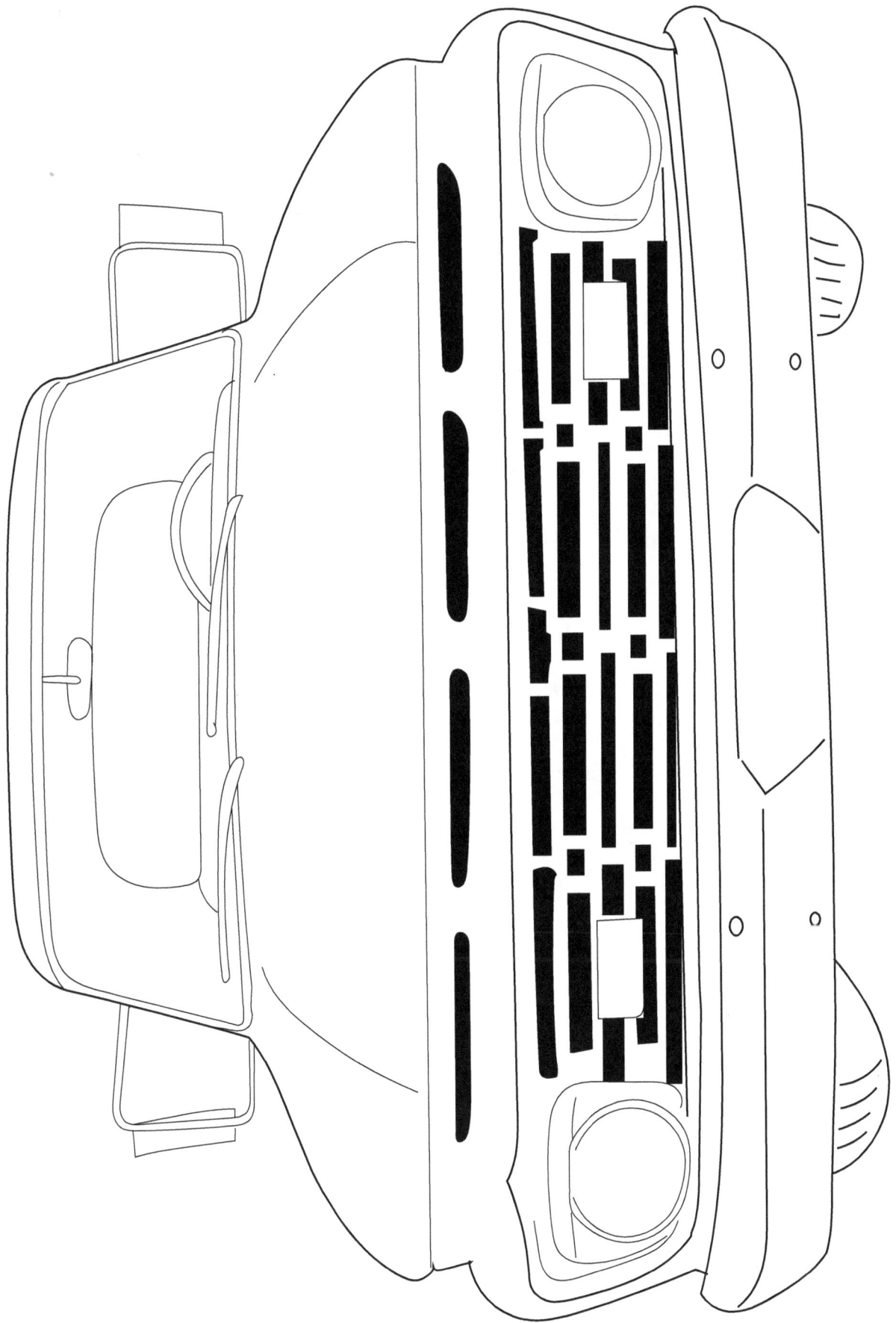

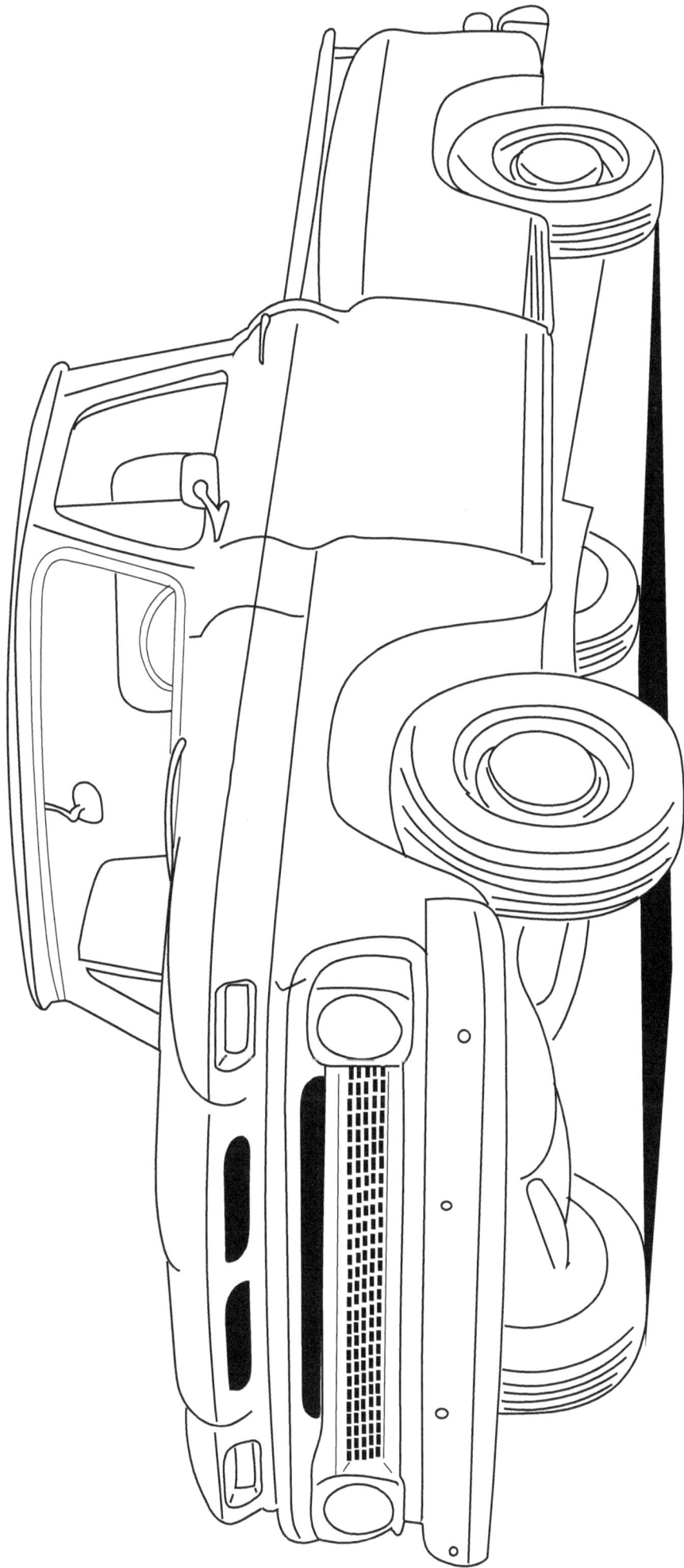

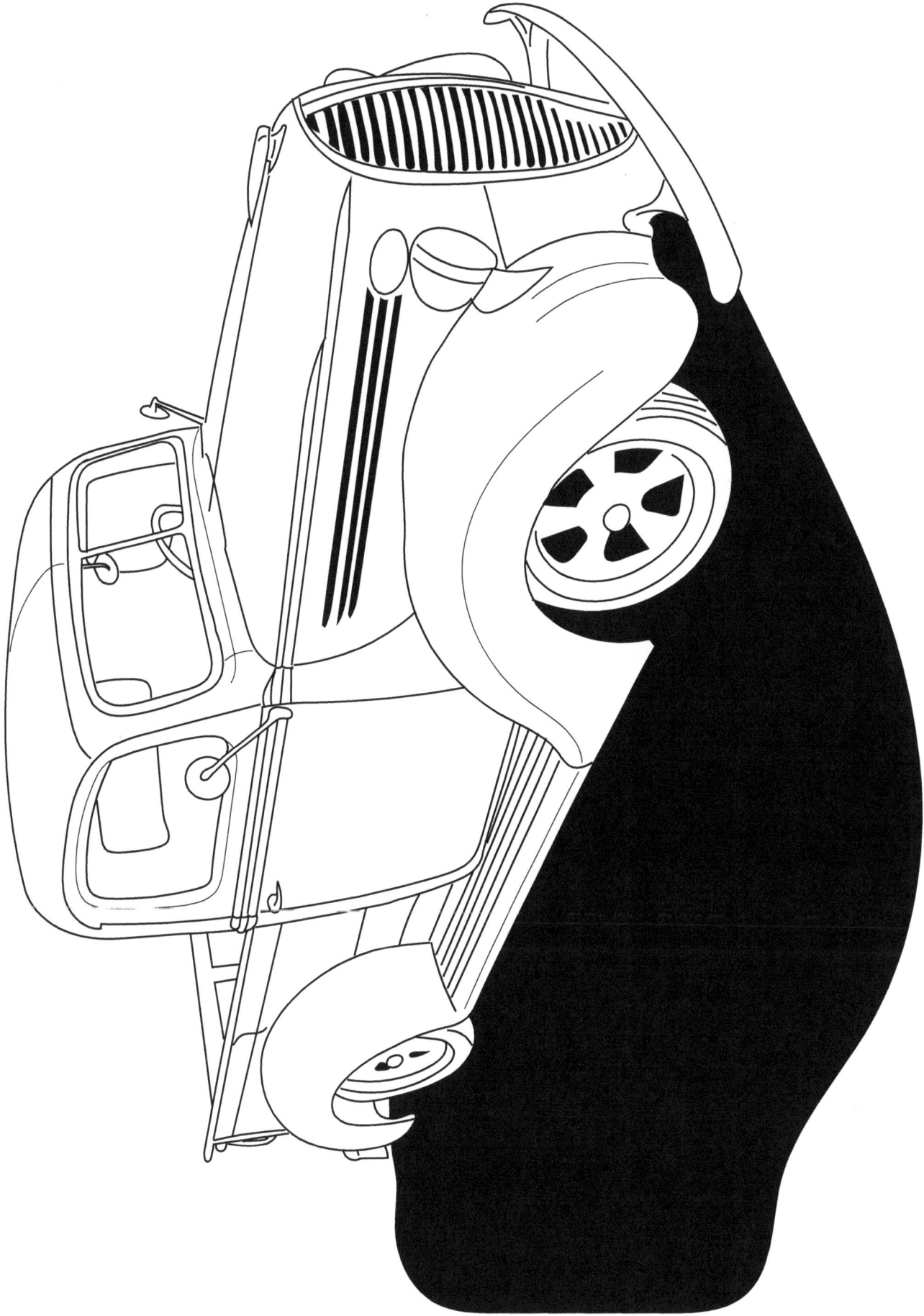

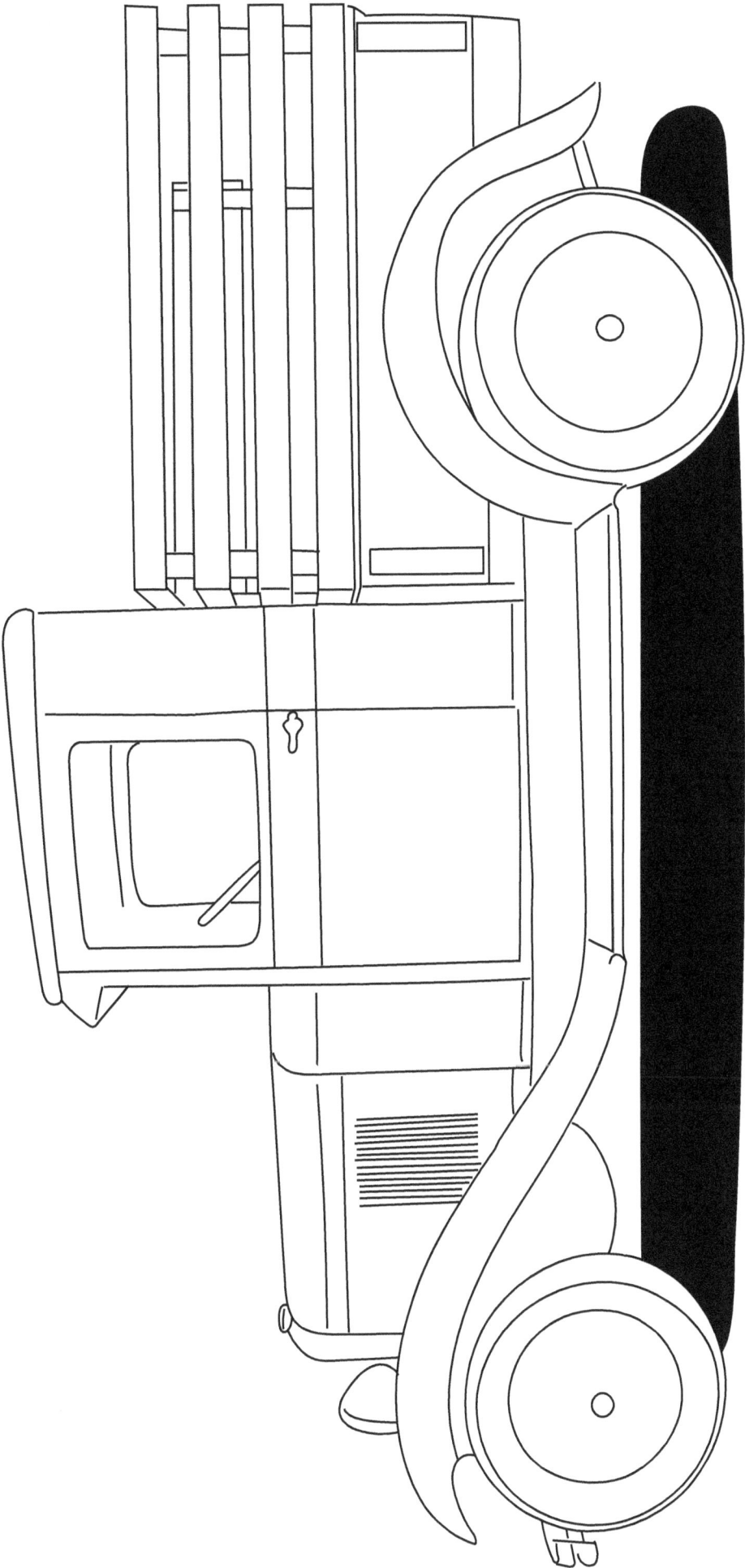

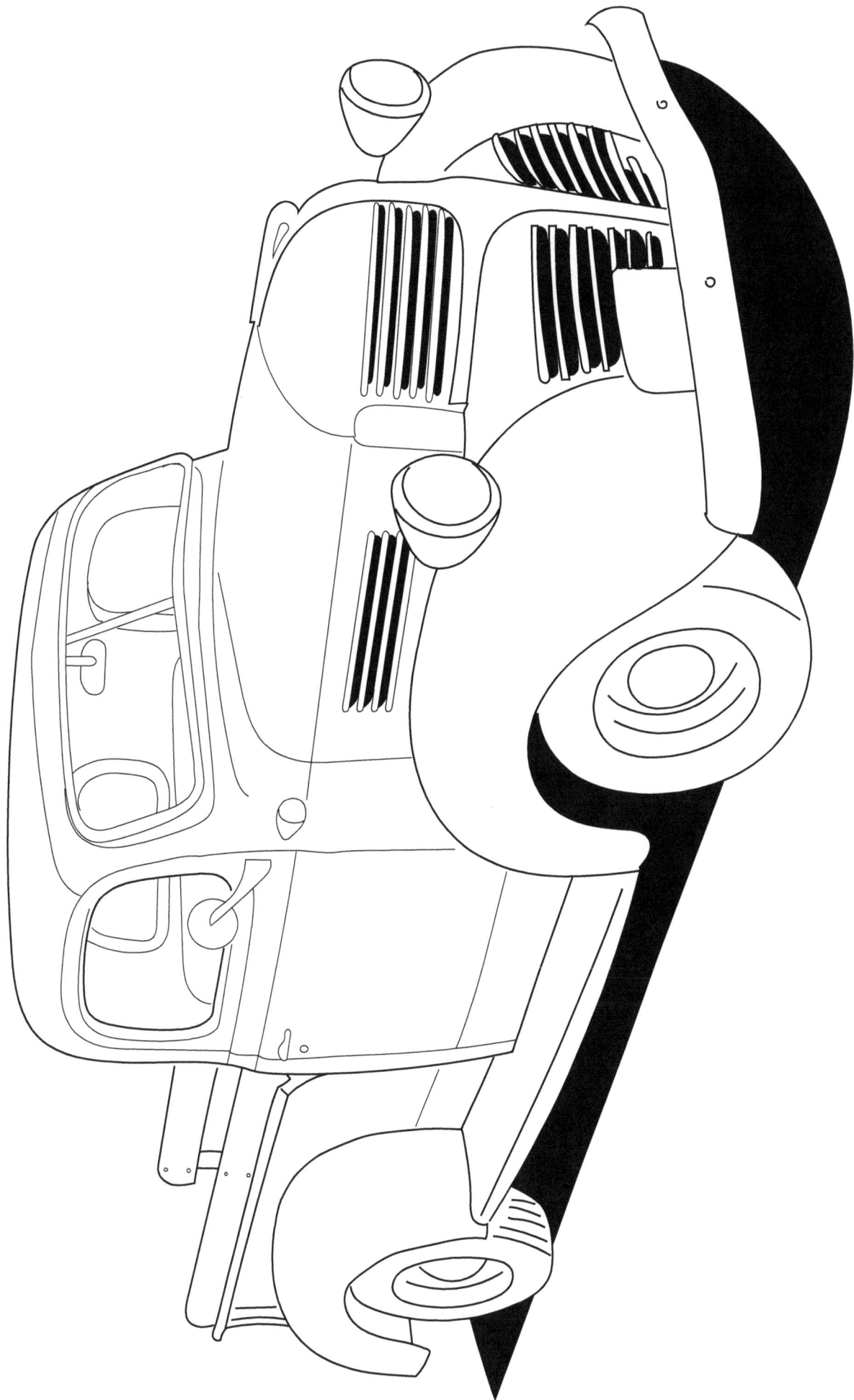

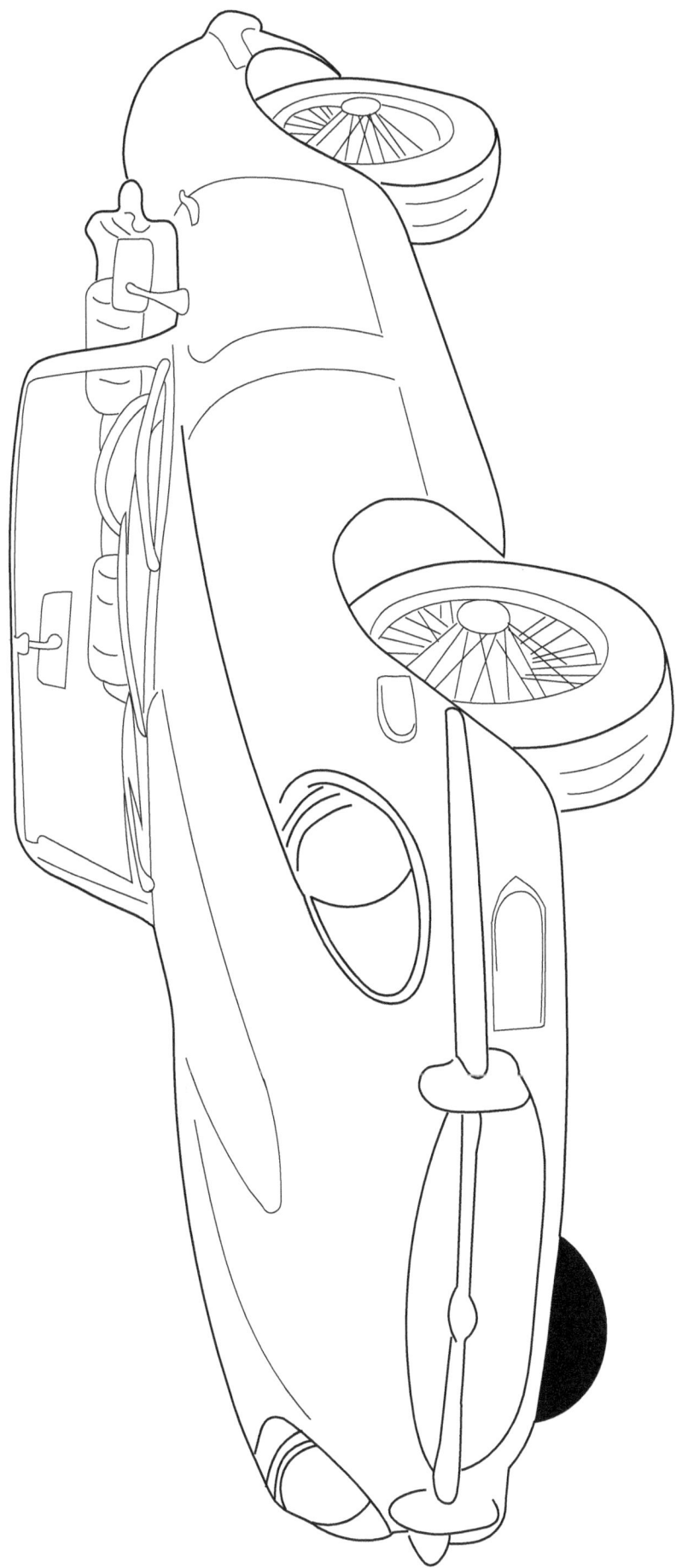

Jaguar XKE

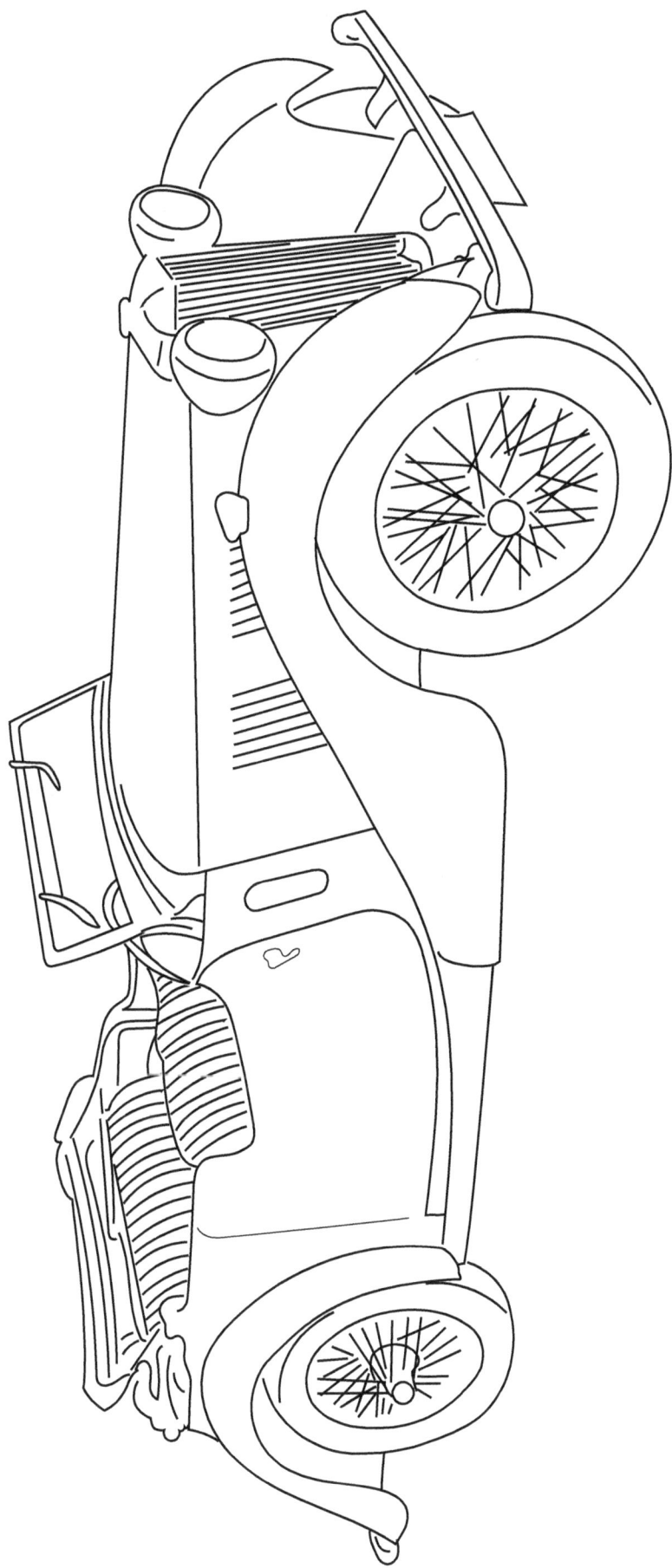

1938 MG ROADSTER

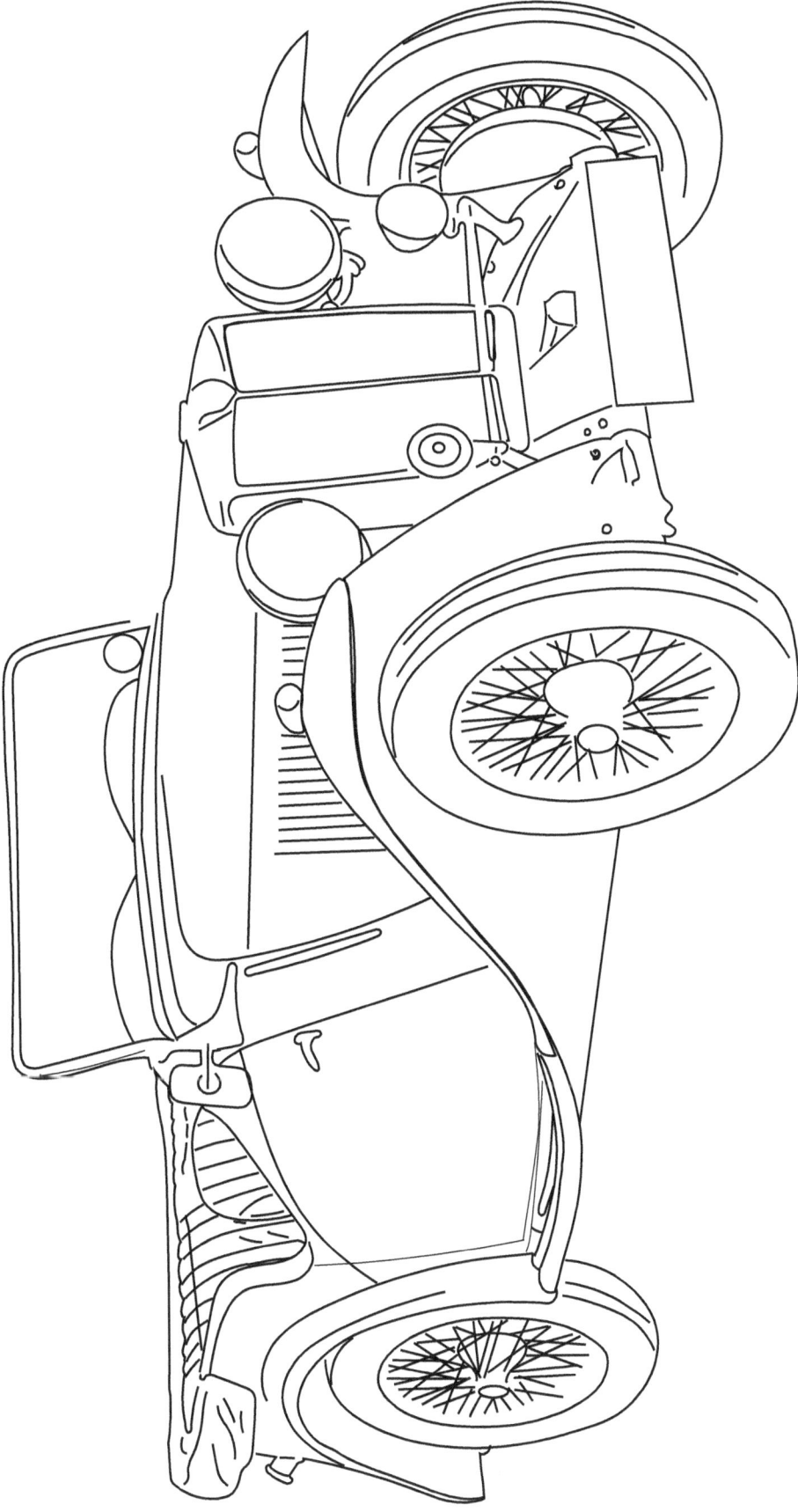

1945 MG TC

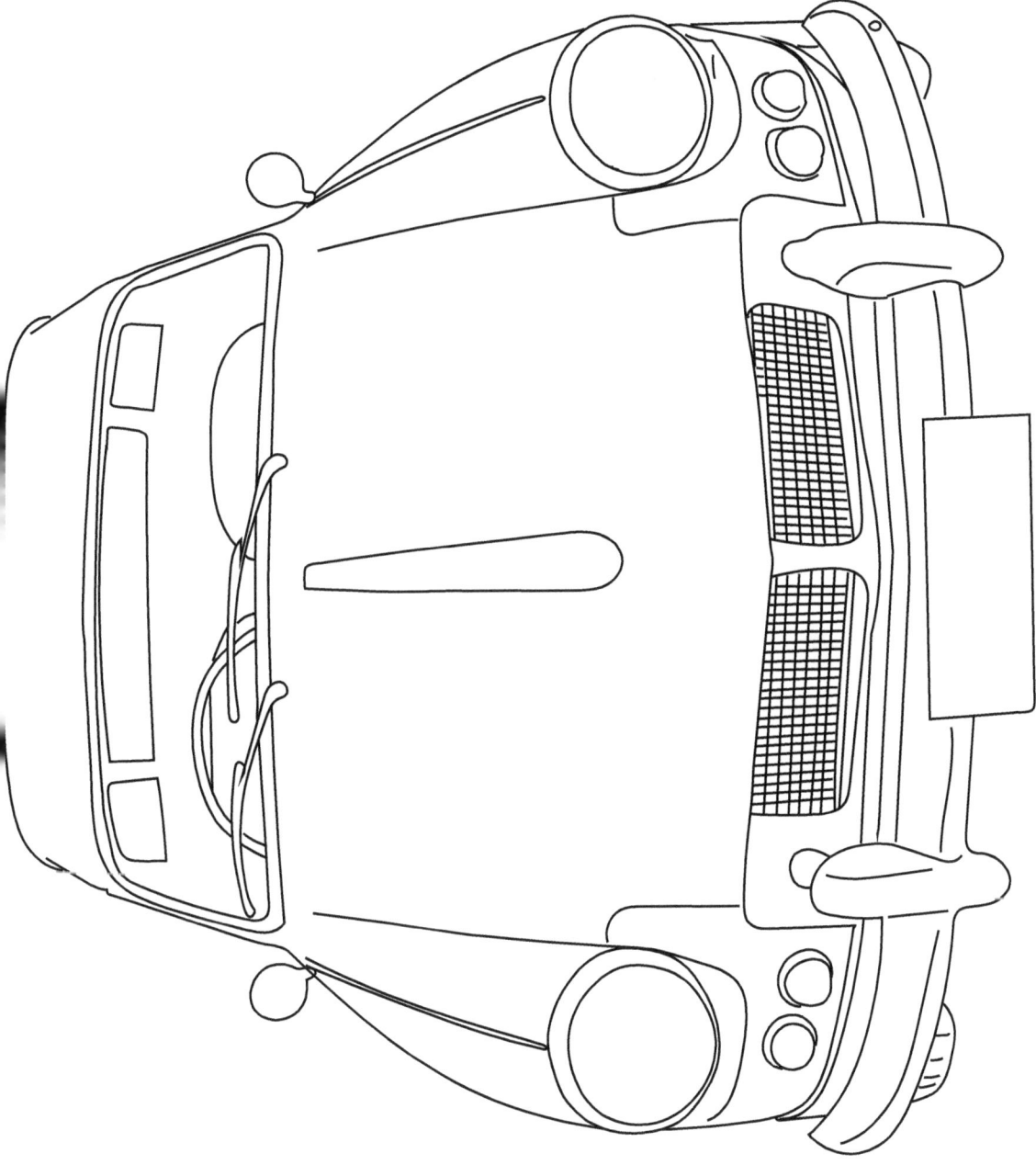

1962 Triumph Spitfire

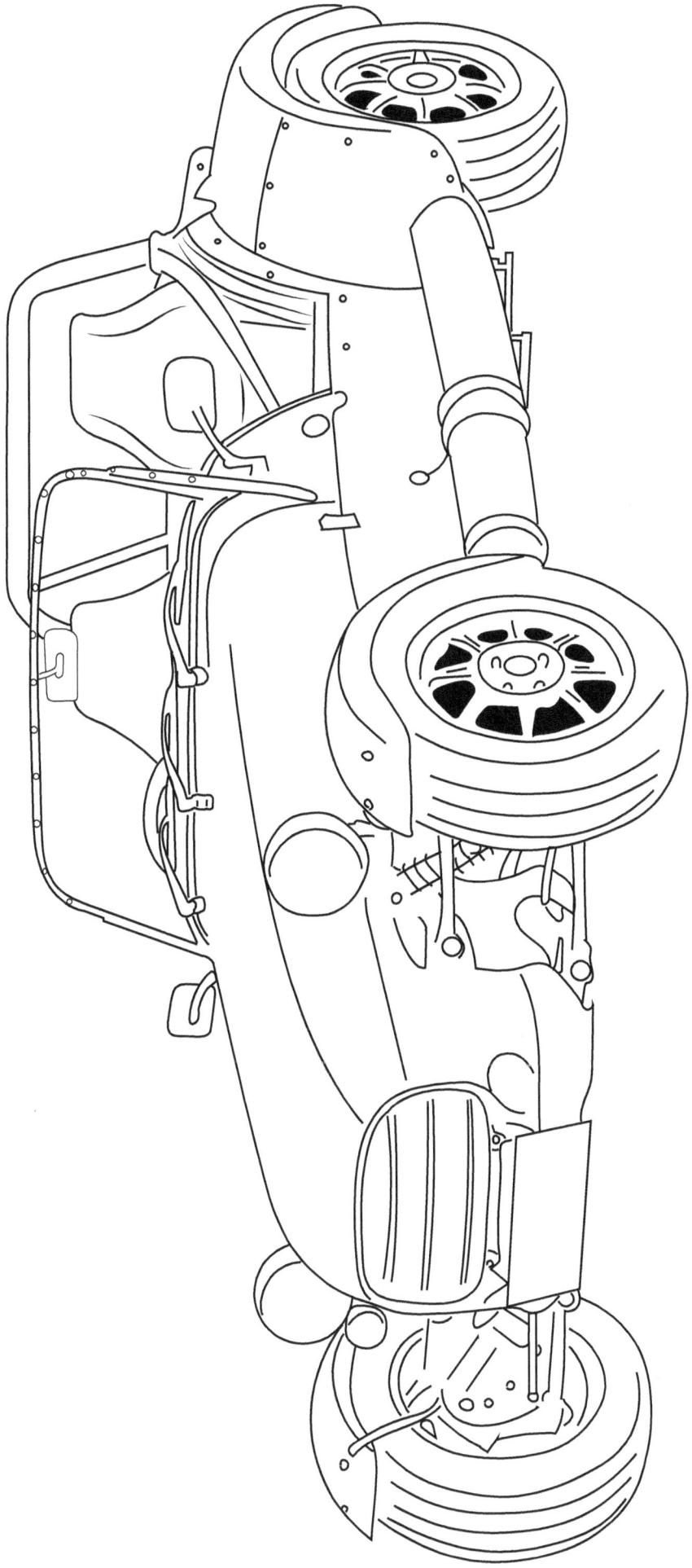

Lotus 7

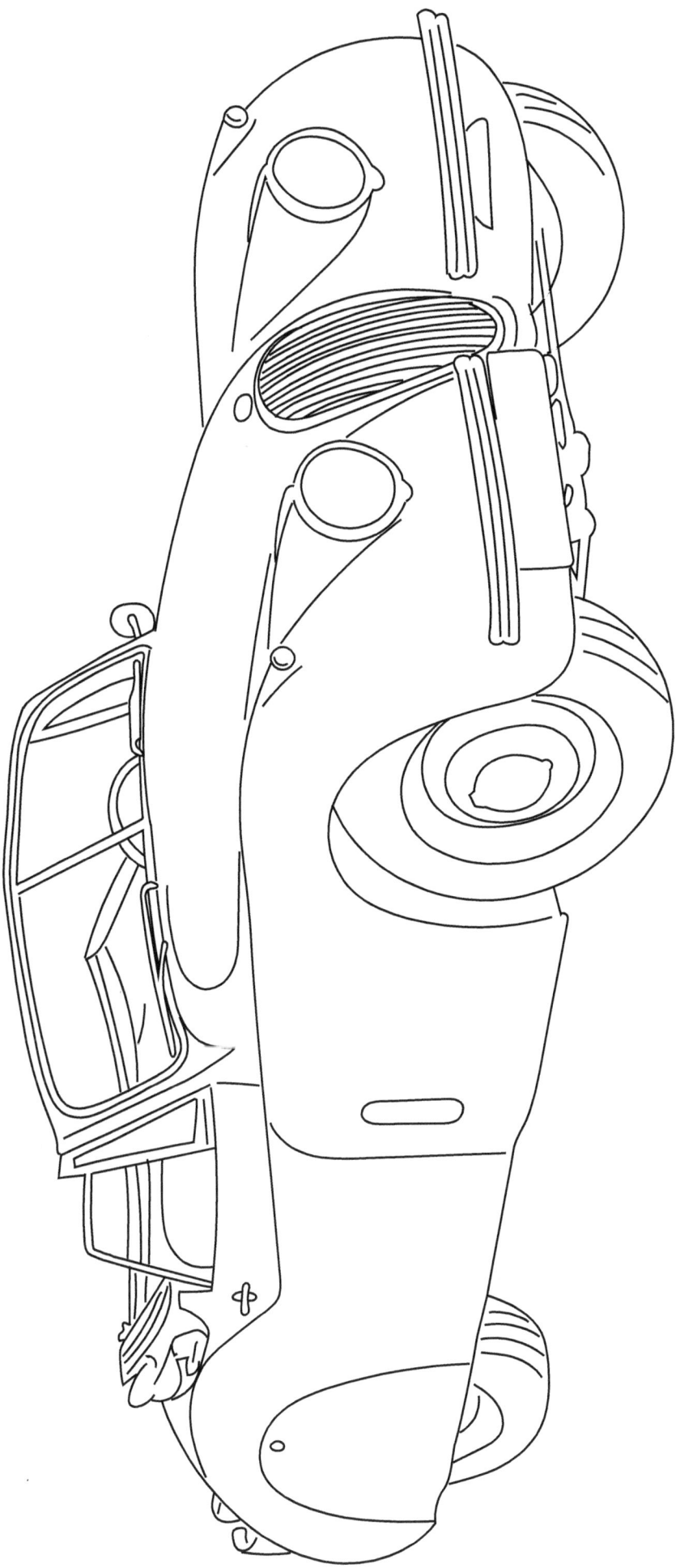

1953 Jaguar XK

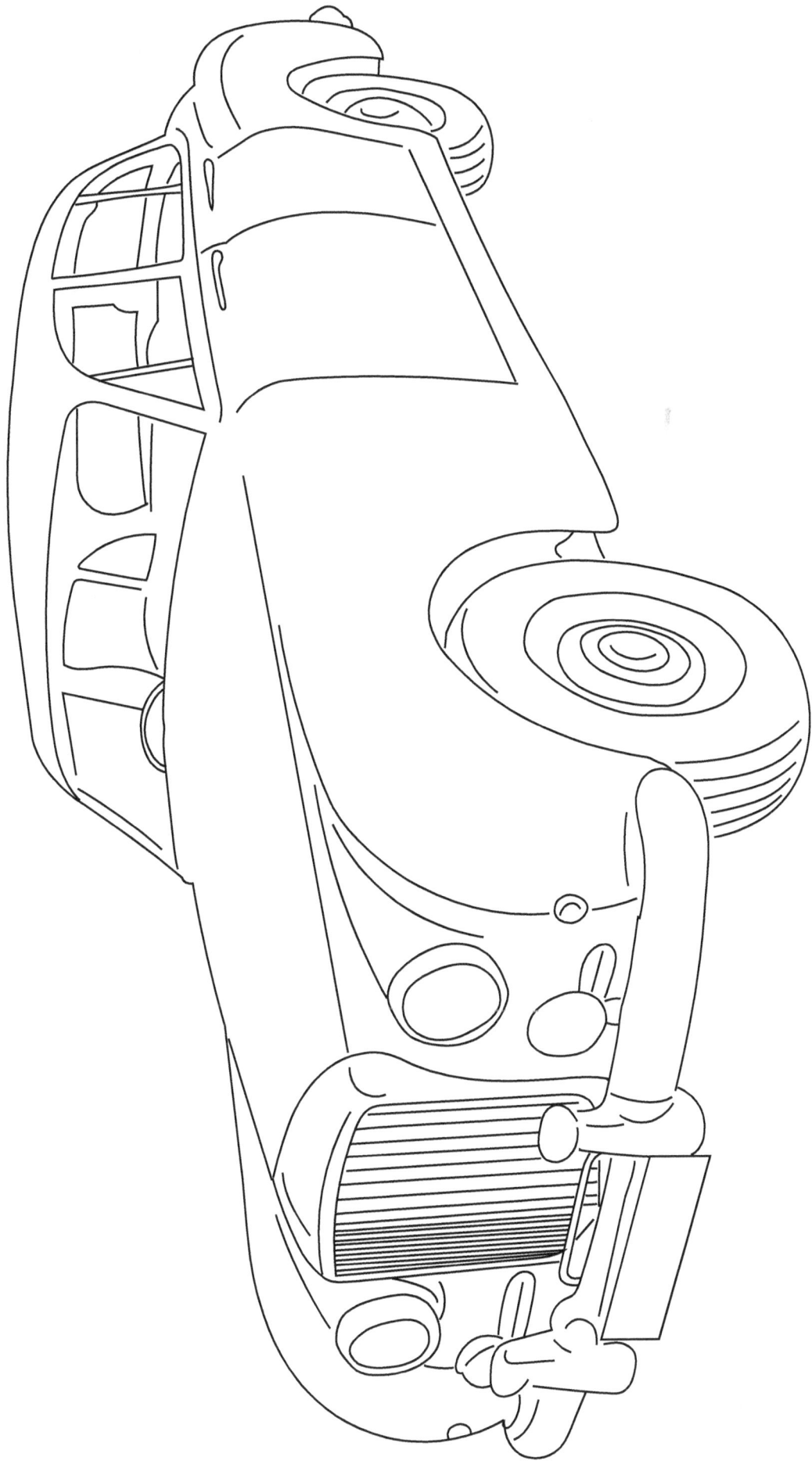

1960 Bentley S2

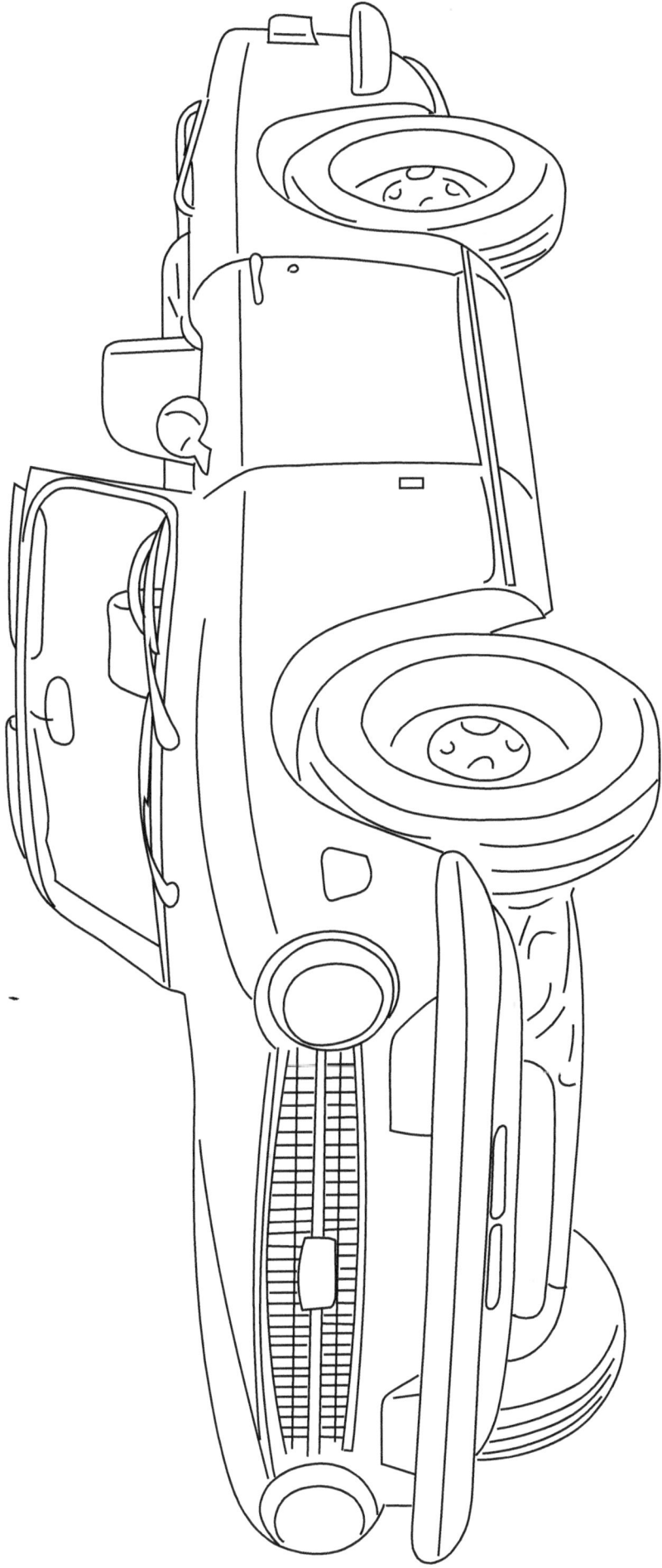

1969 Triumph TR6

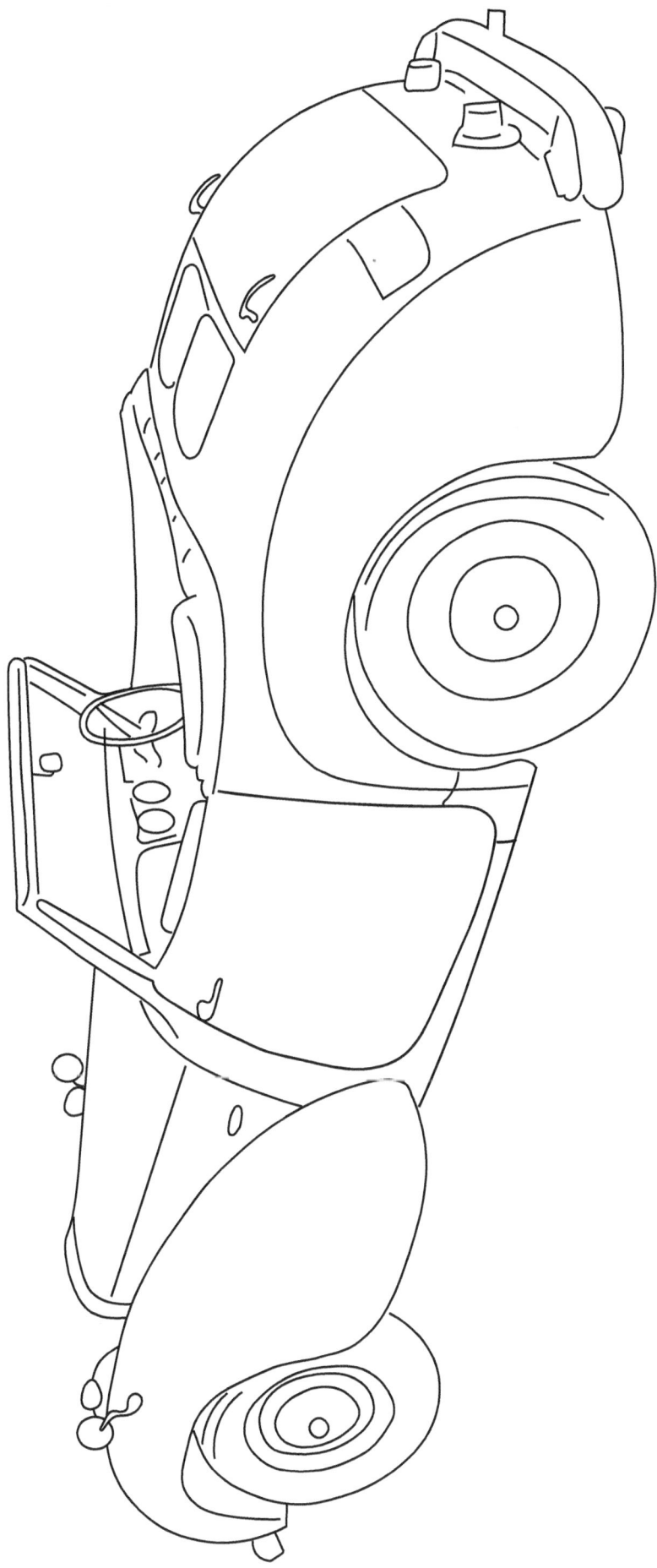

1949 Triumph 2000

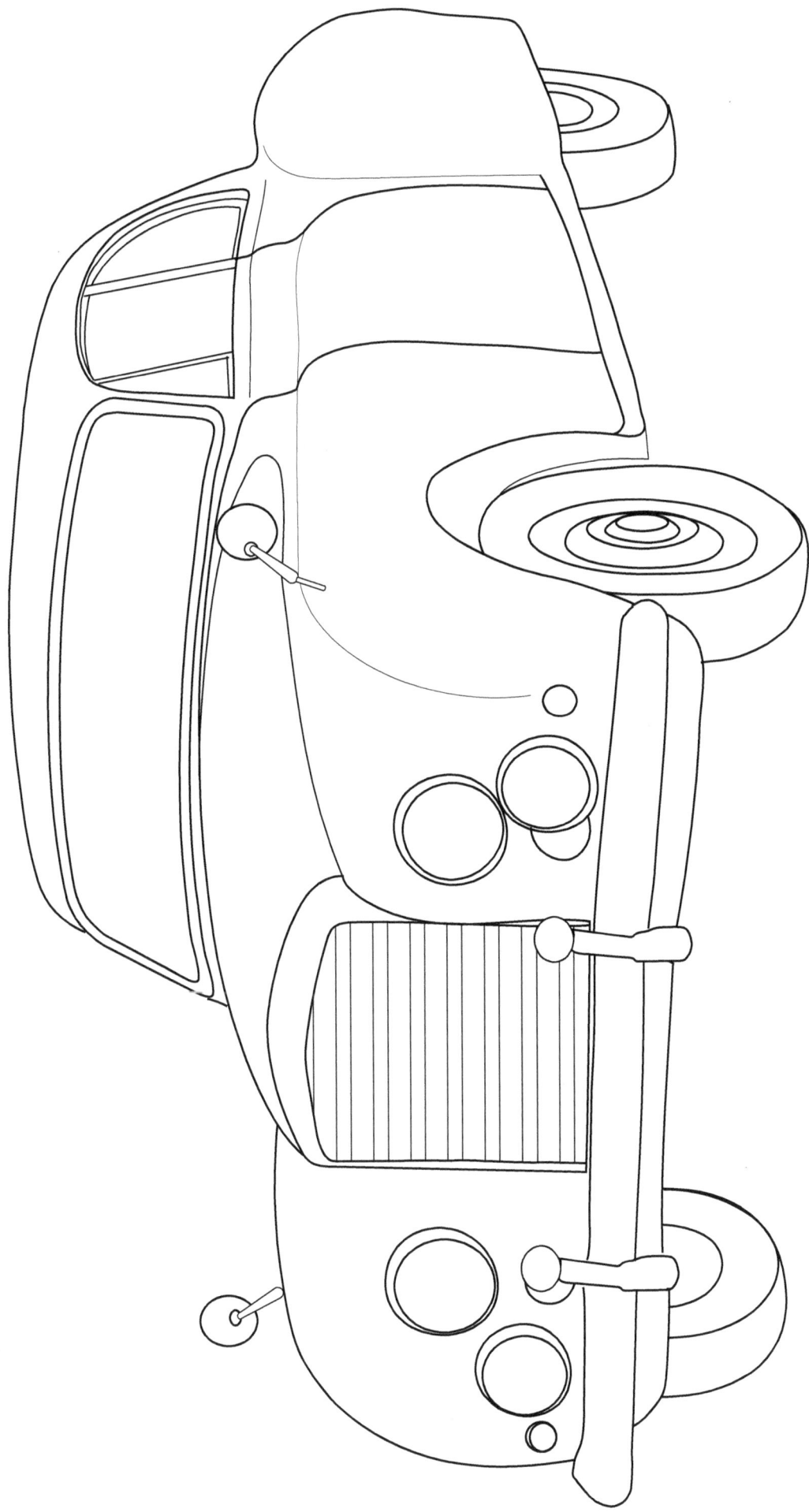

1955 Bentley R Type

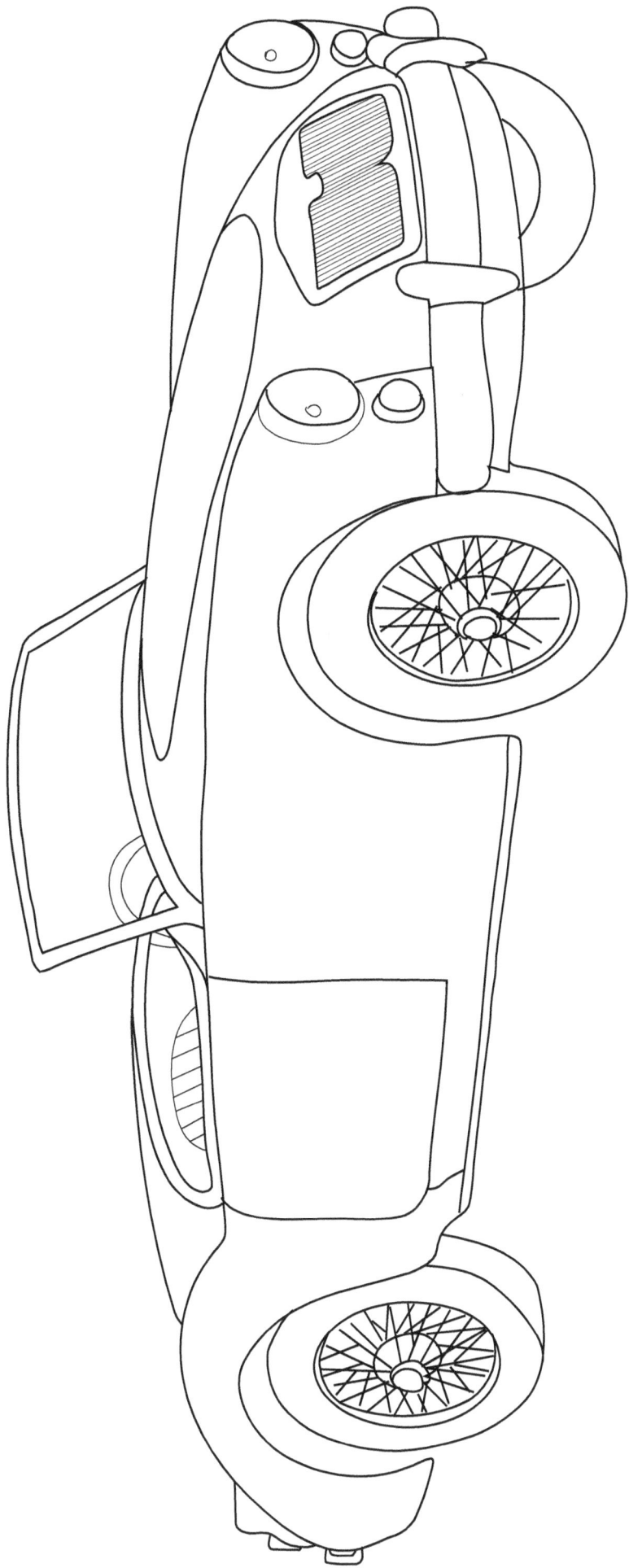

1955 MG MGA

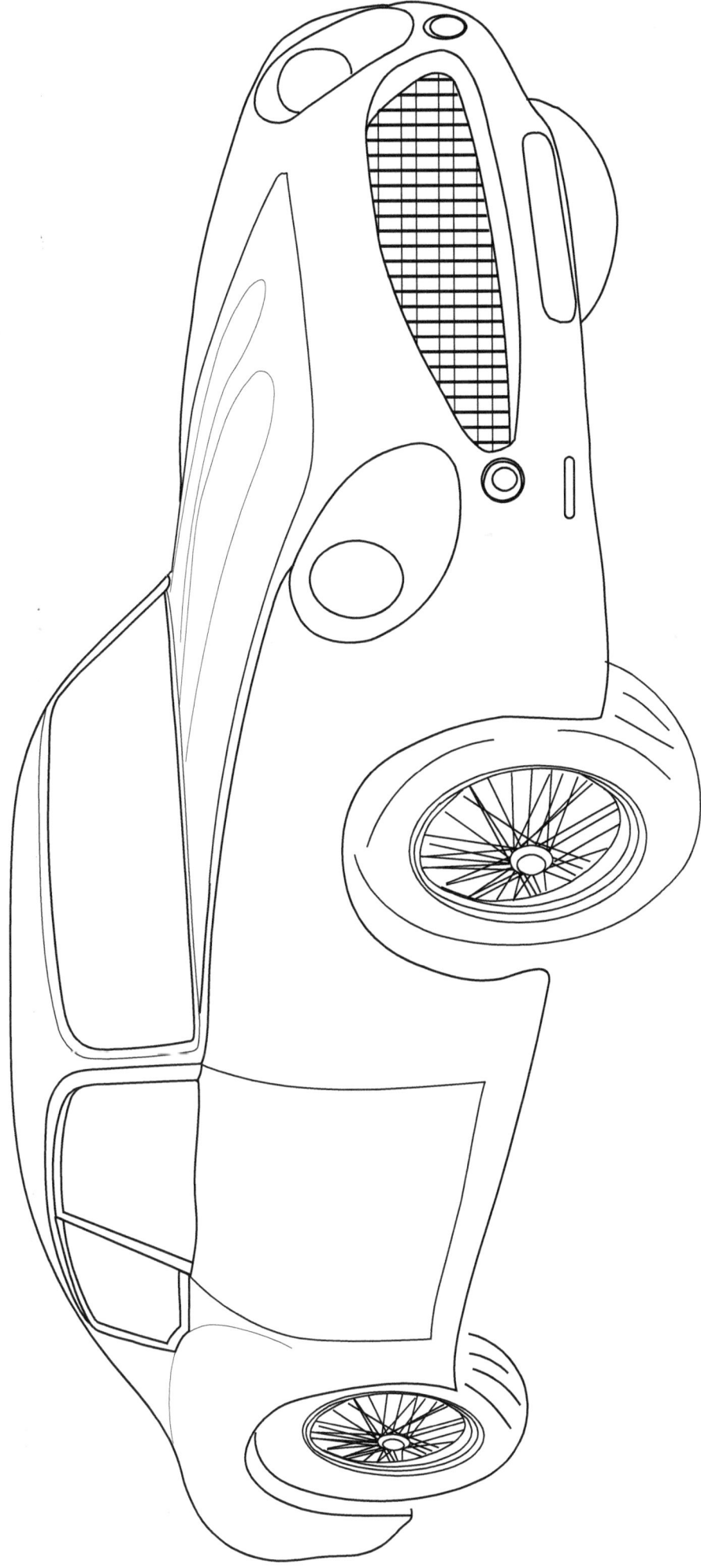

1960 Austin Martin DB4 GTZ

ZAGATO COUPE

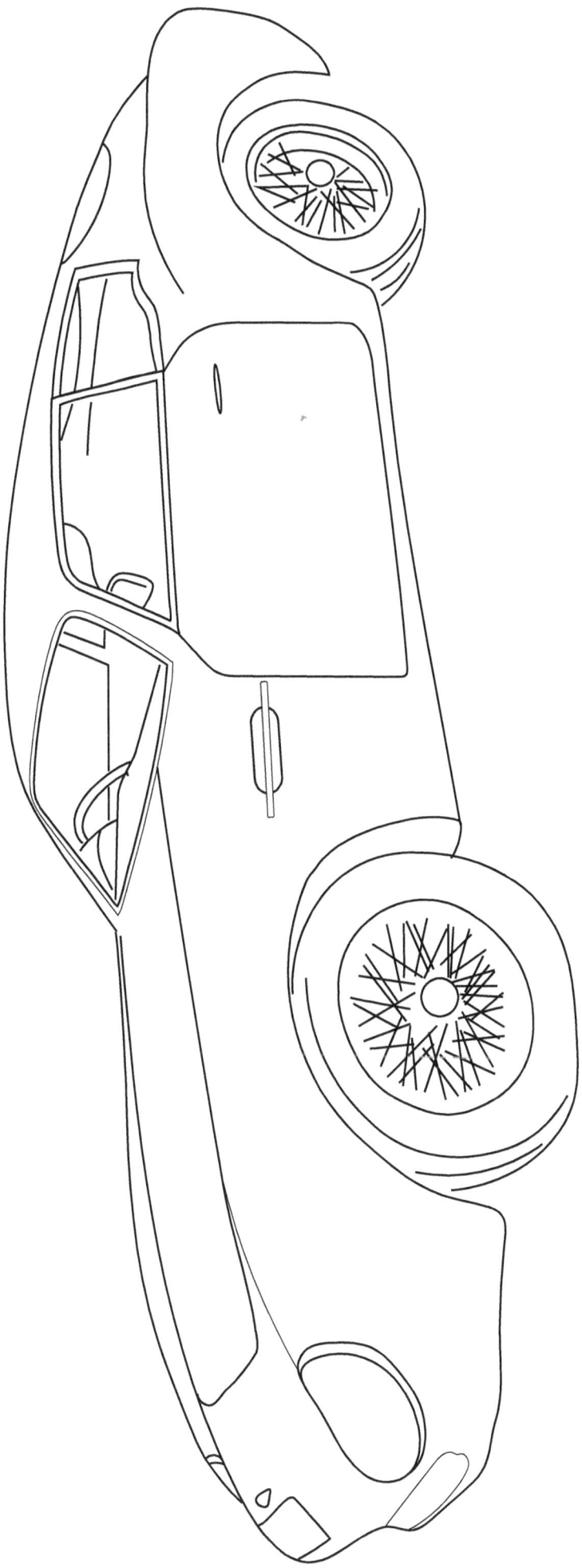

1961 Aston Martin

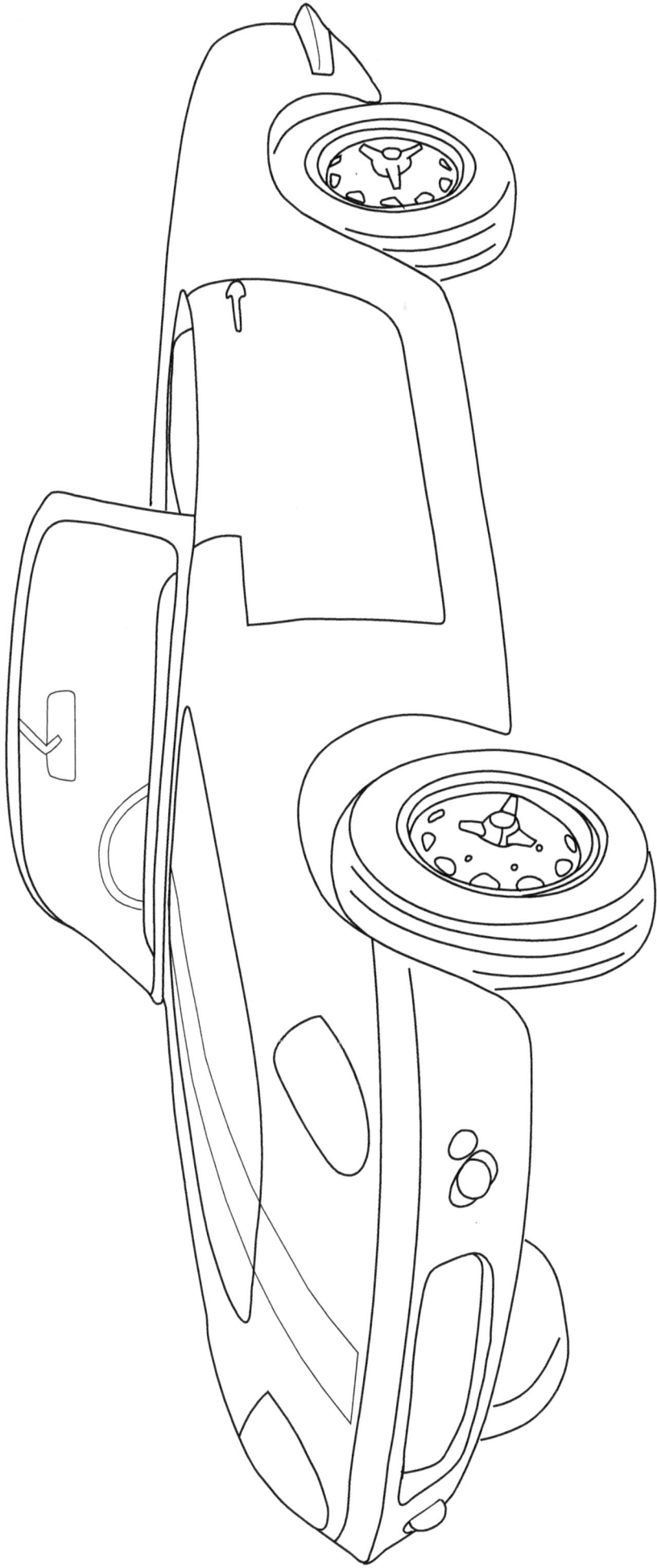

1962 Lotus ELan

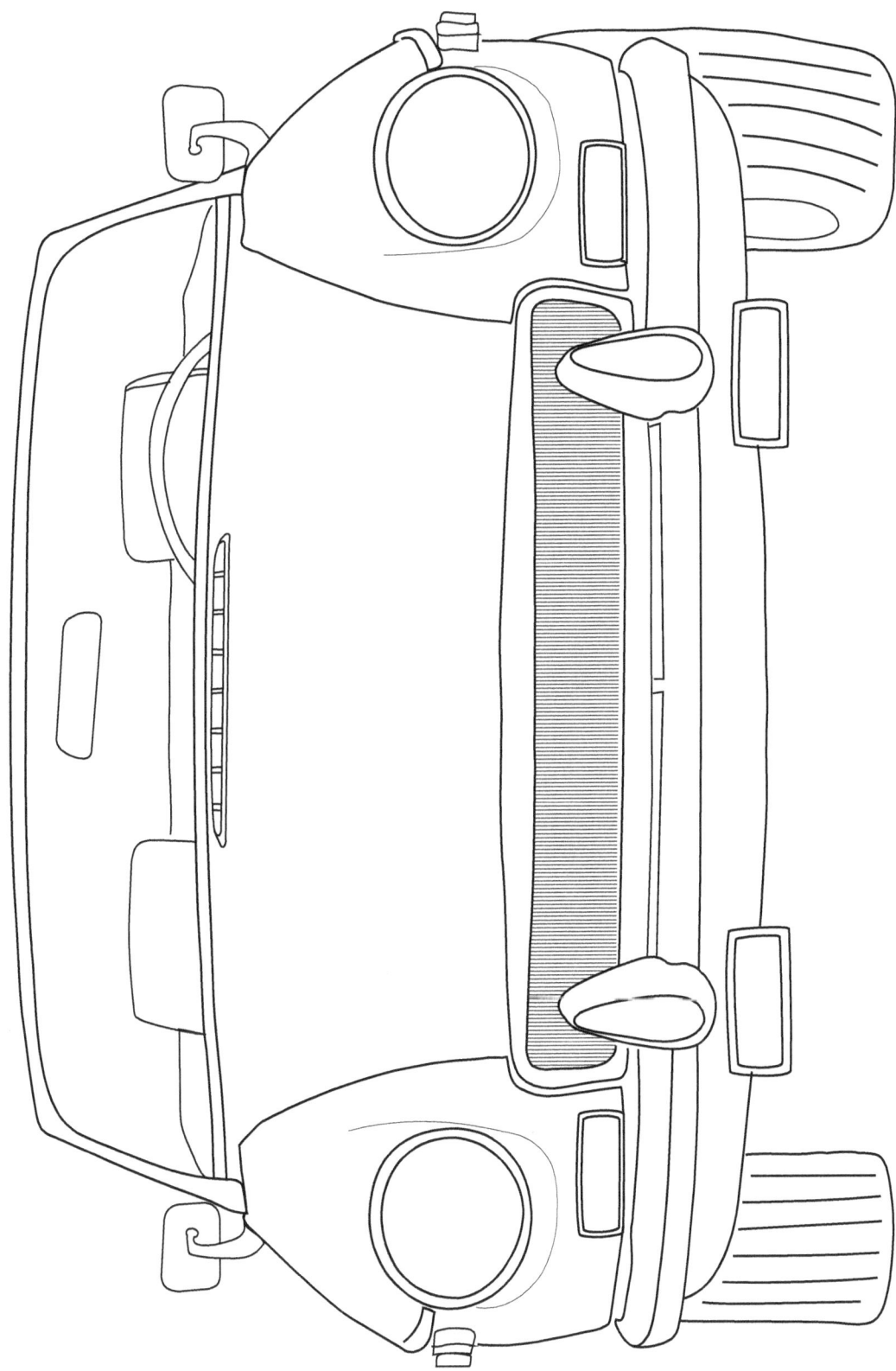

1962 MGB

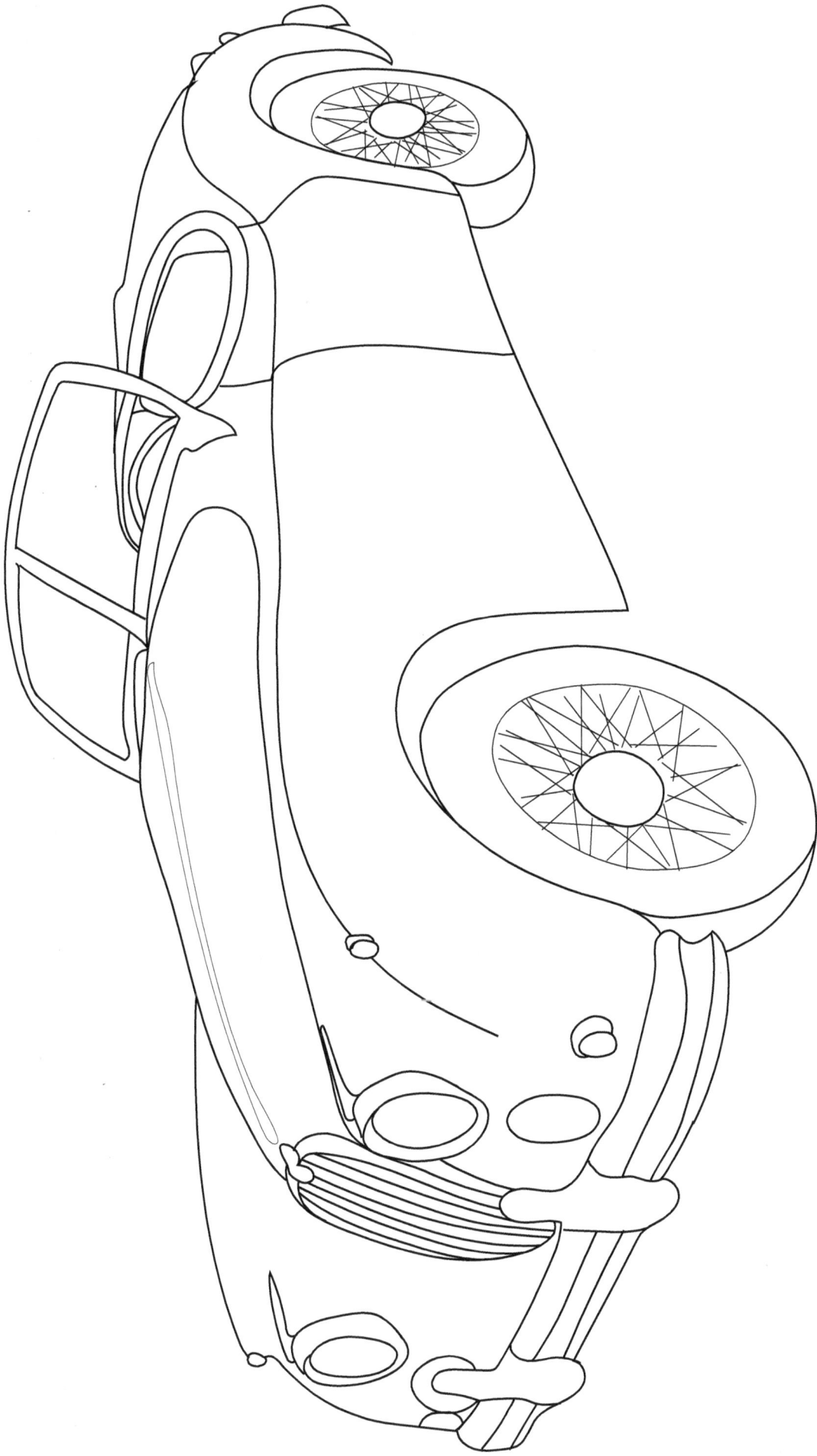

1957 Jaguar

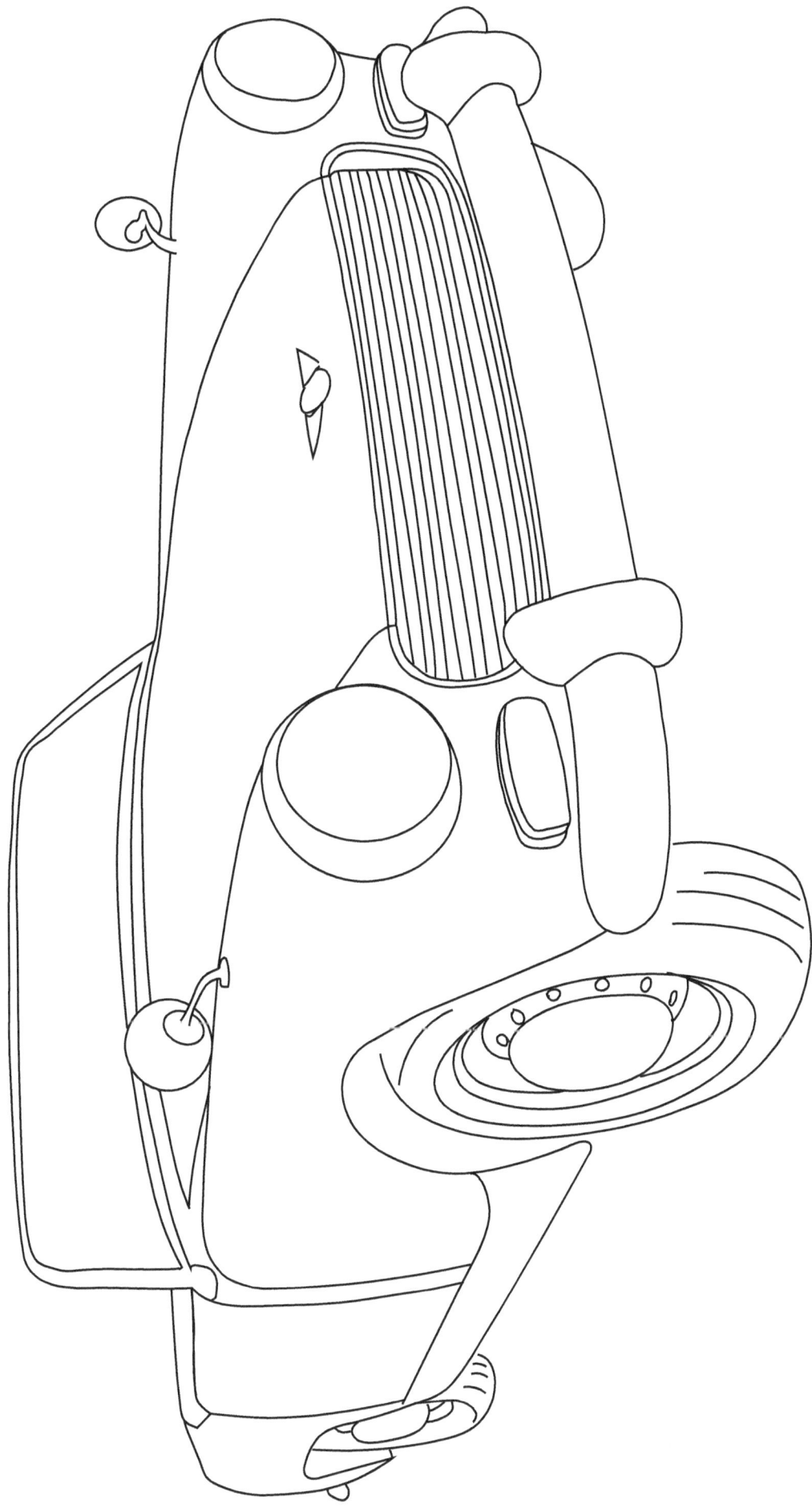

1963 Austin Healey Sprite MKII

1964 Austin Mini

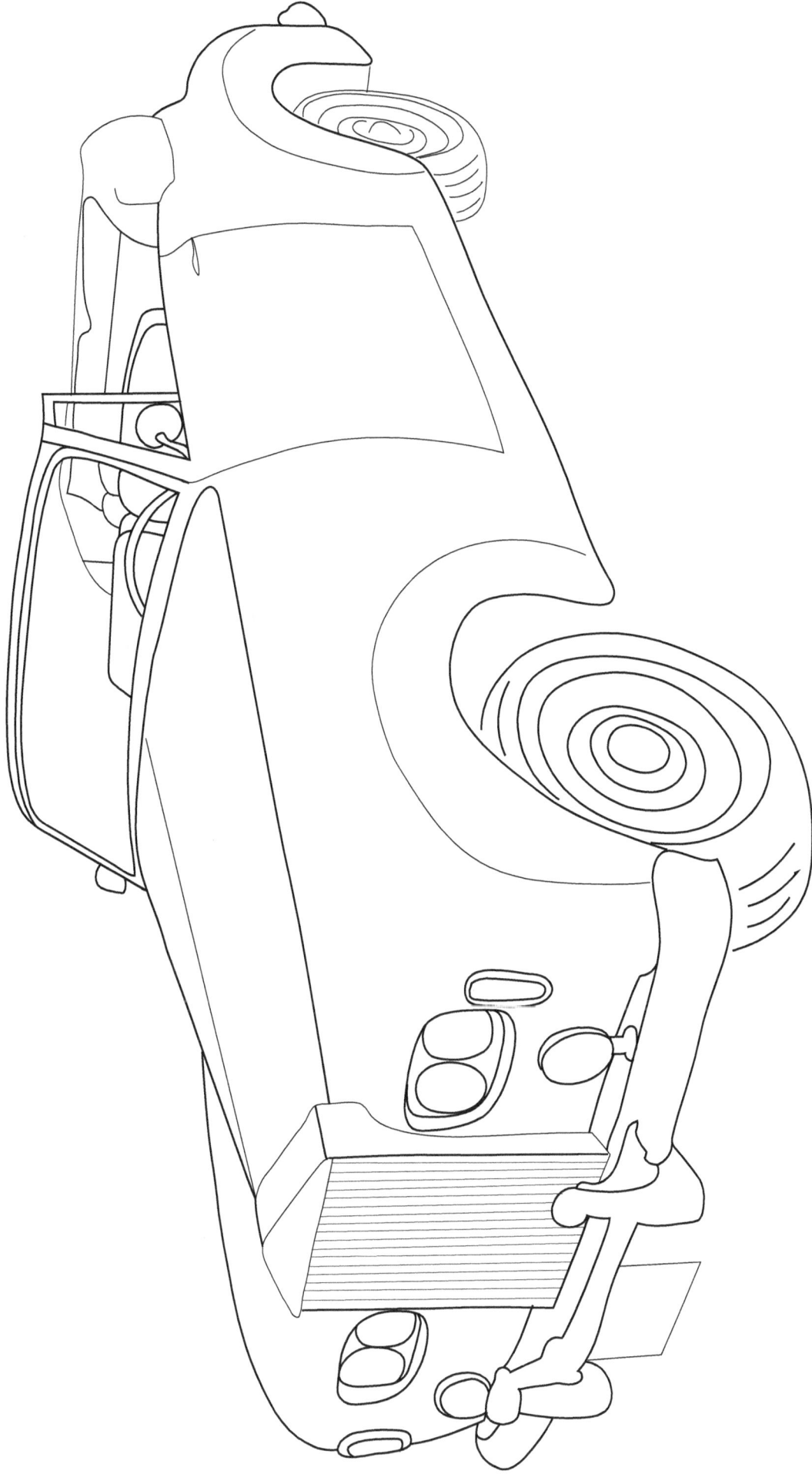

1964 Rolls Royce

1967 Austin Healey 3000 MK III

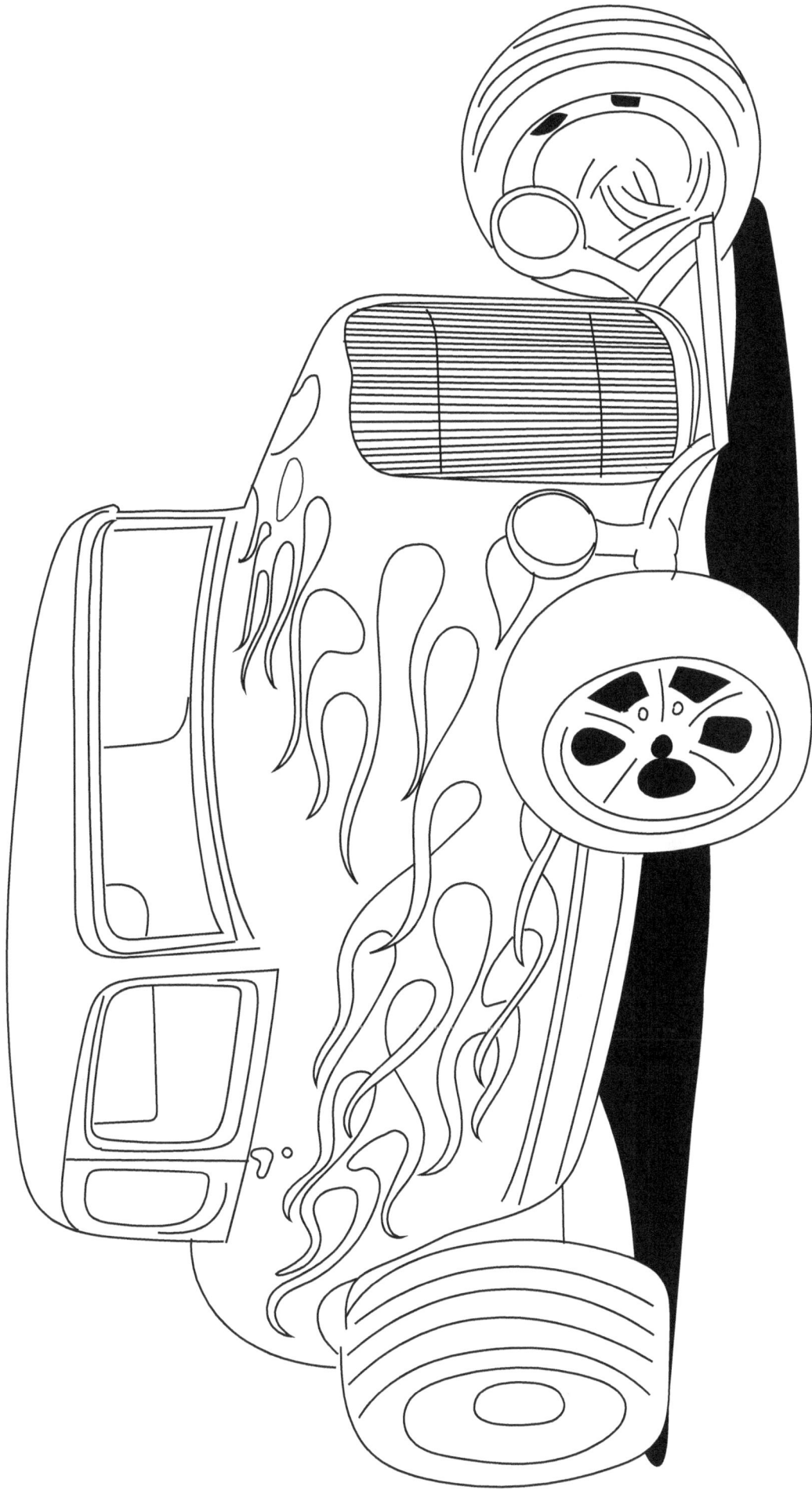

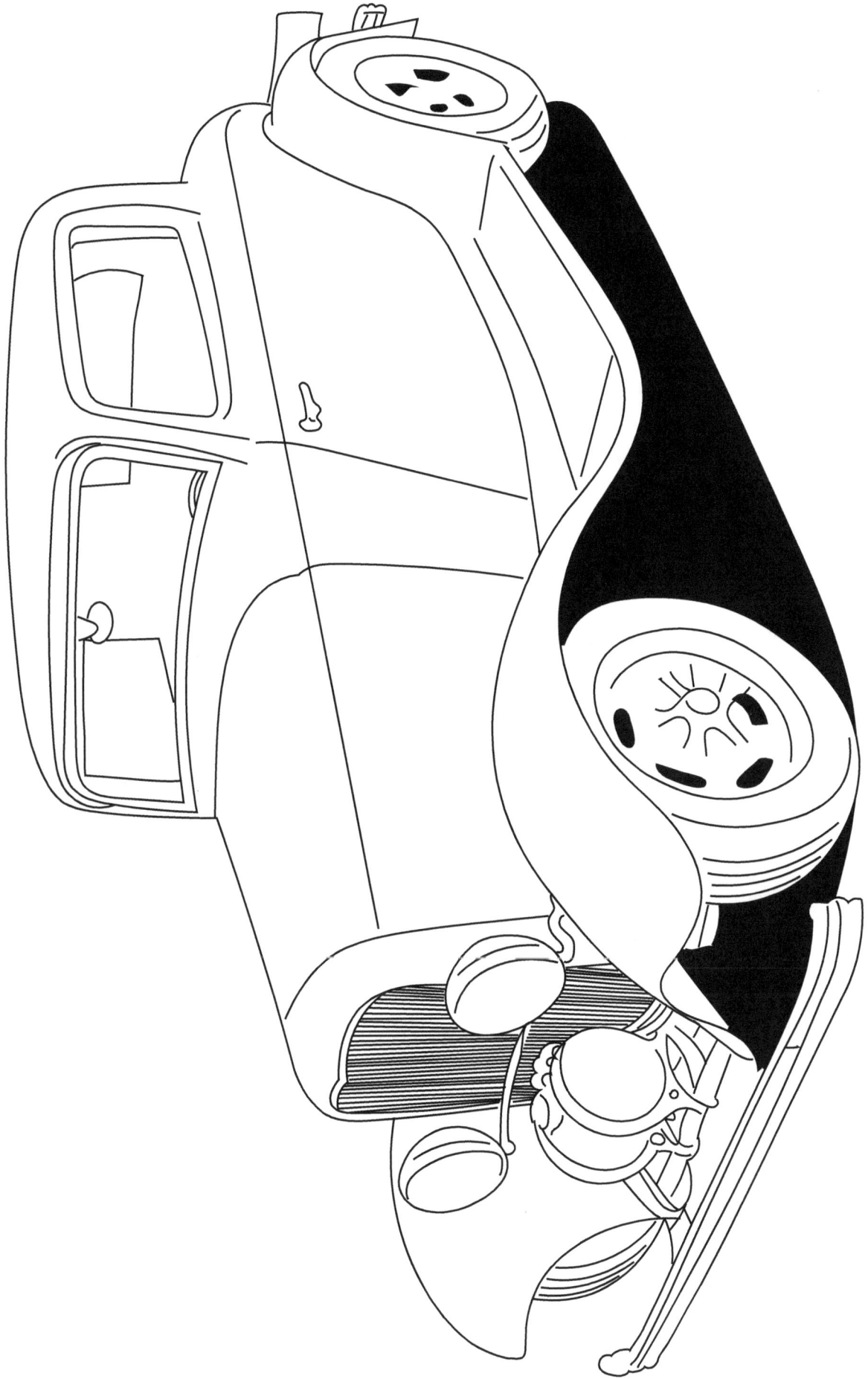

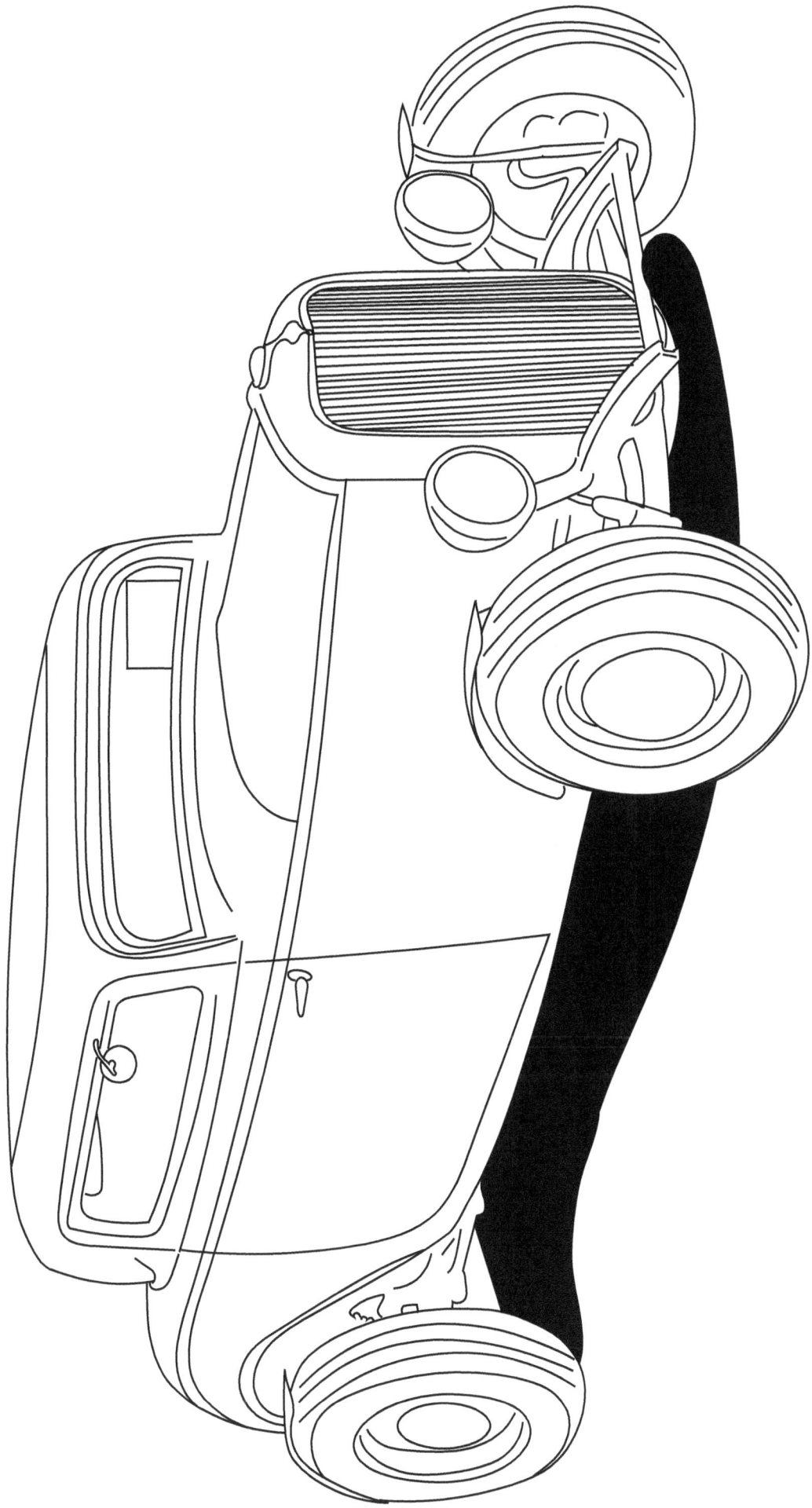

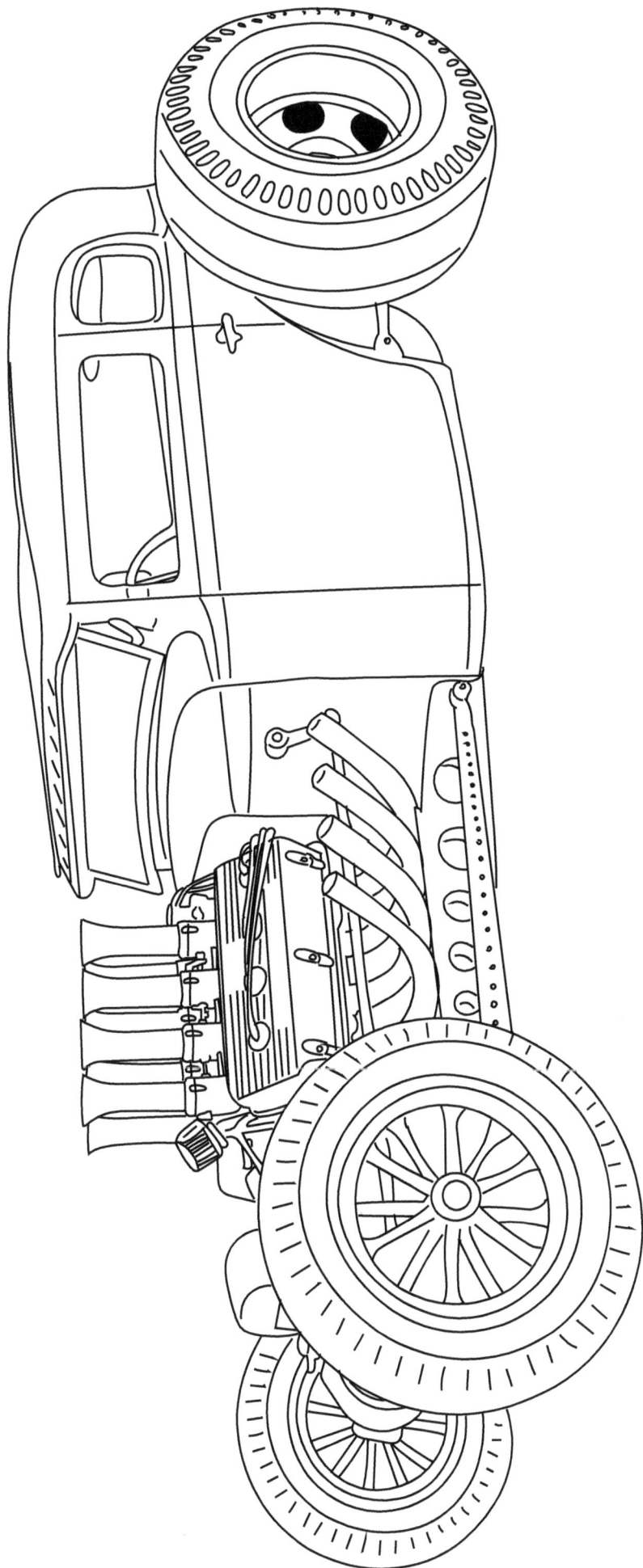

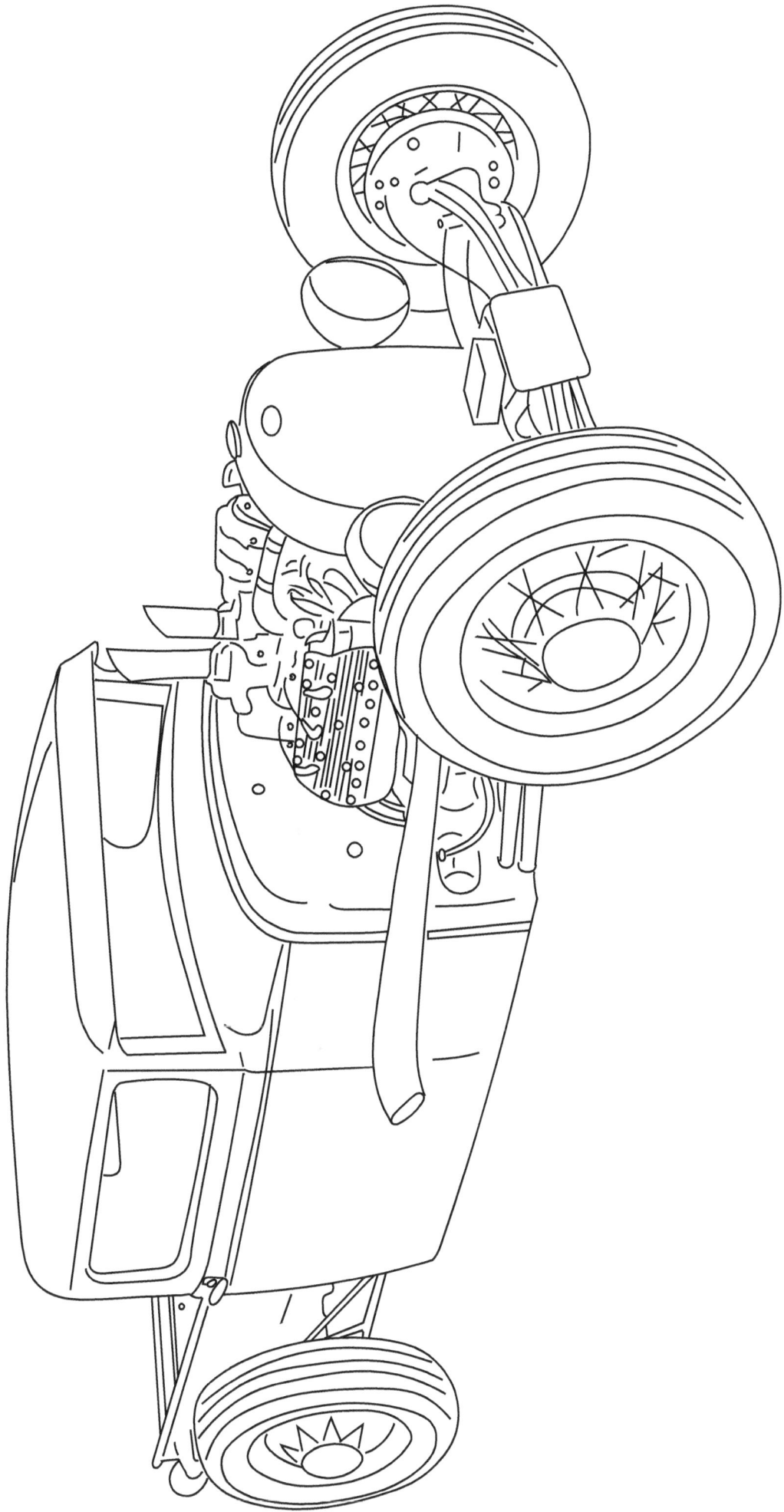

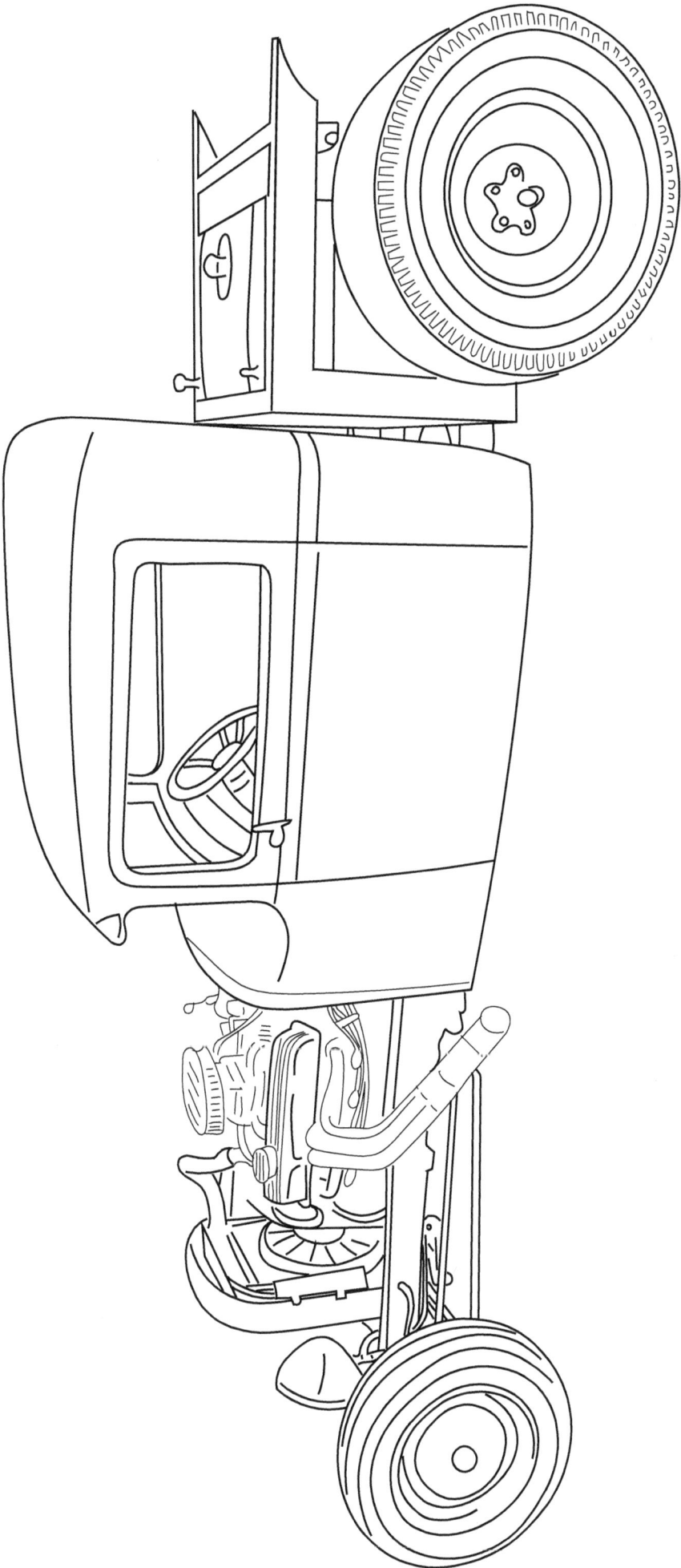

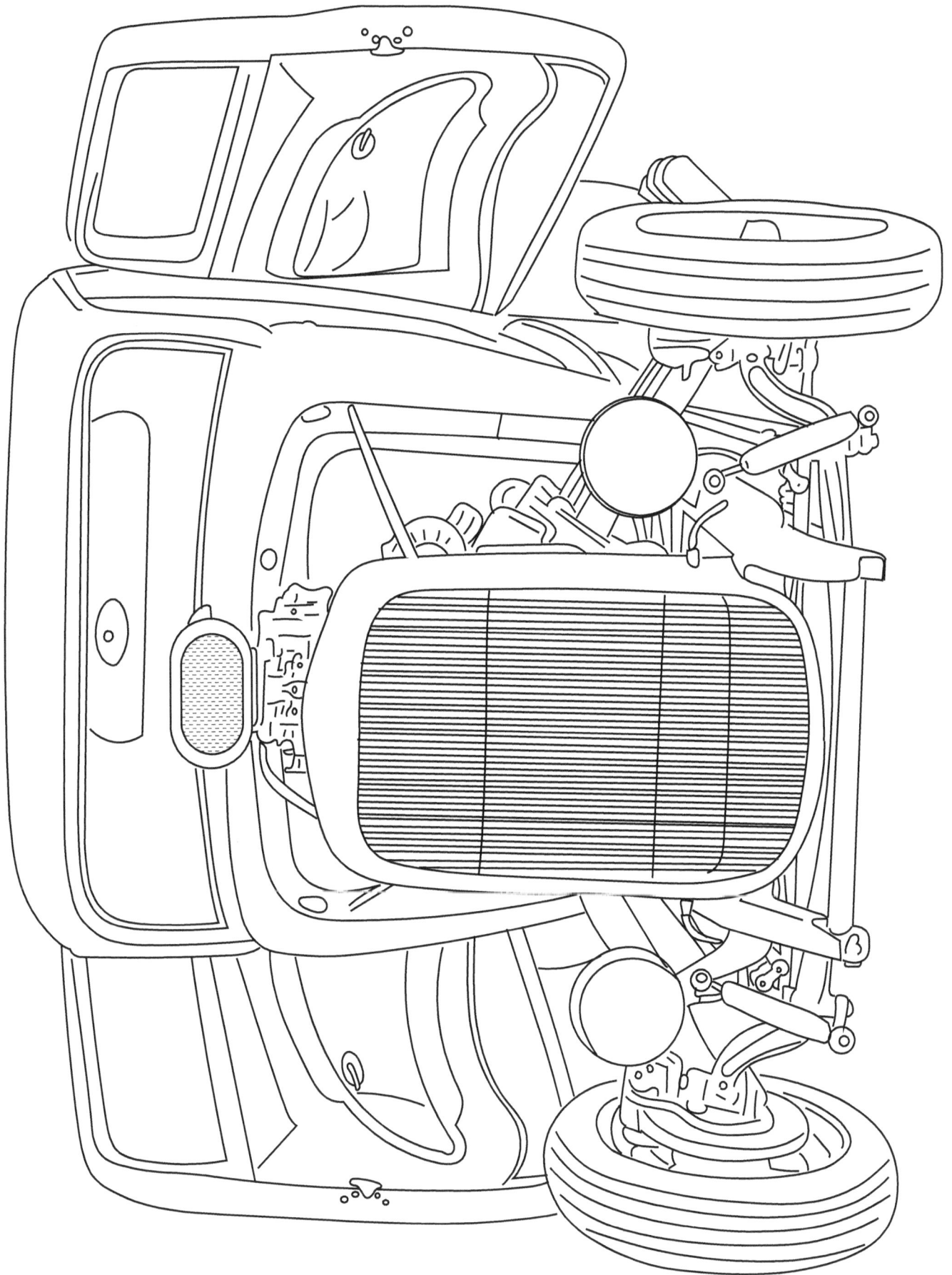

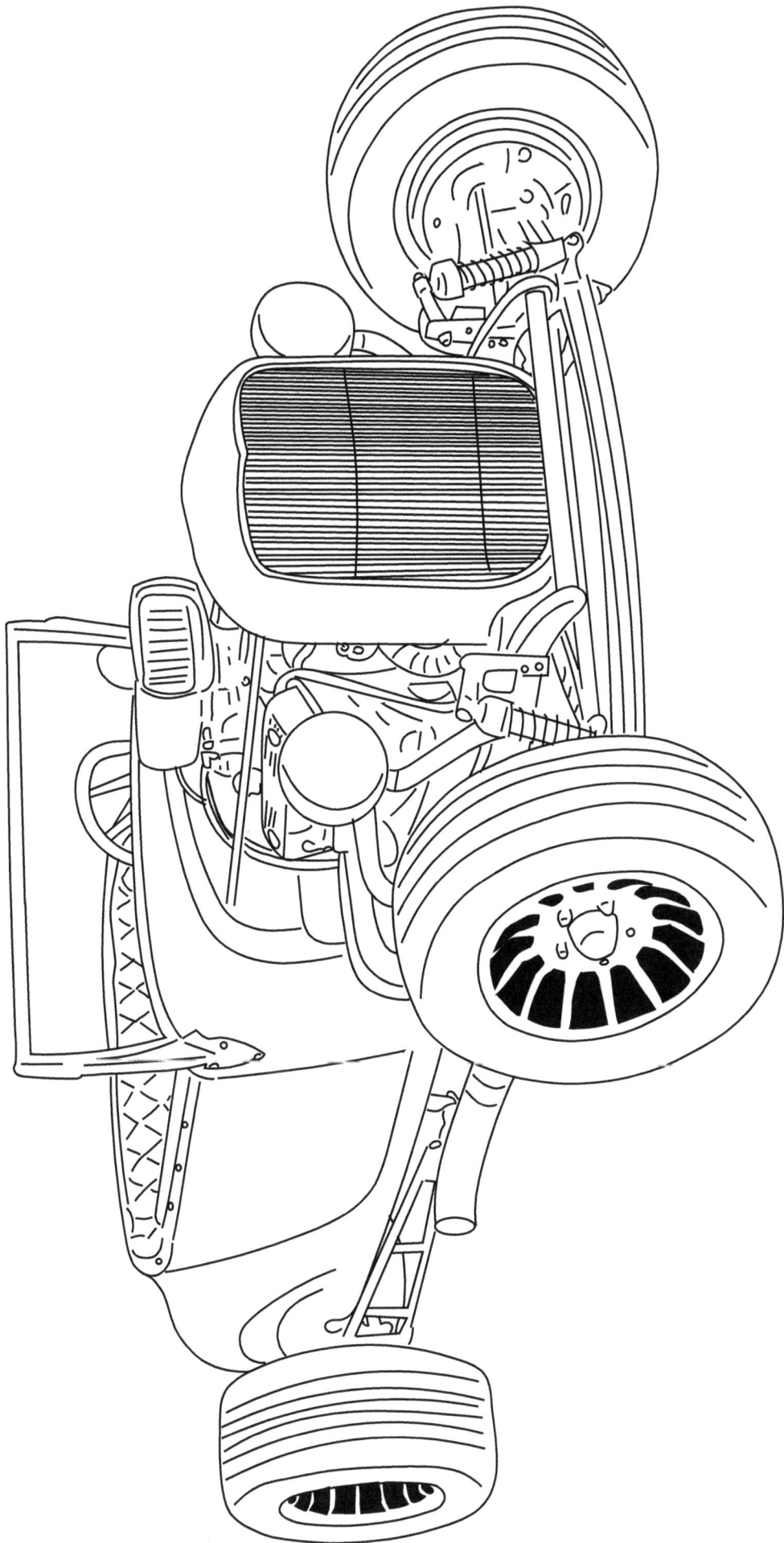

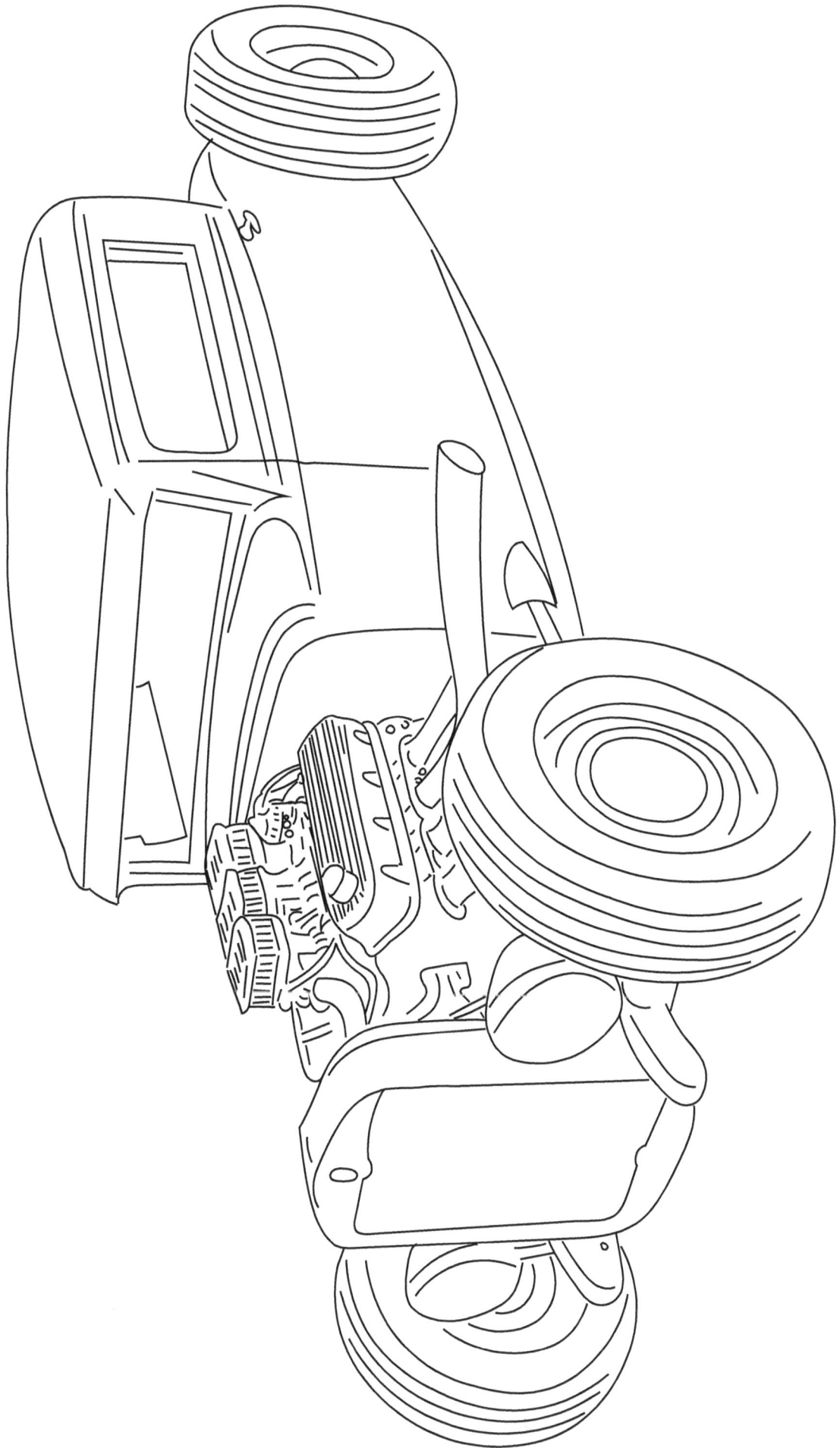

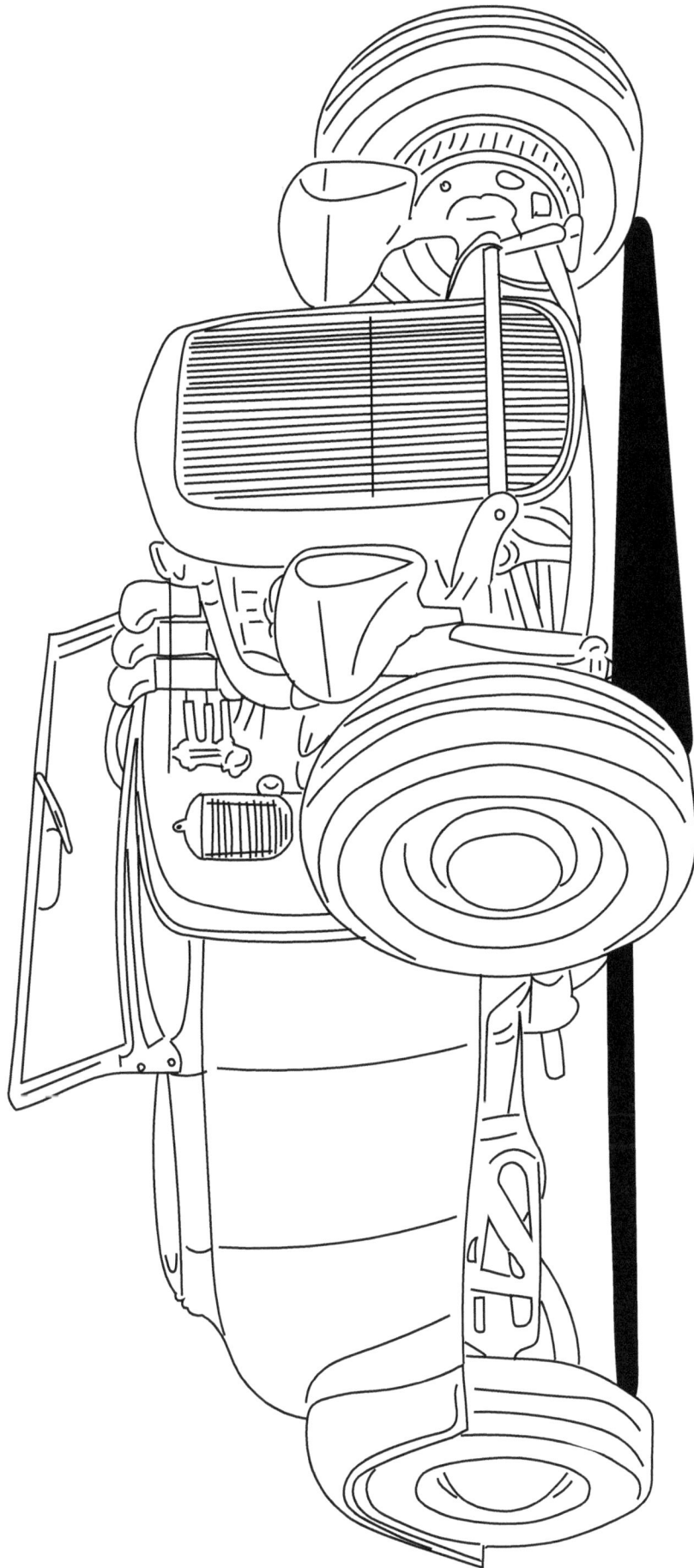

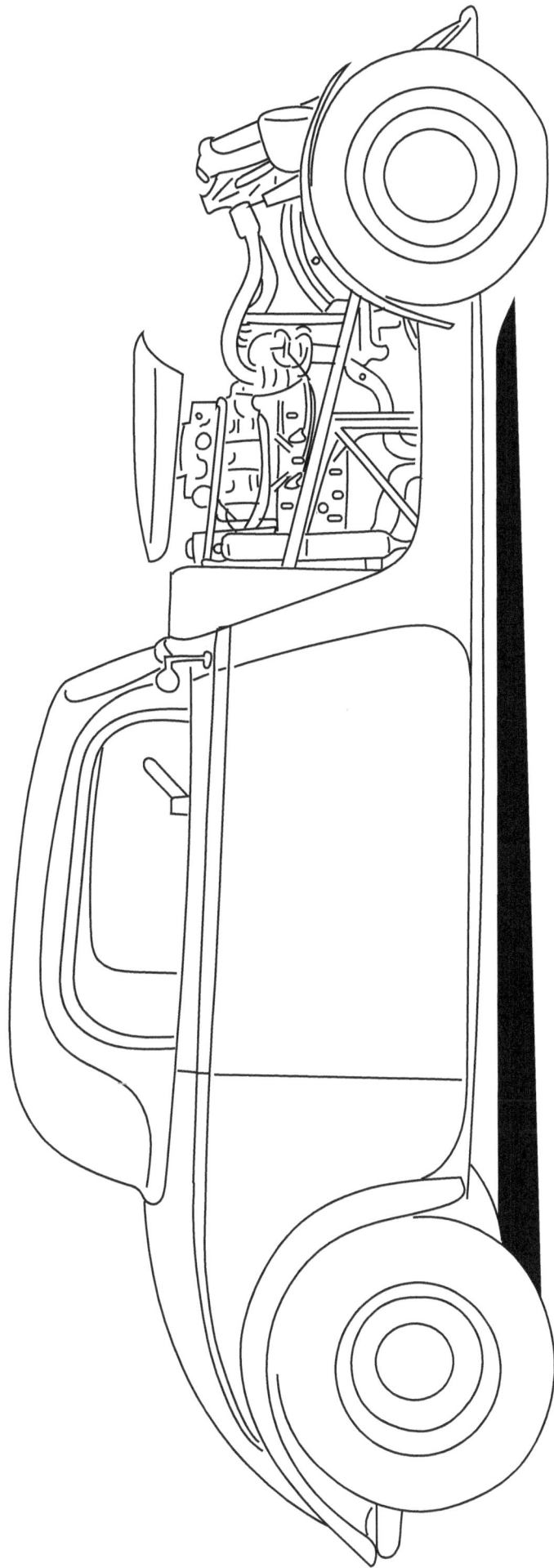

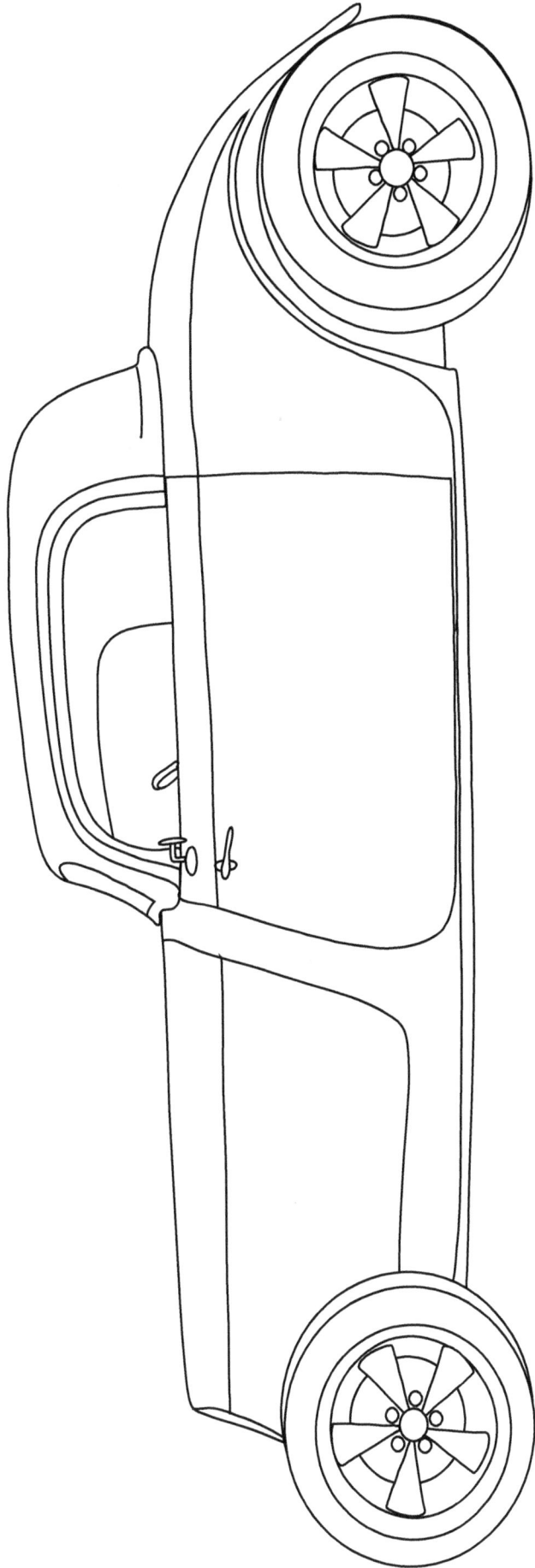

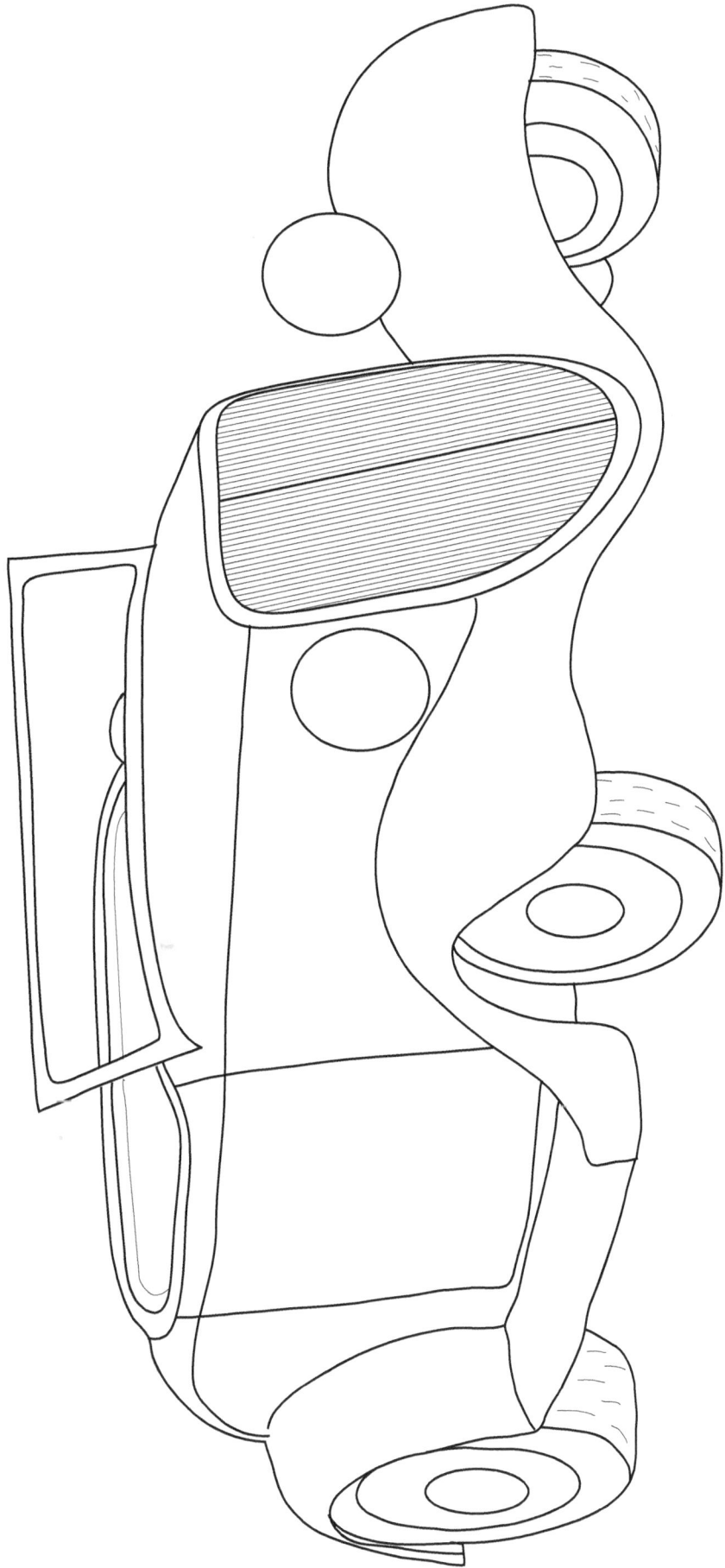

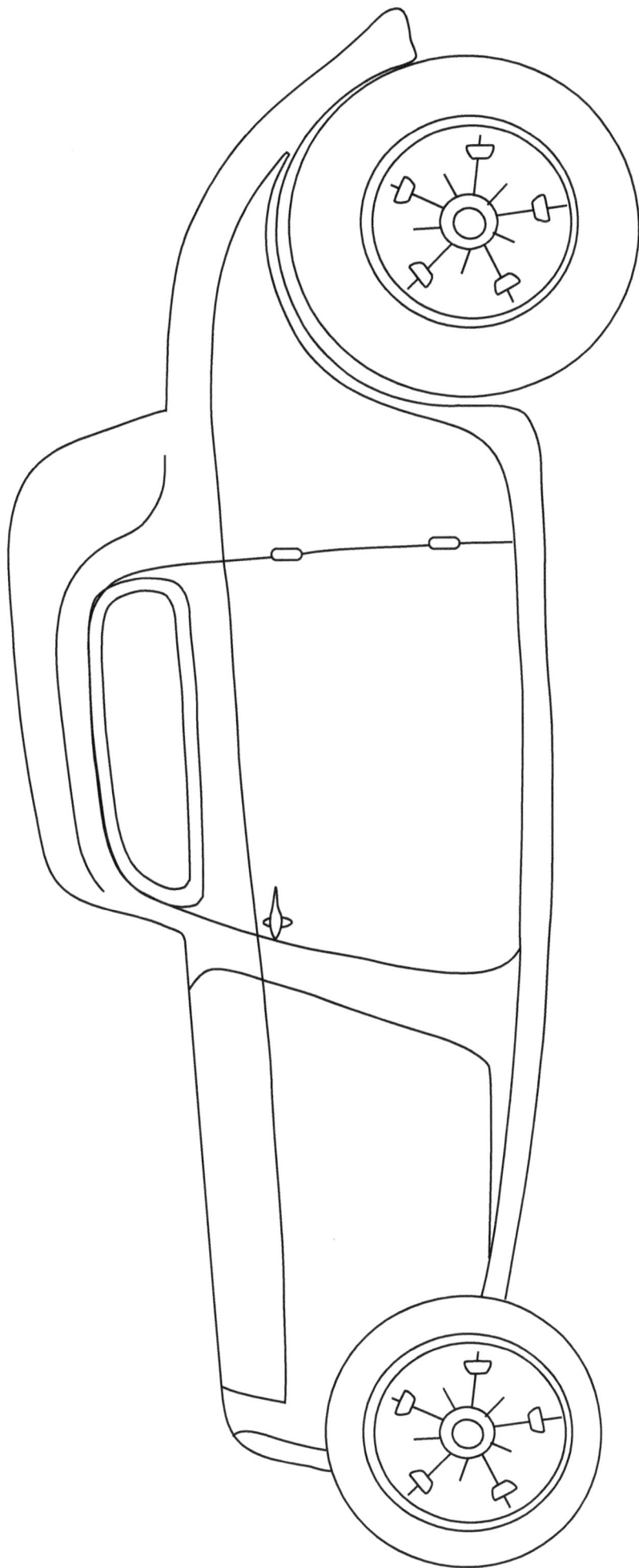

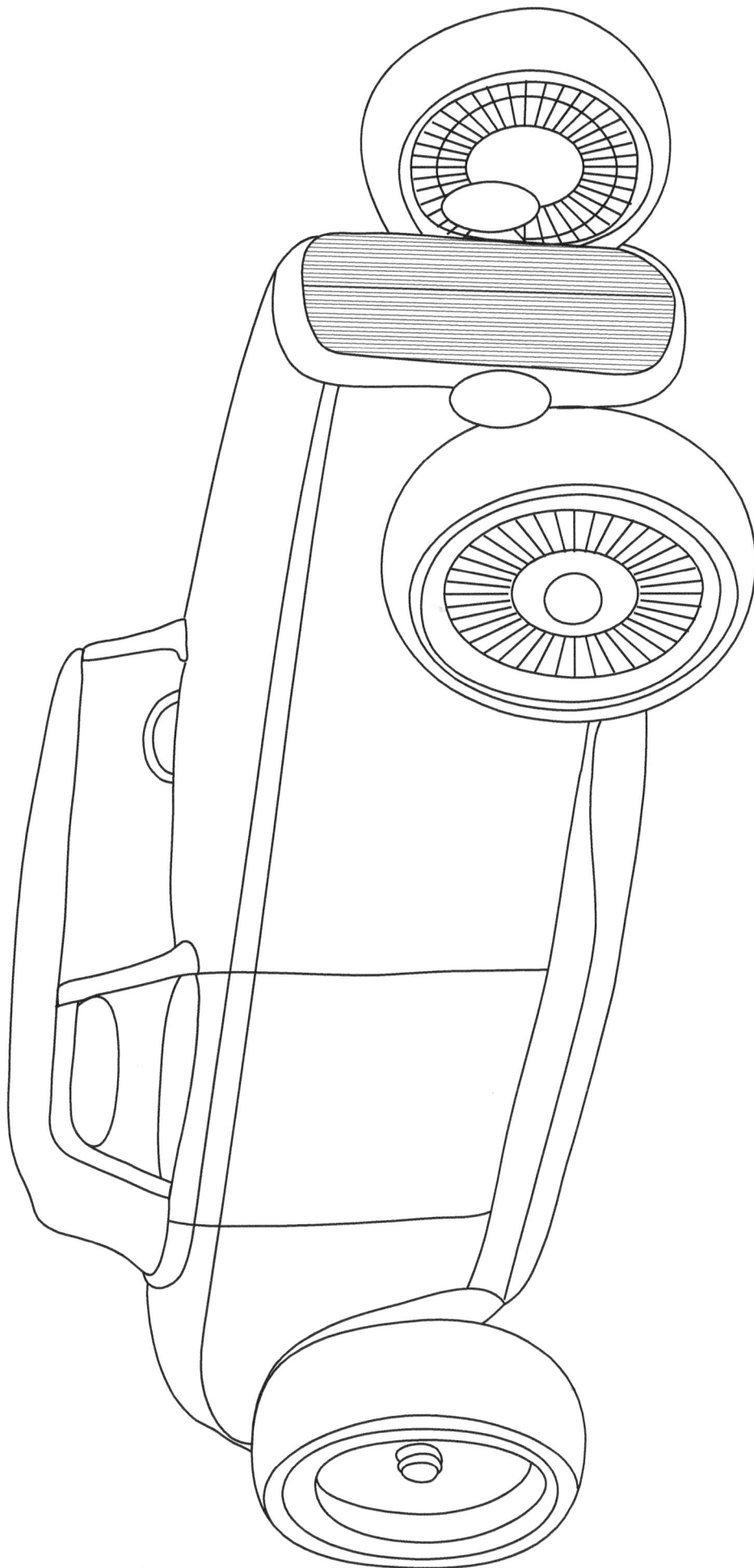

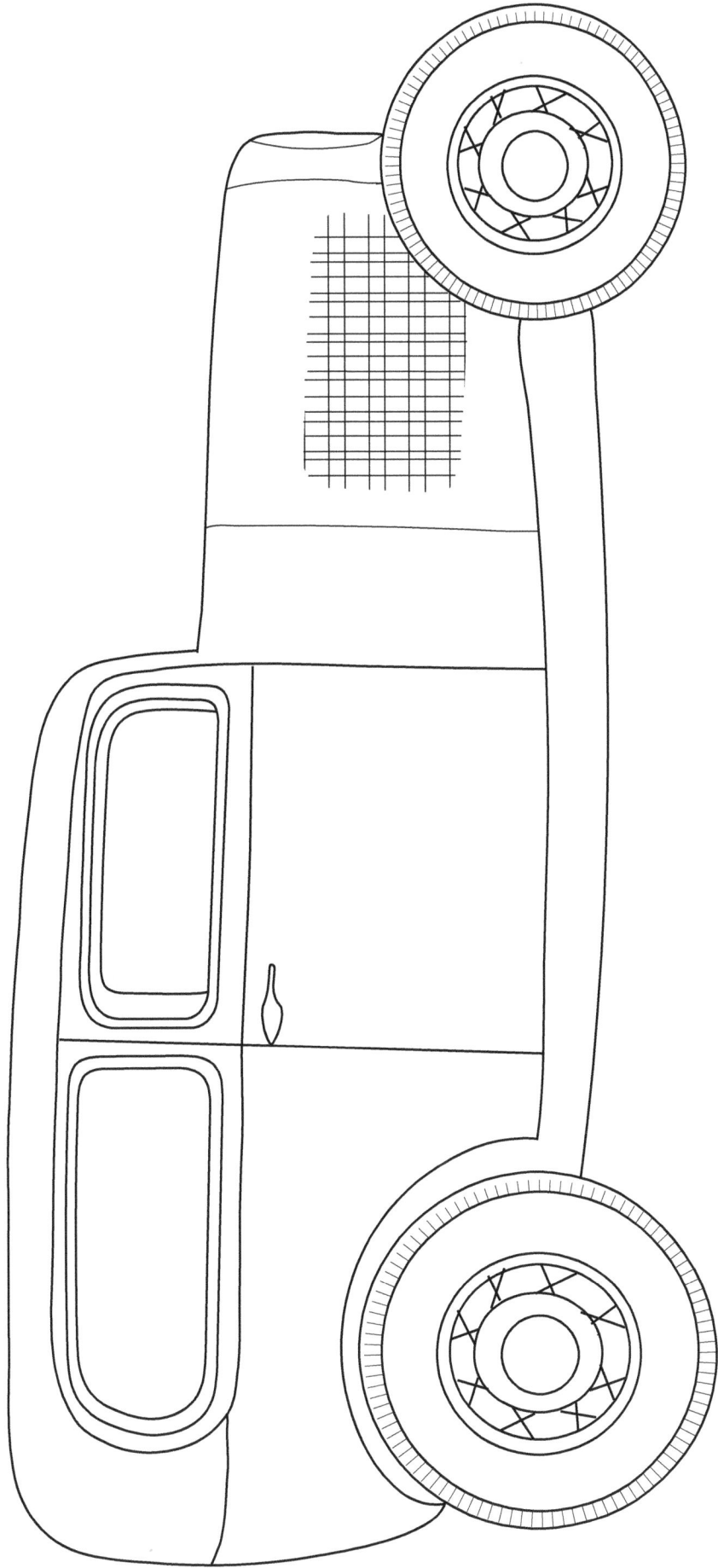

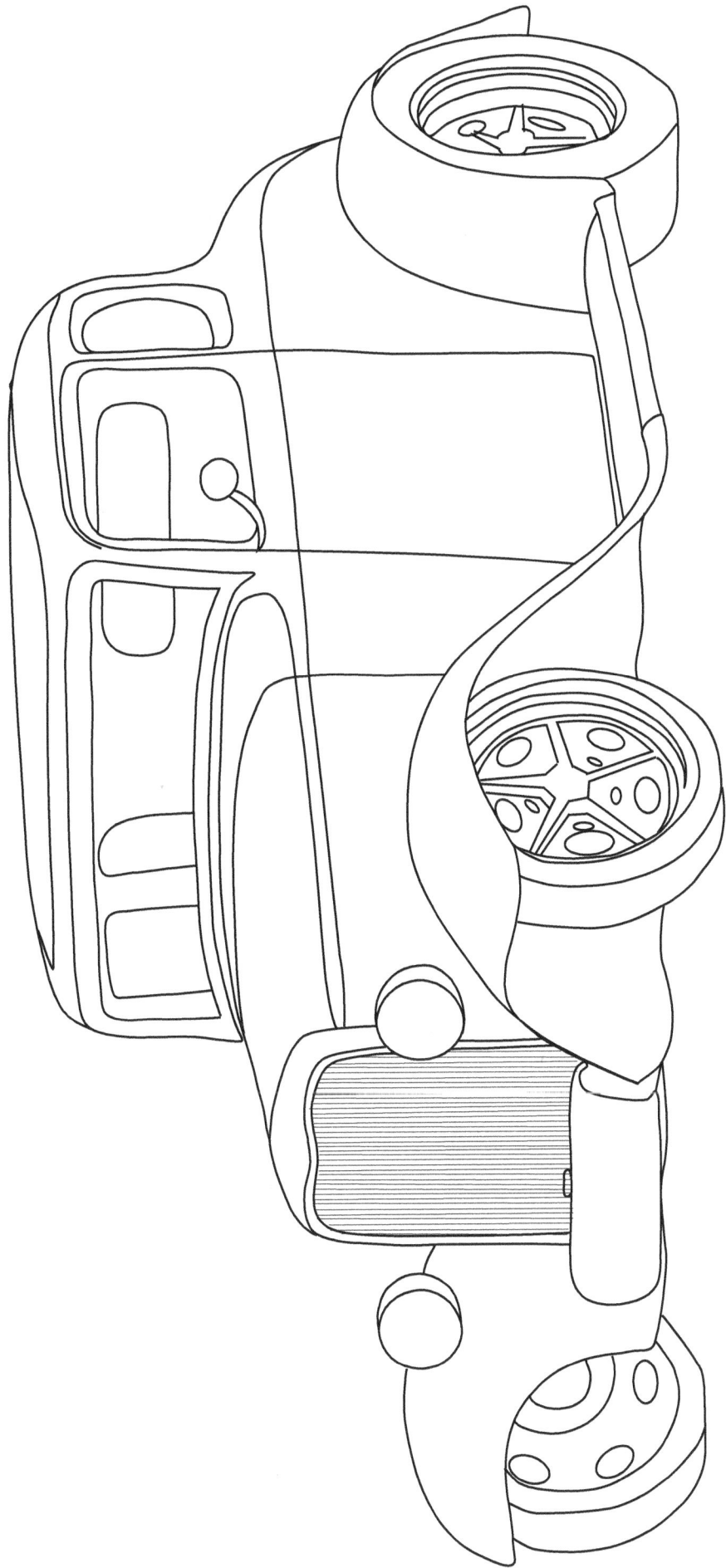

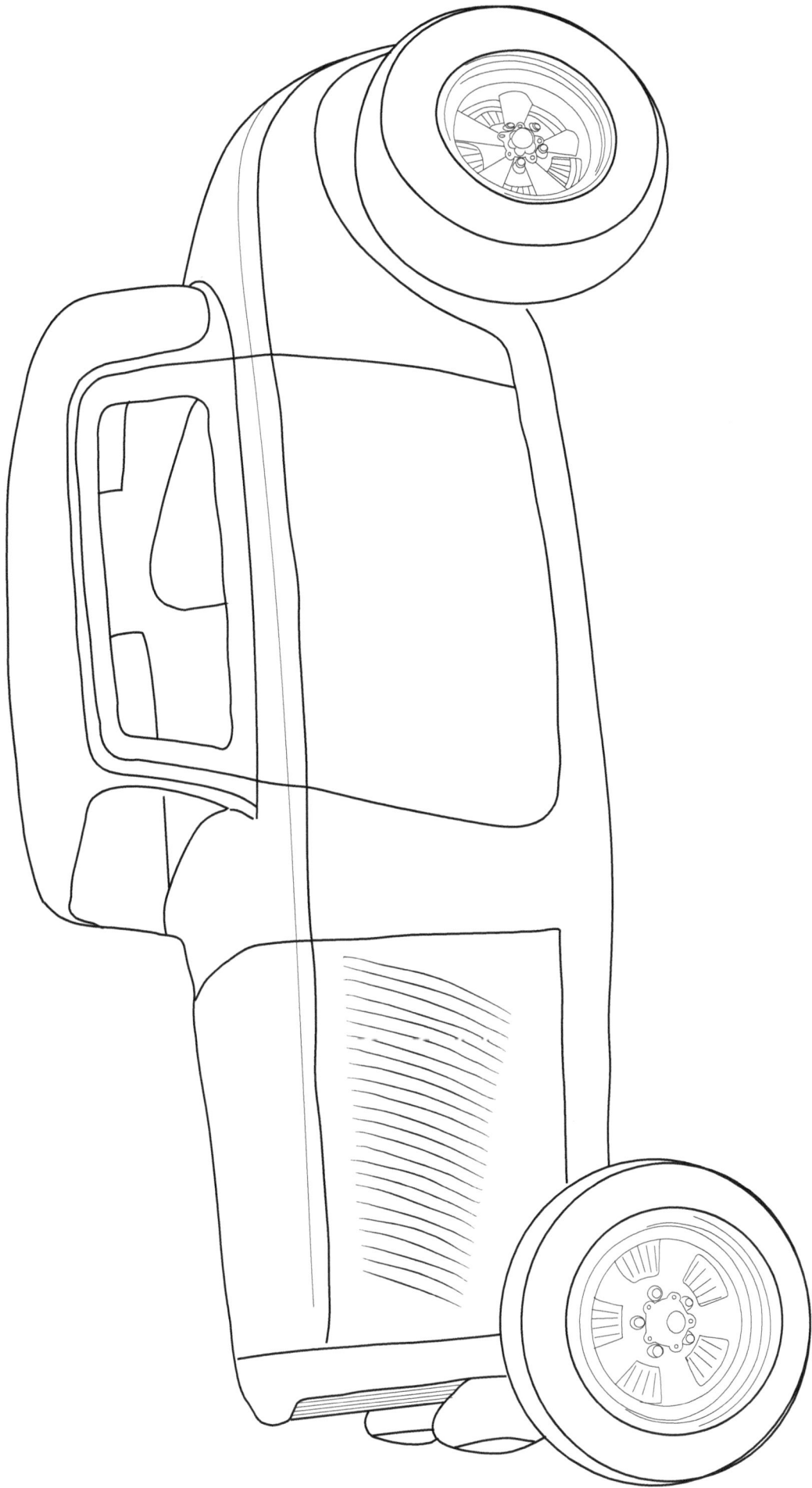

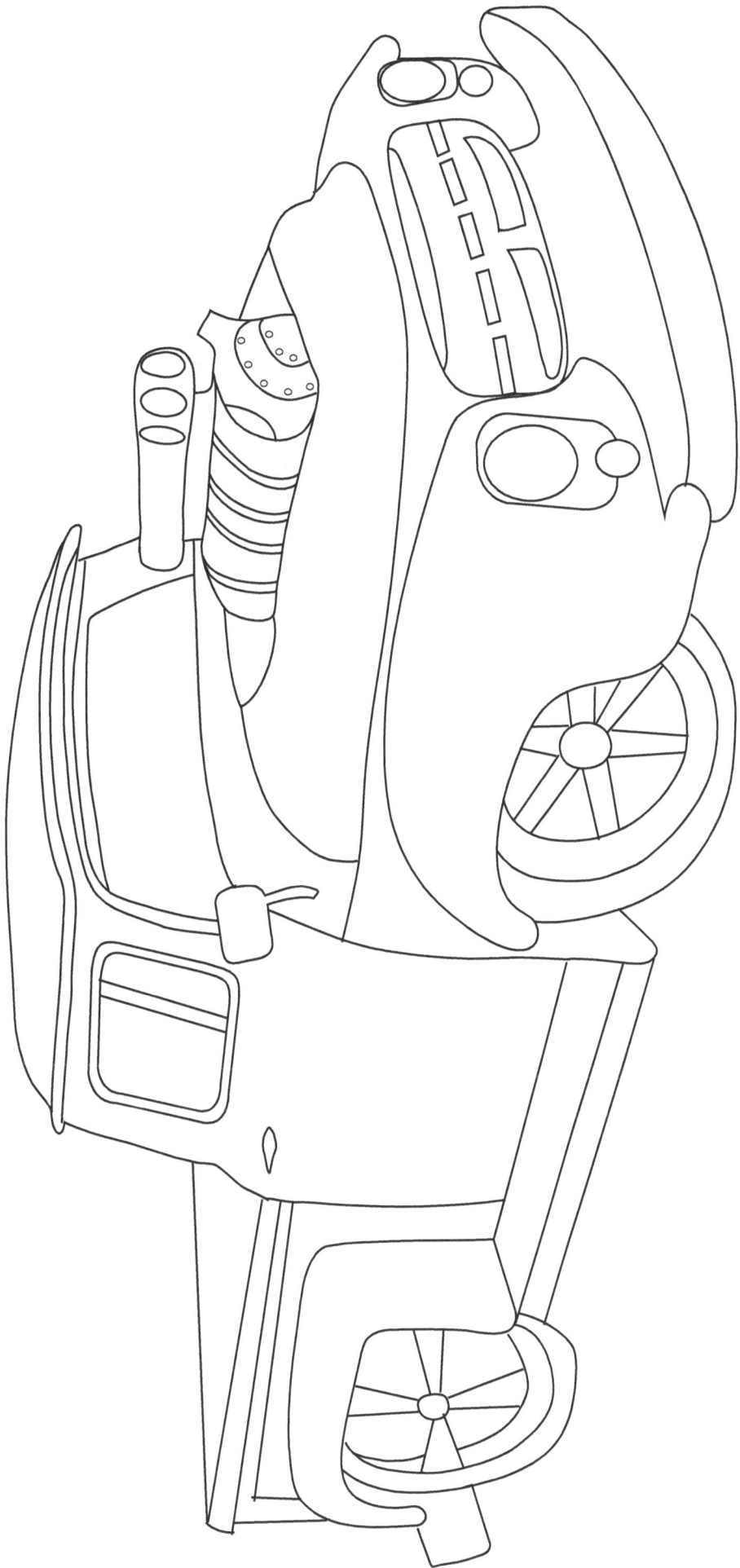

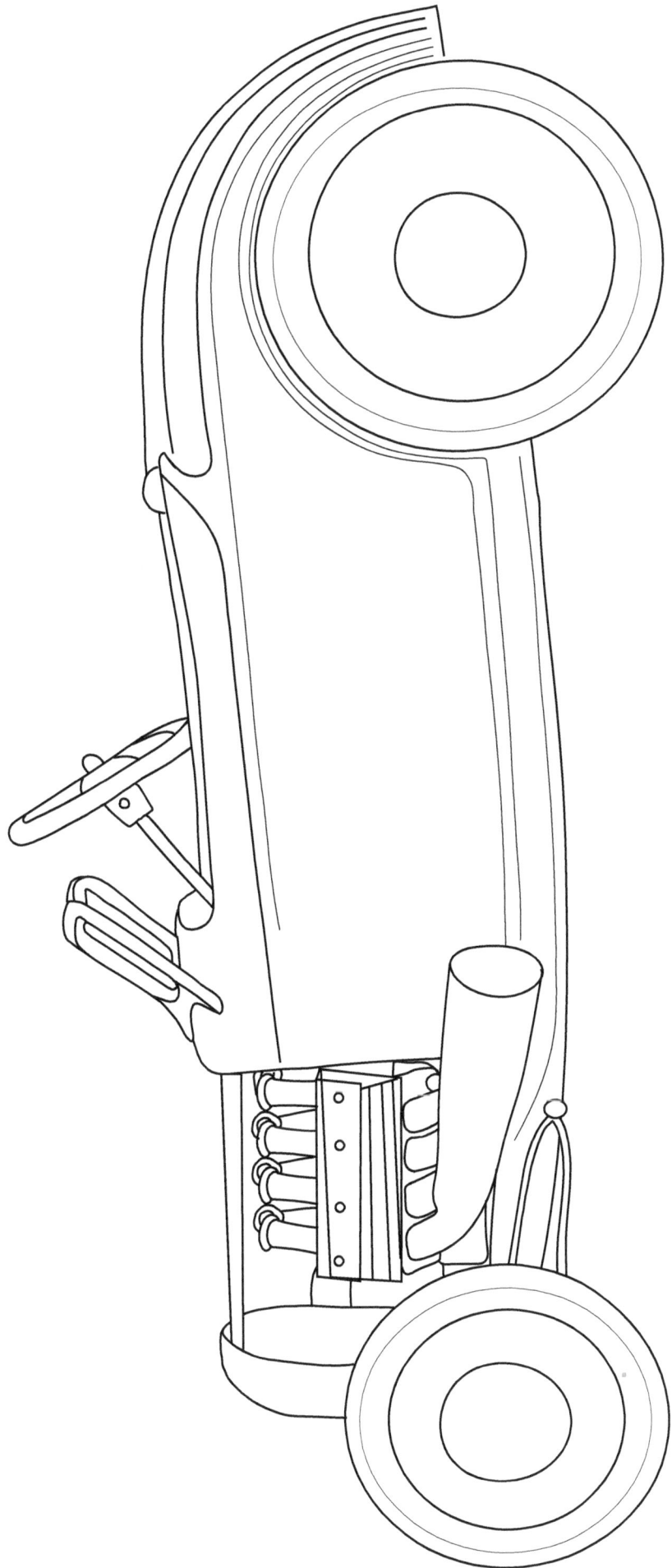

www.ingramcontent.com/pod-product-compliance
Lightning Source LLC
Chambersburg PA
CBHW080540090426
42734CB00016B/3161